Ranging widely through literature, both theological and sociological, about the state of marriage in our world, Bernard Wong will help his readers think about marriage and the household in ways other than those shaped by a late modern commitment to autonomy. Aiming to articulate a Christian vision of marriage and the household, he does not shy away from the hardest and most perplexing questions, and his constructive vision of the family as a school of love deserves attention and careful consideration.

Gilbert Meilaender, PhD
Senior Research Professor, Valparaiso University, Indiana, USA

Beginning from Man and Woman is an important contribution to the literature on Christian marriage and family. Bernard Wong tackles many vital issues in a direct, forthright, and engaging manner, offering invaluable critical and constructive insight. This is a must read for anyone who takes seriously the theological and moral significance of the family, especially as a witness to Christ's love.

Brent Waters, PhD
Stead Professor of Christian Social Ethics,
Director of Stead Center for Ethics and Values,
Garrett-Evangelical Theological Seminary, Evanston, Illinois, USA

Beginning from Man and Woman

Witnessing Christ's Love in the Family

Bernard K. Wong

MONOGRAPHS

© 2017 by Bernard K. Wong

Published 2017 by Langham Monographs
An imprint of Langham Creative Projects

Langham Partnership
PO Box 296, Carlisle, Cumbria CA3 9WZ, UK
www.langham.org

ISBNs:
978-1-78368-270-6 Print
978-1-78368-272-0 Mobi
978-1-78368-271-3 ePub
978-1-78368-273-7 PDF

Bernard K. Wong has asserted his right under the Copyright, Designs and Patents Act, 1988 to be identified as the Author of this work.

All rights reserved. No part of this publication may be reproduced, stored in a retrieval system or transmitted, in any form or by any means, electronic, mechanical, photocopying, recording or otherwise, without the prior written permission of the publisher or the Copyright Licensing Agency.

Unless otherwise stated, Scripture quotations are from the New Revised Standard Version Bible, copyright © 1989 National Council of the Churches of Christ in the United States of America. Used by permission. All rights reserved.

British Library Cataloguing in Publication Data
A catalogue record for this book is available from the British Library

ISBN: 978-1-78368-270-6

Cover & Book Design: projectluz.com

Langham Partnership actively supports theological dialogue and a scholar's right to publish but does not necessarily endorse the views and opinions set forth, and works referenced within this publication or guarantee its technical and grammatical correctness. Langham Partnership does not accept any responsibility or liability to persons or property as a consequence of the reading, use or interpretation of its published content.

CONTENTS

Chapter 1 1
  Introduction
    1.1 From the Beginning 1
    1.2 Marriage in the Contemporary World 3
    1.3 A Christian Response 7
    1.4 Chapter Outline 11

Chapter 2 13
  Uniformity between Man and Woman
    2.1 Farley: Personhood as Self-Transcendence 13
    2.2 Thatcher: Personhood as Love 22
    2.3 Sexual Ethics of Farley: Coming Together of Minds 28
    2.4 Sexual Ethics of Thatcher: Coming Together of Bodies 34
    2.5 The Gendered Ethics of Farley and Thatcher 43
    2.6 Theological Assessment 46
        2.6.1 O'Donovan and Meilaender: Ordering of Sexual Love
            and Procreation 48
        2.6.2 Barth: Creation as Limited and Concrete 53
        2.6.3 Zizioulas: Eschatological Transformation of Sexuality 56
    2.7 Conclusions 59

Chapter 3 63
  Equal-Regard between Man and Woman
    3.1 Critical Familism and Children 64
    3.2 Critical Familism and the Democratization of Family 67
    3.3 Male Problematic and Family Cohesion 70
    3.4 Family as a Liberal Democracy 78
    3.5 Theological Assessment 91
    3.6 Conclusions 100

Chapter 4 103
  Complementarity between Man and Woman
    4.1 Gender Relationship in Complementarianism 104
    4.2 Formulation of "Biblical Manhood and Womanhood" ... 110
        4.2.1 The Descriptive Task 111
        4.2.2 The Synthetic Task 113
        4.2.3 The Hermeneutical Task 115
        4.2.4 The Pragmatic Task 124
    4.3 Theological Assessment 132
    4.4 Conclusions 145

Chapter 5 147
Love between Man and Woman
- 5.1 A Retrospective 147
- 5.2 Dualities of Human Existence as Framework of Gender Relationship 151
- 5.3 Christ's Love as Moral Vision of Gender Relationship 154
- 5.4 The Moral Vision 159
  - 5.4.1 From Just Love to Friendship 160
  - 5.4.2 From Equal-Regard Love to Incarnational Love 169
  - 5.4.3 From Erotic Love to Unfolding Love 180
  - 5.4.4 From Unilateral Love to Mutual Love 191
- 5.5 Conclusions 195

Chapter 6 199
Witnessing Christ's Love: The Ephesian Household Code
- 6.1 A Survey of Contemporary Interpretations 200
  - 6.1.1 Literalist Interpretation 200
  - 6.1.2 Feminist Interpretation 201
  - 6.1.3 Cultural Interpretation 205
  - 6.1.4 Historical Interpretation 206
  - 6.1.5 Theological Interpretation 212
- 6.2. Interpreted through Christ's Love 218
  - 6.2.1 Mutual Subordination 219
  - 6.2.2 Subordination of Wives 225
  - 6.2.3 Love of Husbands 233
  - 6.2.4 Children and Parents 244
  - 6.2.5 Slaves and Masters 250
- 6.3 Conclusions 255

Bibliography 259

Index 277

CHAPTER 1

Introduction

From the beginning of creation, God made them male and female.
(Mark 10:6)

1.1 From the Beginning

The creation of male and female marks the beginning of the human race. In the first creation narrative, simultaneous creation of male and female suggests that neither man nor woman alone can offer a complete portrayal of humanity.[1] Humanity must be known through both man and woman together. Hans Urs von Balthasar avers, "The human being, in the completed creation, is a 'dual duality,' . . . two poles of a single reality, two diverse presences of a single being, two *entia* in a single *esse*, one existence in two lives."[2] It is not coincidental that on the first spacecraft that traveled beyond the solar system, scientists decided to attach a picture of a man and a woman standing side by side as a self-depiction of the human race in case the spacecraft encountered any extraterrestrial intelligence.[3] The dual existence of man and woman is not only essential in understanding humanity. As part of God's creation, it is also pronounced "very good."[4] The second

---

1. Gen 1:27.
2. Hans Urs von Balthasar, *Theo-Drama: Theological Dramatic Theory*, Vol 2: *The Dramatis Personae: Man in God*, trans. Graham Harrison (San Francisco, CA: Ignatius, 1990), 365–366.
3. Richard O. Fimmel, *Pioneer Odyssey*, revised ed. (Washington, DC: Scientific and Technical Information Office, National Aeronautics and Space Administration, 1977), 183–186.
4. Gen 1:31.

creation narrative continues to describe this goodness: a man living "alone" is "not good" and the remedy is to find him a "fitting partner." This partner must not be any other creature but the "woman," who is fashioned from the very bones and flesh of the man.[5] Therefore, the goodness of a human person is predicated upon partnership with fellow human beings who share one's "bones and flesh" yet are not merely duplicates of the self.

This notion of dual existence in Christian theology, however, does not imply that an individual man or woman is an incomplete being so that marriage is the only avenue to wholeness. As I will discuss later, the advent of Christ has released humanity from the imperative to procreate, and singleness has become an equal yet distinct vocation alongside marriage.[6] What the two creation narratives reveal is that the goodness of humanity, in Helmut Thielicke's words, is founded upon "being in fellow-humanity." The relationship between fellow human beings – the *I-Thou* relationship – is emphasized over and against all *I-It* relationships.[7] Sexual differentiation in humanity, argues Karl Barth, serves as the "great paradigm" for relationships between persons: "The fact that he [sic] was created man and woman will be the great paradigm of everything that is to take place between him and God, and also of everything that is to take place between he and his fellows."[8] Man and woman were created simultaneously; both bear the *imago Dei*, are of equal dignity, and share "bones and flesh" with each other. Yet they are also different, occupying the opposite poles of a single reality so that the other is not merely a duplicate of the self, and otherness between persons becomes possible. It is this sameness and difference between man and woman that makes their relationship paradigmatic of all interpersonal relationships. In his discussions of human fellowship, Barth speaks of the paradigmatic man-woman relationship as the "first sphere of fellow-humanity," from which the "second sphere of human fellowship" – between parents and children – arises. Finally, the relationships between

---

5. Gen 2:18–23.

6. See section 2.6.3.

7. Helmut Thielicke, *The Ethics of Sex,* trans. John W. Doberstein (New York: Harper & Row, 1964), 4.

8. Karl Barth, *Church Dogmatics Vol. 3.1: The Doctrine of Creation,* eds. G. W. Bromiley and T. F. Torrance; trans. J. W. Edwards, O. Bussey, and H. Knight (Peabody, MA: Hendrickson, 2010), 186.

one's near and distant neighbors are respectively the "third sphere" and "fourth sphere" of human fellowship.[9] In other words, all human relationships originate from the paradigmatic man-woman relationship. To understand human relationality, we must begin with the relationship between man and woman.

1.2 Marriage in the Contemporary World

After asserting that the man-woman relationship is paradigmatic of all human relationships, Barth continues to argue that marriage is paradigmatic, or the *telos*, of the man-woman relationship, though not every man or woman must marry nor does marriage exhaust the encounter between them. Marriage is paradigmatic because it involves

> the encounter of male and female in which the free, mutual, harmonious choice of love on the part of a particular man and woman leads to a responsibly undertaken life-union which is lasting, complete and exclusive. Whatever happens or does not happen in this sphere, as the encounter between man and woman, has some kind of reference to this form and possibility.[10]

Marriage as the paradigm or the *telos* of human relationality is also expressed in Scripture. The relationship between the first man and woman in Genesis, though primarily infers the importance of human fellowship in general, is nonetheless a marital relationship. The covenantal relationship between God and the nation of Israel is often described in marital languages. Although not all Christians ought to marry, every Christian is a member of the church – the bride of Christ, looking forward to the eschatological wedding. Marriage is thus the paradigm of the man-woman relationship, which in turn is the paradigm of all other human relationships. This implies that the marital relationship is at the center of all human relationships; a culture that fails to nurture good marital relationships would

---

9. Karl Barth, *Church Dogmatics, Vol. 3.4: The Doctrine of Creation*, eds. G. W. Bromiley and T. F. Torrance; trans. A. T. Mackay, T. H. L. Parker, H. Knight, H. A. Kennedy, and J. Marks (Peabody, MA: Hendrickson, 2010), 117, 240, 285.

10. Ibid., 140.

also struggle with other forms of human relationships. Studies show that a stable and harmonious spousal relationship is essential for good familial relationships and the wellbeing of children.[11] Flourishing marriages and families, in turn, contribute to the wellbeing of the society at large.[12]

However, the marital relationship in the contemporary world appears far from ideal. The rates of divorce and cohabitation among western nations rose sharply in the second half of the twentieth century, spawning much concern among scholars. For instance, Don Browning, leader of the Religion, Culture, and Family Project conducted in the 1990s, contends that the modern family is in crisis[13] and advocates a "worldwide revival and reconstruction of marriage."[14] Stephen Post also argues that recovering the traditional norm of stable marriage is imperative for the wellbeing of spouses, their children, and even society.[15] Yet not all concur with their assessment of the recent marital trends. John Gillis argues that despite the high rates of divorce and cohabitation in contemporary societies, people continue to live by the "conjugal ideal" and marriage retains a strong symbolic meaning. He points out that cohabitation is simply a strategy for modern couples to avoid the high costs and expectations associated with the traditional marriage. The prevalence of remarriage after divorce shows that marriage is still perceived as an important avenue to personal fulfillment. Therefore, the decline of the marriage institution does not indicate a deteriorating importance of the conjugal relationship. Gillis says that if the

---

11. John Coleman, "Parenting Teenagers," in *Contemporary Issues in Family Studies: Global Perspectives On Partnerships, Parenting and Support in a Changing World*, eds. Angela Abela and Janet Walker (Chichester, West Sussex: John Wiley & Sons, 2014), 210–211.

12. Nancy F. Cott writes: "Political ordering began in the household and influenced all governance and representation inside the household and out. Marriage itself served as a form of governance." *Public Vows: A History of Marriage and the Nation* (Cambridge, MA: Harvard University Press, 2002), 7.

13. Don S. Browning, *Equality and the Family: A Fundamental, Practical Theology of Children, Mothers, and Fathers in Modern Societies* (Grand Rapids, MI: Eerdmans, 2006), 53.

14. Don S. Browning, *Marriage and Modernization: How Globalization Threatens Marriage and What to Do About It* (Grand Rapids, MI: Eerdmans, 2003), 2.

15. Stephen G. Post, *More Lasting Unions: Christianity, the Family, and Society* (Grand Rapids, MI: Eerdmans, 2000), 5–8.

quality, not the form of the conjugal relationship is our main concern, then there is nothing alarming about the recent marital trends.[16]

Gillis suggests that the health of the marital relationship cannot simply be equated with the health of the marriage institution. In fact, some recent studies show that for countries where cohabitation is practiced widely, the stability and wellbeing of cohabitating couples is virtually the same as that of the married couples.[17] In some European countries, a declining rate of marriage coupled with an increasing rate of cohabitation implies that cohabitation is increasingly considered an acceptable alternative to marriage.[18] However, merely looking at marriage statistics does not give us the whole picture; an approach that surveys the quality of conjugal relationships is needed to assess the health of the marital relationship in the contemporary world. Paul Amato and Lydia Hayes conducted a study that compares married individuals living in the United States between 1980 and 2000. Over this two-decade period, the reported marital happiness remained constant yet the amount of shared activities between couples declined substantially. Now couples have fewer common friends with each other and are less likely to belong to the same clubs and organizations. Amato and Hayes call this kind of happy yet low-interaction marriage "alone together marriage." Since the increase in "alone together marriages" cannot be accounted for by factors such as the duration of marriage, the number of children, the amount of work hours, or the education level, they attribute this trend to general cultural shifts, in particular a shift toward individualism. In the contemporary individualistic culture, they argue, people increasingly emphasize self-development and personal fulfillment over companionship in conjugal relationships. Although couples in "alone together marriages" are often happy and satisfied, their unions tend to be unstable. The lack of shared interests and common friends means that they are likely to split if one or both fall out of love, or if their relationships no longer satisfy their

---

16. John R. Gillis, "Marriages of the Mind," *Journal of Marriage and Family* 66, no. 4 (Nov 2004): 989–990.

17. Jan Pryor, "Marriage and Divorce in the Western World," in *Contemporary Issues in Family Studies*, 50.

18. Turid Noack, Eva Bernhardt, and Kenneth Aarskaug Wiik, "Cohabitation or Marriage? Contemporary Living Arrangements in the West," in *Contemporary Issues in Family Studies*, 27.

personal needs.[19] Amato and Hayes also observe a parallel trend in Europe, where more couples who engage in intimate relationships choose to reside in separate places. While many consider this type of "living apart together" arrangement transitory, some couples consider it a long-lasting alternative to marital or non-marital cohabitation. "Living apart together" is especially attractive to older adults who have invested considerably into their own homes, have experienced divorce, or have responsibilities toward their own children or aging parents. These existing commitments and previous experiences discourage them from establishing shared residence with their new partners. Amato and Hayes suggest that "living apart together" is one feature of the Second Demographic Transition, a phenomenon first described by Ron Lesthaeghe.[20] The transition is characterized by sub-replacement fertility rates, multiple living arrangements besides marriage, splitting of procreation from marriage, and shrinking and aging populations.[21] These trends first emerged in the western countries in the 1950s and have now spread to the rest of the world.[22] The increase in "alone together marriage" and "living apart together" arrangements in recent decades implies that marital relationships have become more fragile and individuals are less likely to remain committed to each other when problems emerge.[23] Besides, recent trends in the western nations do not simply show a gradual replacement of marriage by other forms of conjugal arrangements. Fewer people are now living together as a couple due to more relationship break-ups and fewer people entering into co-residential relationships.[24] Studies also indicate that the quality of conjugal relationships – for both marriage and cohabitation relationships – do not grow strong but decline over time.[25] In

---

19. Paul R. Amato and Lydia H. Hayes, "'Alone Together' Marriages and 'Living Apart Together' Relationships," in *Contemporary Issues in Family Studies*, 32–37.

20. Ibid., 38–42.

21. Ron Lesthaeghe, "The Unfolding Story of the Second Demographic Transition," *Population and Development Review* 36, no. 2 (Jun 2010): 211.

22. Ibid., 244.

23. Amato and Hayes, "Alone Together," 43.

24. Noack, Bernhardt, and Wiik, "Cohabitation or Marriage?" 28.

25. Kelly Musick and Larry Bumpass, "Reexamining the Case for Marriage: Union Formation and Changes in Well-Being," *Journal of Marriage and Family* 74 (Feb 2012): 13.

summary, these studies show that not only is the traditional marriage being undermined, the quality of conjugal relationship is also deteriorating.

1.3 A Christian Response

This book attempts to offer a Christian response to the declining marital relationship. I concur with Amato and Hayes that cultural changes, in particular a shift toward individualism and the factors instrumental to the Second Demographic Transition, contribute to the deterioration. I contend that a moral vision that informs the relationship between man and woman is needed to counter these cultural shifts. My thesis is that this moral vision, based on Oliver O'Donovan's notion of moral order, is *Christ's love* as revealed in his life, death, resurrection, and exaltation.[26] As this love should be practiced by concrete persons living in the world, it must be formulated taking into account the contemporary culture. Lesthaeghe, a proponent of the Second Demographic Transition theory, states that "the motivation during the second transition is adult *self-realization* within the role or life style as a parent or more complete and fulfilled adult. This major shift is also propped up by the innovation of hormonal and other forms of *highly efficient contraception*."[27] Among the factors that contribute to the second transition, two stand out as prominent: "the rise of moral individual autonomy; [and] the availability of highly efficient contraception and enhanced female control over reproduction."[28] In other words, the image of autonomous individuals seeking personal fulfillment through the use of modern technology is characteristic of contemporary culture. Under this cultural climate,

---

26. See Oliver O'Donovan, *Resurrection and Moral Order: An Outline for Evangelical Ethics*, 2nd ed. (Grand Rapids, MI: Eerdmans, 1994).

27. Lesthaeghe, "Unfolding Story," 213. My emphasis.

28. Ron Lesthaeghe, "The Second Demographic Transition in Western Countries: An Interpretation," in *Gender and Family Change in Industrialized Countries*, eds. Karen Oppenheim Mason and An-Magritt Jensen (Oxford: Clarendon, 1995), 57. Davis and Friedman also write: "In his analysis of Western Europe's second demographic transition (SDT), Lesthhaeghe [sic] argued that the SDT was driven by a fundamental 'disconnection' between marriage and procreation supported by a cultural shift that endorsed 'individual autonomy and self-actualization.'" Deborah S. Davis and Sara L. Friedman, "Deinstitutionalizing Marriage and Sexuality," in *Wives, Husbands, and Lovers: Marriage and Sexuality in Hong Kong, Taiwan, and Urban China*, eds. Deborah Davis and Sara Friedman (Stanford, CA: Stanford University Press, 2014), 23.

people unwittingly perceive marital and familial relationships using the technological mindset and the liberal ideal of autonomy to the detriment of their relationships. Christian ethicists are not exempt from these cultural influences. For instance, the sexual ethics of Margaret Farley and Adrian Thatcher are influenced by the late-modern technoculture. Don Browning and his colleagues of the Religion, Culture, and Family Project embrace the ideals of liberalism and autonomous individuals in formulating their family ethics. Besides, Lesthaeghe observes that when a society undergoes a Second Demographic Transition, fundamentalist reactions often arise.[29] In American Evangelism, the complementarianism gender theory which evolved in the past several decades is one such fundamentalist response. To heed the cultural influences on marriage in the contemporary world, these three groups of Christian ethicists – those influenced by the technoculture, those embracing liberalism, and those advocating a fundamentalist reaction – have been selected as the dialogue partners of this book. It is through examining their sexual and familial ethics that the moral vision relevant to the contemporary culture is formulated.

Dialogue with these partners will begin from sex and gender, subjects that pertain to the relationship between man and woman. But as I argue below, sexual ethics is inseparable from marriage ethics, which in turn flows naturally into familial ethics.[30] My discussion that begins with sex and gender will eventually lead to the family and beyond. In fact, the focus of this book gradually shifts to the family as the discussions progress, and this book is concerned with the family as much as with man and woman. I concur with Brent Waters in defining the family as "a mutual and timely place of belonging" that "embodies the natural and social contours" of the relationships among its members.[31] The structure of the family serves as "both a means of safeguarding the nature of procreation, *and* the nature of familial association as a social sphere."[32] Waters points out that there is a procreative as well as a social dimension of the family. Lisa Sowle Cahill

---

29. Lesthaeghe, "Unfolding Story," 245.

30. See section 2.6.1.

31. Brent Waters, *The Family in Christian Social and Political Thought* (Oxford: Oxford University Press, 2007), 182.

32. Ibid., 183. Original emphasis.

chooses to emphasize the procreative dimension of the family and defines it as "an organized network of socioeconomic and reproductive interdependence and support grounded in biological kinship and marriage."[33] Thomas Breidenthal, meanwhile, stresses the social aspect of the family. He avoids the language of the "family" altogether and instead names the familial association a "household," defining it as a place where "two or three people [share] the daily round of life to a significant degree and over a significant period of time, whether the sharing is freely chosen or not."[34] I contend that both the biological and social aspects of the family should be kept in balance; one should not dictate the family discourse nor be neglected altogether. In the book, I assign no distinction between the words "family" and "household" and use them interchangeably.

A word should be said about the social background and the target audience for the book. As mentioned, in my discussions I engage with the late-modern technoculture and liberalism that contribute to the Second Demographic Transition. Consequently, all societies that are going through this transition are my target audience. As a Chinese born in Hong Kong, who spent the majority of my life there, I have this particular city in mind as I write. Similar to other industrialized regions, Hong Kong also shows signs of the Second Demographic Transition.[35] Following the trends of North America and Europe, Hong Kong is transitioning into a society with "a higher age at first marriage, fewer barriers to divorce, declining marital fertility, and greater social acceptance of premarital, extramarital, and same-sex intimate relationships."[36] In recent decades, a higher percentage of both men and women obtained postsecondary education, and the dual-income family gradually replaced the male-breadwinning family as the main family model.[37] Studies show that gender equality in the city has

---

33. Lisa Sowle Cahill, *Family: A Christian Social Perspective* (Minneapolis, MN: Fortress, 2000), x–xi.

34. Thomas E. Breidenthal, *Christian Households: The Sanctification of Nearness* (Cambridge, MA: Cowley, 1997), 2.

35. Lesthaeghe, "Unfolding Story," 234–236.

36. Davis and Friedman, "Deinstitutionalizing Marriage," 3.

37. Kwok-fai Ting, "Continuities and Changes: Five Decades of Marital Experiences in Hong Kong," in *Wives, Husbands, and Lovers: Marriage and Sexuality in Hong Kong, Taiwan, and Urban China*, 147–150.

improved significantly over the past several decades with the implementation of anti-discriminatory laws, equal opportunity to education and work, and the transition from manufacturing to financial and service industries.[38] Although traditional Chinese patriarchy still exerts influence in certain social locations, the city has moved from a traditional patriarchal society to a generally egalitarian society. Therefore, gender equality – equal dignity between the sexes and no fixed gender division of labor – is presupposed in my discussions. But the assumption and rhetoric of gender equality alone is inadequate. In a recent study that examines the perspectives of Hong Kong men on gender relationships, interviewees feel that they need to relate to women in ways different from their fathers. They use the discourse of "gender equality" to establish their identity against their patriarchal predecessors and also to try to meet the social expectations and act responsibly toward women. At the same time they seek to realize their own personal desires against the rising status of women. These different desires contradict one another, with the result that some men develop a sense of bitterness toward women, become involved in multiple sexual relationships, or avoid marrying altogether.[39] Another study reveals that Hong Kong women with high educational and professional achievements find it more difficult to seek a partner or to have children even if they hope to do so.[40] The experiences of these women and men in Hong Kong show that the rhetoric and attainment of gender equality alone is not adequate for sexual ethics. As man and woman are not merely duplicates or mirror images of each other, gender and marital ethics must address the differences between the sexes. One purpose of this book is to address these differences under the purview of gender equality. Although this book does not aim to offer specific recommendations directed toward the matters in Hong Kong discussed above, the notion of Christ's love developed in this book will, nevertheless,

---

38. See Eliza W. Y. Lee, *Gender and Change in Hong Kong: Globalization, Postcolonialism, and Chinese Patriarchy* (Honolulu, HI: University of Hawaii Press, 2003); Katherine P. H. Young, *Understanding Marriage: A Hong Kong Case Study* (Hong Kong: Hong Kong University Press, 1995), 122.

39. Petula Sik Ying Ho, "An Embarrassment of Riches: Good Men Behaving Badly in Hong Kong," in *Wives, Husbands, and Lovers: Marriage and Sexuality in Hong Kong, Taiwan, and Urban China*, 182–183.

40. Ann Brooks, *Gendered Work in Asian Cities: The New Economy and Changing Labour Markets* (Hampshire, UK: Ashgate, 2006), 92–94.

shed light on how we conceive of the man-woman relationship in our contemporary world.

1.4 Chapter Outline

After this introductory chapter, chapter 2 presents a dialogue with Farley and Thatcher. Both of their sexual ethics are influenced by the late-modern technoculture, a culture characterized by the will to master over human and nonhuman nature. I argue that their theories are predicated upon a mind-body *dualism* that subjugates the body under the superior mind. The resulting sexual ethics undermine the biological and procreative dimension of the family and jeopardize the flourishing of human persons as concrete men and women. Instead of a *dualism*, I argue that the mind-body relationship should be conceived of as a *duality*. Recovering the importance of the body suggests that sex should not be severed from procreation and the conception of gender should be linked to, but not dictated by, the biological characteristics of the sexes.

In chapter 3, Browning's critical familism is examined. While his family ethics rightly emphasize procreation and gender differences, the weakness in his position stems from conceiving the family as a liberal democracy where members are free to enter and exit in accordance with their desire for personal fulfillment. As a result, the "equal-regard" ethics that Browning advocates cannot be reconciled with his aim of encouraging family cohesion for the sake of children. Undergirding his theory is the assumption that persons are discrete individuals who resist associating with one another. In other words, a split, or *dualism*, is assumed between man and woman so that their relationship is intrinsically antagonistic. From the notion of "one-flesh union," I argue that man and woman are in original union; they should be conceived of as persons occupying different poles of a single *duality*. Instead of an agglomeration of discrete individuals, the family should be conceived of as a community that arises from the outflow of love between the couple who are called by God into marital union.

In chapter 4, I dialogue with the fundamentalist gender theory of complementarianism. While this theory affirms that marriage and family are a matter of God's calling, advocates of complementarianism err in elevating roles and functions as the definitive aspect of familial relationships. As a result, one particular form of gender expression – the breadwinner-homemaker gender division of labor – is hailed as divinely ordained and universal. Complementarianism therefore abstracts gender relationships from the concrete economic and political circumstances in which people live. It is predicated upon a split, or *dualism*, between individuals and their culture and community. Besides, redemption in complementarianism is a return to the original creation instead of a fulfillment of God's creation in the eschaton. The lack of eschatology in their theory precludes any free expression of gender roles, rendering the ethics incapable of responding to the changing culture. The dialogue with complementarianism suggests that sex and family ethics should heed the *duality* between the individual and the community, as well as the *duality* between the present age and the future eschaton.

I contend that the *dualities* developed in chapters 2–4 constitute the *framework* for gender ethics. They form the boundary beyond which gender and family ethics should not transgress. A *moral vision* within the framework that informs marital and familial relationships is needed. My thesis is that *Christ's love* is this moral vision. In chapter 5, I formulate this notion of love through another series of dialogue with the three groups of conversation partners. I argue that friendship, incarnational love, and unfolding love – as conceived of in the life, death, resurrection, and exaltation of Christ – are aspects of Christ's love pertinent to the different familial relationships. Through practicing these different aspects of Christ's love in the family, Christians bear witness to Christ vis-à-vis one another and in front of the world. The family is a "school of love" in which members are trained to practice Christ's love. As all familial relationships are special relationships where mutuality is the *telos* of these relationships, the family is inadequate and must be complemented by the eschatological community of the church where the disinterested love of agape is practiced.

In chapter 6, I interpret the Ephesian household code (Eph 5:21–6:9) using the concept of Christ's love developed in the book. I first argue that any adequate attempt to apply the household code to our contemporary world requires a notion of Christ's love. Then the notions of friendship, incarnational love, and unfolding love are used to interpret the texts and to draw out moral implications relevant for today. This hermeneutical exercise enhances our understanding of the household code, and clarifies and enriches the meanings of the different aspects of Christ's love.

CHAPTER 2

Uniformity between Man and Woman

In contemporary ethical discussions concerning the relationship between man and woman, some ethicists are apprehensive about accentuating sexual differences. Two main reasons underlie their apprehension. First, it is assumed that underscoring sexual difference leads to gender essentialism and a strengthening of the existing patriarchal structures. Second, it is believed that reifying biological differences implies fixed forms of sexual expressions and is detrimental to human freedom. As a result, these ethicists avoid explicit discussions of sexual differences; in their sexual ethics, man and woman are assumed to be more or less uniform. In this chapter, I examine the sexual ethics of two such Christian ethicists: Margaret Farley from the Roman Catholic background and Adrian Thatcher of the Anglican tradition. First, I will introduce their views of human personhood and sexuality. Then I will explore how these views contribute to their sexual ethics. I argue that the late-modern mind-body *dualism*, where the body is subjugated under the superior mind, undergirds their theories. It is demonstrated that sexual ethics that do not respect the body are inadequate. Finally, a theological assessment of their sexual ethics is offered, giving directions and guidelines for the construction of sexual ethics in chapter 5. To counter mind-body *dualism*, I suggest that Gilbert Meilaender's notion of *duality* should instead characterize the relationship between the mind and the body.

2.1 Farley: Personhood as Self-Transcendence

The sexual ethics of Margaret Farley aims at human flourishing. In an essay written in 1983, she identified four major problems that jeopardize human flourishing within the modern western family: (1) family violence;

(2) "structural" problems such as gender roles and absent parent; (3) family breakdown and the escalating rate of divorce; and (4) connection between family and society.[1] She discussed the issue of family breakdown in her book, *Personal Commitments: Beginning, Keeping, Changing*, first published in 1986.[2] She investigates the necessity and meaning of commitments, as well as the grounds to remain in or to secede from obligations. She proposes the notion of "just love" as the principle of sexual ethics, and she further explicates this notion in *Just Love: A Framework for Christian Sexual Ethics*.[3] In this latter work, her discussion is broadened to include sexuality, patterns of relationships, gender, and social justice.

Experience plays an important role in Farley's moral thinking. Although other sources such as Scripture, tradition, and secular disciplines all inform Christian ethics, she argues that experience is the most important as it contributes significantly to each of these sources and is a key factor in using and interpreting them.[4] For sexual ethics, Farley contends that we should start with the body, as it is more basic than sex or gender. Focusing on the body through experience leads to an awareness of the mind or the spirit,[5] for "humans are complex beings who experience themselves as bodies but not only as bodies, as spirits but not only as spirits." We are "embodied spirits" and "inspirited bodies;" mind and body are unified yet distinguishable.[6] Embodiment is thus an essential aspect of human nature. Yet a closer look at her discussions reveals that the relationship between mind and body is rather unequal. She argues that human embodiment is "transcendent" embodiment; human beings need to self-transcend, to be potentially more

---

1. Margaret A. Farley, "The Church and the Family: An Ethical Task," *Horizons* 10, no. 1 (Mar 1983): 52.

2. Margaret A. Farley, *Personal Commitments: Beginning, Keeping, Changing*, rev. ed. (Maryknoll, NY: Orbis, 2013). First edition by Harper & Row, 1986.

3. Margaret A. Farley, *Just Love: A Framework for Christian Sexual Ethics* (New York: Continuum, 2006).

4. Margaret A. Farley, "The Role of Experience in Moral Discernment," in *Christian Ethics: Problems and Prospects*, eds. Lisa S. Cahill and James F. Childress (Cleveland, OH: Pilgrim, 1996), 135–136.

5. Different writers use different words to denote the non-bodily aspect of human nature, such as "spirit," "soul," and "mind." I do not distinguish between these words; they are used interchangeably to describe the same non-bodily aspect.

6. Farley, *Just Love*, 116.

than what they are. This self-transcendence is expressed in two ways: "free choice" and "relationships to others." While "free choice" means self-determination and the capacity to bring something new, "relationships to others" means opening up the self to others.[7] Farley acknowledges that these two expressions of transcendence are normally associated with the mind and not the body, but she argues that free choice entails action and relationships involve the body, so they are also bodily expressions. She further explains:

> Whatever transcendence is ascribed to the spirit, then, must also be ascribed to body – for they are intimately one. There are boundaries to transcendence; there *are* "givens" that we cannot transcend – whether biological, ontological, or socially constructed – and we remain human throughout. Yet we not only yearn to become what we imagine we can yet be; we choose to become what we want to be.[8]

This statement appears to assign parity to the body and the spirit; both are ascribed transcendence. However, it is difficult to see how the body can transcend itself by "yearning," "imagining," "choosing," and "becoming." In the end, it is the mind that imagines, yearns, chooses, becomes, and opens up the self for relationships. As the body is "intimately one" with the mind, it must then tag along with whatever the mind chooses. The body is still important; without it, we cannot become what we want to be. Yet the mind-body unity is more fitfully described as a partnership where the mind decides and the body follows.

It is quite natural for Farley to arrive at this mind-body relationship since her theory of embodiment is based solely on experience. The relationship between a human being and her experience is that all her experiences are received through her body and interpreted by her mind. Upon interpreting the experiences, the mind makes decisions to be carried out by the body. When experience is the sole basis of a theory, only the functions of the constituents stand out. The instrumental nature of the body and the interpretive nature of the mind dominate the theory. A unity of body

---

7. Ibid., 128–130.
8. Ibid., 130. Original emphasis.

and mind then becomes a unity of receptor and processor of experiences, as well as a unity of maker and executor of decisions. The body is then perceived of as an instrument to receive experience for the mind, as well as a means to carry out actions, also for the mind. The body is always instrumental, serving the mind.[9] An instrumental view of the body also means that the body only exists to perform functions but has no intrinsic worth. The good of the body is totally dependent on and a derivative of the mind. Therefore, the body is *necessary* for human existence, but it is not *good* in itself. To attain human flourishing – the good of self-transcendence, the mind must then navigate around the bodily necessity and limitation. As the body does not offer a vision of the good, it cannot participate in moral deliberations. The body then becomes silent.

Silencing of the body is reflected in Farley's view on the relationship between man and woman. As mentioned above, one issue she addresses is divorce, which prompts her to contemplate the meaning of personal commitments. She thinks that making commitments is difficult, as it entails letting go of other possible desires and actions, limiting our future freedom.[10] This is antithetical to being a human being, as Farley considers that freedom is at the "center of . . . personality."[11] She recognizes that when a man and a woman fall in love, they desire to commit themselves to each other and form an enduring relationship. It is almost impossible, however, for them to stay together for a long period of time, as human relationships are fragile.[12] The problem arises when love between them expires. Without the motivation of love, they would find it difficult to keep their commitment to one another. Farley contends that if love is purely spontaneous and uncontrollable, then they can do little about it. Yet she thinks that love can be directed by free choice. Love is both active – affirming the other – and passive – responding to the lovableness of the other. We can certainly

---

9. One may argue that our mind also wishes to serve our body. An example is that we often desire bodily comfort. But if we focus on experience alone, bodily comfort becomes an experience. Our desire for bodily comfort is our desire for pleasant experiences to be received by the body and interpreted or "enjoyed" by the mind. The body still serves the mind.

10. Farley, *Personal Commitments*, 22–23.

11. Ibid., 35.

12. Farley, "Church and the Family," 68.

will and direct the active part, but the passive part is not entirely out of our control. Whether the other is lovable can be influenced by the free choice of the lover, as a person can choose to attend to whichever reality she wants. She can choose to discover and believe in the lovableness of the other, or she can choose to blind herself from this reality. Love is therefore a matter of choice within the power of freedom, so is the keeping of commitment that is predicated upon the presence of love.[13] Another reason couples drift apart, according to Farley, is their failure to hold onto past promises. The issue is not just the partners' forgetfulness of their promises, but that their relationship keeps changing over time. Yet she argues that how we are changed can again be affected by our own choice: "insofar as I make choices about my love, including choices to remember and to hope in 'us' – in our relationship, its past and its future – I change myself and the meaning of the relationship."[14] In the end, how we exercise our free choice can have a real influence on our love and how we keep commitments. It is notable that in her discussions on personal commitments, the focus is purely on freedom and choice, an exercise of the mind. The body is silent in the whole conversation. Underlying her discussion, the body is necessary. She argues that the passive aspect of love is a response to the "lovableness" of the other. This "lovableness" is experienced, and the body must be present as an instrument to receive the experience. She also says that our love is awakened by the "original vision" of beauty. The way to keep love alive is not to will oneself to love but to "keep seeing . . . keep looking . . . keep watching."[15] Experience – and the body – is again involved. Although the body is not mentioned in her contemplation, it is nevertheless important as experience is crucial for one to make free choices. Consistent with her view of embodiment, the body only serves an instrumental function. The body is *necessary*, but it does not offer a vision of the *good* in keeping the marriage commitment. Therefore, it does not need to speak.

When we compare Farley's thinking on marriage commitment and Aquinas's discussions on the indissolubility of marriage, her silencing of the body becomes conspicuous. Aquinas gives seven reasons why the marriage

---

13. Farley, *Personal Commitments*, 39–42.
14. Ibid., 74.
15. Ibid., 62, 69.

bond should not be broken. First, human infants are fragile and require long periods to mature. Their survival depends on the cooperation of both parents, who must then stay together for the good of procreation.[16] Second, divorce leads to injustice to the wife. Third, the man needs to be certain that the woman's children are biologically his for him to invest in them. This need for paternal certainty demands indissoluble monogamous marriages. Fourth, the longer the couple stays together, the better the friendship between them. Fifth, by staying together, the couple can help each other in their daily life. Sixth, the indissoluble union between Christ and the church represents the marriage union, thus marriage bonds should not be broken. Seventh, indissolubility encourages constant mutual love and good household conducts.[17] It must be recognized that Farley and Aquinas write under very different contexts and many of Aquinas's reasons are no longer applicable today. For instance, the much more egalitarian culture today renders Aquinas's argument about divorce causing injustice to the woman obsolete. Besides, longer marriages do not necessarily entail better relationships. Now we often observe the opposite of what Aquinas thinks: the longer a couple stays together, the worse their friendship becomes. This is exactly what prompts Farley to contemplate on keeping commitments. Despite the contextual differences between Aquinas and Farley, they share the same approach to ethics. Their ethics are both teleological, aiming at human flourishing. The *telos* of marriage, for Aquinas, involves both spiritual and bodily dimensions. Among his seven reasons for the indissolubility of marriages, the good of procreation, the need for paternal certainty, and the benefit of mutual assistance in daily living are directed towards the body. Meanwhile, the *telos* of marriage for Farley only involves the spiritual dimension; she looks at committed relationships only through the lens of human self-transcendence. This skews her discussions toward free choice and relationality, and her concern becomes narrower. Her discussions of personal commitment only touch on two out of seven of Aquinas's concerns: friendship and mutual love. Despite her emphasis on embodiment,

---

16. Thomas Aquinas, *Summa Contra Gentiles*, trans. Dominican Fathers (London: Burns Oates & Washbourne, 1928), 3, ii, 112–113.

17. Ibid., 115–117.

Farley's experiential approach in fact leads to the exclusion of the body from moral deliberation.

Perhaps it is their distinctive cultural contexts that bring about the differences between Aquinas and Farley. North America in late-modernity is drastically different from medieval Europe in many respects, and multiple factors contribute to the differences in their discussions. If we focus on Aquinas's arguments on marriage permanence pertaining to the body, it becomes obvious that modern technology is the major driving force behind the cultural shift from the middle-ages to late-modernity. Technology radically eases the hardship of daily living and childrearing. Now the father is not always physically or economically needed for a child to survive and grow up. As a result, paternal certainty and mutual assistance are no longer reasons for married couples to stay together. The availability of contraception and abortion can even eliminate any concern the couple has about procreation, and Aquinas's arguments for marriage indissolubility that grow out of the body are no longer applicable today. All that is left to think about are the spiritual aspects such as friendship and love. The influence of modern technology extends deeper than freeing the mind from the limitations of the body. George Grant says that we are a "technological civilisation [sic]" in a way that we encompass and are encompassed by technology.[18] Modern technology gives us a new account of knowing and making. In pre-modern civilizations, science aims at knowledge. In modernity, knowing and making have conflated – or "co-penetrated" – into a single notion. *To know* entails *to make*. If a law of physics is discovered, we ought to use it to master over nature; when a new species is discovered, we should investigate what it can offer for the benefit for human beings. This mode of thinking also permeates into the knowledge of ourselves.[19] The human genome project, an aggressive attempt to understand human nature, is a milestone on our way to conquer diseases. Modern economics, argues Jacques Ellul, serves to regulate human behavior.[20] When human biology and psychology become sciences, the ideal of scientific and technological

---

18. George Grant, *Technology and Justice* (Concord, Ontario: House of Anansi, 1986), 11.

19. Ibid., 13–16.

20. See Jacques Ellul, *The Technological Society* (New York: Vintage, 1964).

mastery straddles both nonhuman and human natures.[21] Under this technological paradigm of knowledge and mastery, the mind that knows must maintain a certain distance from the objects that are known and mastered. This mode of thinking also influences how we conceive of the mind-body relationship: in order to control the body, the mind first splits itself from the body then elevates itself above it. Human nature, including our body, is lowered to the same category as nonhuman nature. Consequently, the technological mindset not only frees the mind from limitations of the body, it also subjugates the body to the superior mind. Yet the body remains important – not in itself but as an instrument to serve the mind. Despite Farley's insistence on the importance of the body, her theory of body and gender reflects a late-modern ideal of mind-body dualism. Brent Waters offers a succinct description of the late-modern subjectivity which aptly characterizes Farley's view of personhood:

> [The] self is premised on two requisite qualities. First, there must be a sufficient means for obtaining experiential input. This is achieved through the various senses. Hence [late-moderns] are sensually embodied. Second, there must also be a sufficient means for interpreting, expressing and assigning value to experiential inputs. This is achieved through various cognitive abilities. Hence [late-moderns] are embodied minds.[22]

"Sensually embodied" and "embodied minds" are fitful descriptions of Farley's notion of embodiment. Her sexual ethic is predicated upon a late-modern mind-body dualism which assigns instrumental value to the body and recognizes the sensual or experiential importance of the body. For matters of sexual ethics, the mind is to make decisions for its own flourishing though the decisions must heed the limitations of the body.

One corollary of this mind-body dualism is to conceive of gender as having no biological or bodily basis. It should be noted that gender, as a cultural phenomenon, is a construction of the individual mind or the collective culture. The issue here is whether gender construction has a

---

21. George Grant, *Technology and Empire* (Concord, Ontario: House of Anansi, 1969), 115–116.

22. Brent Waters, *From Human to Posthuman: Christian Theology and Technology in a Postmodern World* (Burlington, VT: Ashgate, 2006), 33.

biological basis or not. Farley argues that the presence of intersexuals – people of ambiguous sexual identity – destabilizes the traditional view that gender is based on biological difference.[23] As gender is not related to biology, its construction is free from the body and can enhance flourishing of the mind. Gender should not be used to set men against women, to restrict them into prescribed roles, or to differentiate their rights. Gender only matters when we are struggling against the problems of gender, and when it serves to bring in different experiences in human relationships.[24] When gender hampers human flourishing, we can eliminate it as it is a construction of the mind to begin with. For instance, when intersexuals are forced to conform to the binary sexual division, much harm is done to them. A culture less preoccupied with gender differentiation would be more congenial to their flourishing.[25] Farley's notion of "just love" is also devoid of sexual difference. She argues that love alone should not be the norm for sexual ethics, for love can be wise or foolish, good or bad. Love must be supplemented with justice. Love is "just" when "it is a true response to the reality of the beloved, a genuine union between the one who loves and the one loved, and an accurate and adequate affective affirmation of the beloved." Simply put, the beloved should be loved as a "*person,* not a *thing.*"[26] To love a person "as a person" is to attend to and affirm her "concrete reality." Although Farley includes bodily needs and existential contexts into a person's "concrete reality," she highlights two features of human personhood as "basic:" *autonomy* and *relationality.*[27] Autonomy means that a person has the capacity for free choice. Relationality points to one's capacity to reach beyond oneself to other persons. It is the capacity to transcend oneself and "radically open" oneself through knowing and loving others.[28] Again, aspects of the body are absent in these "basic features" of personhood. Our existence as male or female need not enter the discussion, as bodily difference does not affect how autonomy and relationality are understood. These

---

23. Farley, *Just Love*, 149.
24. Ibid., 156–158.
25. Ibid., 151.
26. Ibid., 198. Original emphasis.
27. Ibid., 211. Original emphasis.
28. Ibid., 212–213.

two features of human personhood find parallels in her dual expression of "transcendent embodiment" mentioned earlier: free choice and relationships to others. Therefore, Farley's view of human flourishing, whether starting from the experience of the body or from contemplating the relationship between persons, gravitates toward the exercise of free choice and expression of relationality. These two features, while requiring the body for experiential input and execution of free choice, are essentially exercises of the mind. How Farley's emphasis on the self-transcendence and the delinking of gender from biology influence her sexual ethics will be examined later. I will now turn to the Anglican theologian Adrian Thatcher and his theory of personhood.

2.2 Thatcher: Personhood as Love

Thatcher shares with Farley an experiential approach to sexual ethics and an emphasis on embodiment.[29] Unlike Farley who draws significantly on resources from social and cultural studies, he uses explicit theological language to discuss the body and human personhood. He recovers the importance of the body through countering "dualisms" in the western traditions. The different conceptions of dualisms in ancient Greek and Christian thoughts, he says, lead to rationalism, androcentrism, patriarchy, and the disparagement of the body and sexuality. The incarnation and eucharistic presence of Christ counters this dualism and affirms the holiness of the physical and the body. Christ's incarnation does not confine God's revelation in the human figure of Jesus but enables us to encounter God through the body. Therefore, bodily experience is a source of spirituality and the body becomes an avenue to commune with God.[30] Trinitarian theology expresses that God is relational and the divine persons are in loving relationships. Human persons take on this relationality and are summoned to share in this loving life of God.[31] At the center of human personhood is love – not human love that is prone to fail, but God's love. Although agape

---

29. Adrian Thatcher, *Liberating Sex: A Christian Sexual Theology* (London: SPCK, 1993), 12.
30. Ibid., 30–44.
31. Ibid., 52–53.

is usually associated with divine love, it is not the only form of divine love. In fact, an over-emphasis on agape has resulted in its distortion and abuse, leading to oppression of the powerless. Friendship and eros, or desire, also belong to God's love and can balance the misuse of agape. God's love is "a blend of agape and eros together."[32] Yet this "blend" of love, in Thatcher's later discussions, seems to be dominated by eros. In his recent book, *God, Sex, and Gender: An Introduction*, he builds a theology of sex and gender entirely out of desire – our desire for God, God's desire for us, and our desire for one another. Thatcher distinguishes between the constructive and destructive sides of desire. Lust – an inordinate enjoyment of pleasure – and greed – wanting what is not ours – are harmful to the self, the one desired, and the society and must be avoided. But it is wrong to over-emphasize the negative side of desire and equate desire with evil or sin, for the constructive side of desire lies within the fabric of the created world, even within God. This desire does not arise out of lack, for God lacks nothing. Instead, it comes from a yearning for union with the object of desire, as God desires us. Thatcher substantiates this claim by arguing that *Song of Songs* in Scripture reveals that God desires to unite with us. Furthermore, this constructive side of desire, even for God, is intricately linked with the material and the body. In Christ's incarnation, God is shown to communicate through a human body to other human bodies. God's desire for us, the healthy side of desire which we are invited to share, is expressed through the body.[33] Now since we are called to share in God's love as desire, and since God expresses this desire through the body, human personhood is founded upon an expression and reception of desire through the body. How do we express and receive this desire? Here Thatcher makes a crucial claim: we do it through sex. As love desires the beloved, desire longs for union, and union is expressed in the body; then love is necessarily sexual. Thus, he approvingly quotes Mario Costa: "the relationship between the gods and humans is an erotic one."[34] Thatcher suggests that if we think of God and humanity not through their differences and oppositions but through their

---

32. Ibid., 59–60.
33. Adrian Thatcher, *God, Sex, and Gender: An Introduction* (Chichester, West Sussex: Wiley-Blackwell, 2011), 57–74.
34. Ibid., 66.

relationship, we can say that God also desires bodily and sexual union with human beings. He substantiates this claim by arguing that the Eucharist resembles love making. They both involve the giving and receiving of one's body. Similar to consuming the bread and wine in the Eucharist, sexual intimacy also implicates the eating of the body of the beloved, while participants rejoice in the sensations of taste and smell. The Eucharist is in fact God's erotic communion with human beings. In the same say, God incarnates in our physical expressions of love with one another.[35]

Recovering the importance of the body, for Thatcher, means that sexual expression and intimacy should be at the center of human personhood. Yet it does not mean that we must heed the body as a *given* biological entity. Although sexual expression is crucial for human beings, "[how] men and women think about their relations with each other should not be based on biology, and when appeals to biology are made, the inferences drawn are likely to be misleading."[36] He is correct to point out that biological difference has been abused to subjugate women, and he thinks that the solution should be to eliminate bodily difference from sexual ethics. Instead of viewing humanity as a polarity of two sexes – male and female, we should think of all human beings as belonging to one sex. This "one sex" does not mean a fixed biological entity but a "single continuum." The biological sex of male and female occupies the opposite ends of this spectrum, with intersex and transgender people located between the two ends. To think of everyone belonging to this "one-sex" spectrum means that there is no sexual difference but only gender difference. Gender is only a cultural construct which has no biological basis. The advantage of the "one-sex" model, contends Thatcher, is that we can always deconstruct and reconstruct gender, and thus we are not limited by biology but can decide what we want to become.[37] This "one-sex" model does not attempt to sever gender from sex; Thatcher does not deny that gender is somehow linked with sex.[38] Instead, the model tries to disconnect sex from biology, thus freeing gender from

---

35. Adrian Thatcher, *Liberating Sex: A Christian Sexual Theology* (London: SPCK, 1993) 89–90.
36. Thatcher, *God, Sex, and Gender*, 18.
37. Ibid., 10–13.
38. Ibid., 21.

biology. However, this "one-sex" model is logically inconsistent. The notion of sex is predicated upon the presence of male and female. Without the distinction between male and female in biology, there would not be the notion of sex. Differences in biology associated with the human reproductive function necessarily entail the notion of sex: faced with this biological difference, human beings need to name it, and sex is the notion assigned to this existential phenomenon. Thatcher's "one-sex" model, while predicated upon the notion of sex, attempts to eliminate the notion of sex itself. It other words, it presumes the notion of sex based on biological difference, then it turns a blind eye on it and argues for the disappearance of this very biological difference in thinking about sex. This is why the name "one-sex" is logically inconsistent. Perhaps a more fitting name would be "one-type" model, where all human beings belong to a single "type," whether they are biologically male, female, or others. By replacing "sex" with "type," the notion of sex still remains, albeit within the overarching "type." An alternative would be to conceive of a "multi-sex" model. For instance, Anne Fausto-Sterling suggests a "five-sex" model based on genital configuration, including true, pseudo-male, and pseudo-female hermaphrodites in additional to the traditional male and female sexes. This would challenge and destabilize the male-female binary model.[39] Neither alternative will do for Thatcher, though, because naming the model "one-type" or "multi-sex" does not eliminate the notion of sex as based on biology. Yet no matter what language we use to describe the phenomenon of sexual difference, the concept of sex is always present and is firmly related to biology. Elaine Graham, upon surveying an array of anthropological, biological, and sociology theories on gender, concludes that a balanced view of gender should consider biology, social conditioning, and individual consciousness as intertwined in its formation. Although it is difficult to differentiate between these elements, we must recognize the importance of each in describing each specific cultural construction of gender. A "dialectical account of

---

39. Anne Fausto-Sterling, *Sexing the Body: Gender Politics and the Construction of Sexuality* (New York: Basic Books, 2000), 78–79.

gender" should be adopted.[40] If she is correct, Thatcher's view of gender ignores the biological factor and is inadequate.

The philosopher Roger Scruton also argues for a biological basis of gender. He defines sex – the biological distinction between male and female – as the "material concept of sexuality" and gender as the "intentional concept of sexuality." These two concepts must not be confused. Gender, a construction, should not be entirely based on sex, a given. Otherwise the phenomenon of gender would be reduced to biology and become deterministic. This reduction has been proven wrong by experience and the different and sometimes disparate cultural expressions of gender. Yet the construction of gender is not entirely arbitrary. He points out the two semantic meanings of gender: first, it is the concept by which we understand sex, and second, it is the artifact we construct in response to this understanding.[41] The second meaning – gender as artifact – is firmly rooted in the first meaning – our understanding of sex, which is predicated upon biology. He then demonstrates the connection through our experience as embodied sexual beings. In the experience of sexual desire, he contends, a person is "overwhelmed . . . by his [sic] sex. It is this bodily condition which comes to the surface, and which takes command of him [sic]."[42] In these instances of sexual desire we are nearly indistinguishable from animals and our existence as embodied creatures becomes evident. This animal nature of ours, this biology that marks our body, reminds us of the physiology that divides male from female, man from woman. As embodied beings, we are inseparable from our sex. Gender is our response to this sexual difference experienced from sexual desire and sexual act, and is our intentional construction that separates us from the animals. Exactly because we are not animals, we experience ourselves not just as a "self" but also as a "moral kind" in sexual intercourse. Social mores and behavior are developed to redeem ourselves from the arbitrariness of animalistic sexual desire. These mores and behavioral patterns are culturally dependent, and contribute

---

40. Elaine L. Graham, *Making the Difference: Gender, Personhood, and Theology* (Minneapolis, MN: Fortress, 1996), 90–91.

41. Roger Scruton, *Sexual Desire: A Moral Philosophy of the Erotic* (New York: Free Press, 1986), 254–258.

42. Ibid., 265.

to the specific construction of gender. While sex is common to all animals including human beings, gender is unique to humanity. Gender is an "elaborate prelude" to sex, and is also the revelation of sex which, as human beings distinct from animals, must be hidden from sight. This revelation takes the form of gendered clothing observed in all traditional cultures and, more recently, is taken up by the body when men and women shape themselves into sexually appealing bodies. Men and women also develop separate characters, separate virtues and vices, and separate social roles. When the layers of gender phenomena are peeled off, what is disclosed is sex.[43] Our gender perception arises from our experience of sexual desire and the sexual act, which are universal experiences. But gender is not determined by it. Hence, the *conception* of gender is cultural-specific but the *concept* of gender is universal, for the biological distinction between male and female is universal. Although the conception of gender varies from culture to culture, each conception is never arbitrary as it is based on the culture's understanding of sex, a phenomenon that is universal.

Both Scruton and Thatcher develop their views of sex and gender from experience, in particular, from the experience of sexual intimacy. Thatcher concludes with a "one-sex" model that delinks gender from biology but Scruton insists that gender arises from biology, though not determined by it. It is worth seeing what contributes to this difference. Embodiment, for Thatcher, is important as the body is crucial to the expression of love as desire, the center of human personhood. We attain personhood through sexual intimacy. Yet biology is not important as long as a person can experience sex. The body as male or female only means that a person occupies a certain location confined within a single "one-sex" spectrum beyond which biology is unimportant. The body should not break away from this confinement and enter into the realm of gender construction. In other words, bodily difference is an *adiaphora* – a matter of indifference – in gender and sexual ethics. Scruton, meanwhile, does not start from love but from the embodied experience of sexual intimacy. In this embodied experience, we recognize our animal nature. As human beings, we transcend this nature through gender construction. Human transcendence is not freedom from

---

43. Ibid., 265–269.

the body but is founded upon the very nature of the body. Gender is not constructed solely by our free will or free choice but must be constructed through attentive listening to the body. Thus the body is significant in gender and sexual ethics. This comparison shows that despite Thatcher's emphasis on embodiment, he does not really listen to the experience of the body in sexual intimacy. Instead, his primary concern is love, an aspect of the soul yet requiring the experience of the body. The body serves as an indispensable instrument in the performance and experience of sexual intimacy. This notion of the body is strikingly similar to that of Farley's. For both, the body is an instrument to receive experience for the soul and to carry out actions, also for the soul. While Farley locates the center of personhood in self-determination and relationality, Thatcher locates it in love as desire for union. Both place human personhood on aspects of the mind. Both see the body as necessary, but neither allows the body to speak in its own terms in gender construction or moral deliberation. Waters's description of late-moderns as "sensually embodied" and "embodied minds" also characterizes Thatcher's theory. Underlying Thatcher's rhetoric of embodiment is, again, a late-modern mind-body dualism not unlike Farley's. While he tries to counter the "dualisms" with his notion of embodied personhood, his own thinking is plagued with the mind-body dualism that silences the body.

2.3 Sexual Ethics of Farley: Coming Together of Minds

Both Farley and Thatcher attempt to retrieve the Christian traditions in their construction of sexual ethics in the late-modern context. Traditions of the church, they claim, need not be abandoned but should be revised vis-à-vis the changing culture, scientific discoveries, and modern technology. One common argument between them is that they both advocate for some form of framework or institution such as marriage as applicable to today's sexual relationships, although others have abandoned marriage as archaic or hopelessly patriarchal.[44] Our discussions show that their views of

---

44. See Adrian Thatcher, *Marriage after Modernity: Christian Marriage in Postmodern Times* (New York: New York University Press, 1999), 61–66; Farley, *Just Love*, 260.

personhood are undergirded by the late-modern mind-body dualism and the technological mindset, resulting in the subjugation of the body, the delinking of gender from biology, and the undermining of the procreative function. How they construct their sexual ethics within this framework is discussed below.

Farley advocates the notion of "just love," that is, treating others as a person and not an object. Out of this notion she proposes seven norms for sexual ethics: do no unjust harm, free consent, mutuality, equality, commitment, fruitfulness, and social justice. All of these norms are deemed necessary for the couple to respect each other's autonomy and relationality. Several of them safeguard the importance of the body, as the body is understood as an indispensable instrument of the self: one should not harm the other's body or mind; free consent involves how the body is used; and sexual intimacy should practice mutuality. Other ethical norms tend to emphasize the flourishing of the mind over respecting the bodily or biological framework. For instance, commitment is no longer tied to heterosexual marriage or the procreative order but becomes a means to fulfill the couple's potential for relationality. Fruitfulness is redefined from procreation to extending the couple's love toward others so that those who cannot procreate biologically can still be fruitful. Even for fruitfulness defined as procreation, it is not necessarily predicated upon the body and thus limited to fertile heterosexual couples. Modern reproductive technologies such as *in vitro* fertilization and surrogate motherhood can now enable other partnership types to procreate.[45] Under these ethical norms, sexual intimacy, the body, and the reproductive capability are all instruments to serve the mind. When the body is silenced, gender also vanishes. Of the seven norms, none considers any sexual or gender difference between man and woman. This is curious as they are norms of *sexual* ethics. As discussed above, the notion of sex is predicated upon the presence of male and female; without sexual difference there would be no notion of sex. But in these norms for sexual ethics, the identity and difference between male and female are purged. Perhaps it should not be a surprise when a person is essentially her mind while her body is only an instrument to be used

---

45. Farley, *Just Love*, 215–228.

and mastered by technology. For late-moderns, sexual ethics becomes the ethics of the coming together of minds which happen to have bodies that are designated as male, female, or some other categories, and these designations can be deconstructed and reconstructed at will. The coming together of persons is solely governed by their free choice and motivated by their need for relationality. Sexual ethics then tends to diffuse with social ethics. For this reason, it is not a coincidence that the seventh and final norm of Farley's sexual ethic is social justice. She contends that "just love" between sexual partners is normative for all other types of relationships, and thus "this norm obligates us all."[46]

The absence of gender specificities and the priority of free choice and relationality are also apparent in Farley's discussions on marriage and family. Human flourishing, she considers, does not require fixed family forms. Any family configuration that "works" should not only be accepted but also welcomed. What is important is the relationship between family members. She contends that familial relationships involve commitments and obligations not found in other relationships. The institution of marriage and family should still be advocated, as institutional frameworks may help us keep our promises and hold us accountable to one another. Yet these frameworks and commitments must abide with the norm of justice. Although the traditional Christian marriage ideals of monogamy, sexual exclusivity, and permanence are not normative and ought not to be universalized, experience tells us that they are congenial to human flourishing and should therefore be desired.[47] Yet the reasons for desiring these ideals have changed. In the Christian tradition, monogamy symbolizes the faithful relationship between Christ and church. Polygamy has also been associated with unbridled lust and monogamy is preferred.[48] Now monogamy is, from experience, considered the best arrangement to encourage love, intimacy, companionship, and friendship between the couple, as well as affection for children. Sexual exclusivity has traditionally been assumed as necessary for monogamous marriage. Now experience tells us that betrayal leads to harm and deep pain, so fidelity remains a condition for just love

---

46. Ibid., 228–230.
47. Ibid., 259–263.
48. Ibid., 253.

within marriage. As discussed above, Christian tradition names procreation and cooperation in daily living among others as reasons to support permanent marriages. Currently, lifelong commitment is still desired as it is the path to the "goals of marriage," that is, the experience of "embodied and inspirited love [in] greatest joy."[49] In advocating these Christian marriage ideals, Farley replaces the traditional theological and natural law languages with the language of experience. This is necessary as she aims to make the ethics of just love accessible to "those who stand in diverse faith traditions or no faith tradition at all."[50] Since her target audience is situated in late-modernity, the language of experience she uses is also the language of late-modernity. Perhaps the mind-body dualism that underlies her theory is necessary for an ethic that is palatable to late-moderns.

The question, for us, is whether the sexual ethics developed from this framework are adequate. Is the language of experience and mind-body dualism adequate, even for late-moderns? Is freeing the mind from bodily limitations by technology always good? Is human flourishing only a matter of self-transcendence, self-determination, and relationality? Must we maintain the significance of sexual and gender difference in thinking about sex and sexual ethics? Lisa Sowle Cahill, who also emphasizes the role of experience in sexual ethics, offers an argument which pinpoints the inadequacy of ethical thinking that ignores bodily differences. She insists that sexual ethics must consider human physiology such as sexual differentiation and procreation, because women and men experience the body differently:

> Surely women's diffuse and receptive sexuality, cyclic reproductive capacity, and deeply connective relation to their children both born and unborn, contribute to women's sense of self. Women's embodied experience could not be identical to that afforded by men's sharply focused but uneasily controlled sexual response, perennial but momentaneous capacity to impregnate; the necessity to do so by means of an externally borne and hence vulnerable member; and a man's need to work out a social relation to his children without the easy

---

49. Ibid., 264–265.
50. Ibid., 212.

and ready support of natural bodily relations (pregnancy and lactation) . . ."[51]

The experience of "motherhood" is distinctive to women and is shared by all mothers. It does not mean that women are defined primarily by motherhood; yet motherhood is "in many cultures, and perhaps universally, an avenue of fulfillment and flourishing for women."[52] By the same token, fatherhood is also an important experience for men and can lead men into flourishing lives. Stephen Post writes that "There is nothing in the experience of men quite like becoming a father. Fatherhood is a new way of being in the world. Many fathers still fail; but many succeed in becoming responsible and caring and, in some cases, morally and spiritually resurrected."[53] To hope for human flourishing, we must then hearken to our concrete reality as embodied beings, as men and women. Cahill observes that sexual ethics and gender construction that consider biological differences does not necessarily lead to inequality or patriarchy; it can instead offer opportunities for human flourishing, for both the individuals and the family.[54] Therefore, human flourishing – whether through free choice, relationality, or love – is achieved not by overcoming our bodily limitations or using our bodies as instruments, but is attained within the very framework and structure of our bodily existence. The body, as God's creation, is in itself good. The late-modern mind-body dualism that subjugates the body under the mind is inadequate and we ought to listen to the body in thinking about man and woman and the relationship between them.

Recognizing the importance of our physiology not only allows man and woman to flourish, it is also imperative for the wellbeing of children. Many studies have concluded that two-parent families where both parents are involved in caring for their children provide the best environment in which children should grow. In single-parent families, economic, emotional, and communal resources can be scarce for children, resulting in their reduced academic achievement, difficulties in employment, and early childbearing

---

51. Lisa Sowle Cahill, *Sex, Gender, and Christian Ethics* (Cambridge, UK: Cambridge University Press, 1996), 85.
52. Ibid., 89.
53. Post, *More Lasting Unions*, 104.
54. Cahill, *Sex, Gender and Christian Ethics*, 89–90.

which perpetuates the vicious cycle of single parenthood.[55] Single parenthood mostly results from divorce, separation, or the father abandoning the mother and the child. As discussed above, Farley is concerned about the escalating rates of divorce. She identifies the problem to be a lack of commitment, and proposes ways to exercise our free choice so that our commitments to personal relationships can be strengthened. However, the absence of gender specificity in her approach prevents her from addressing the fact that it is mostly the father who is absent from the children. While I will discuss the issue of the absent father in more detail in the next chapter, it is worth pointing out that simply because women carry and give birth to children, men are usually the ones who drift away. Although Farley's contemplation on marital commitment through free choice and love is helpful, only focusing on the mind is inadequate to address the issue of the absent father. An analysis of sexual difference in reproductive strategy and gender difference in constructing motherhood and fatherhood is necessary. For instance, David Blankenhorn argues that the cultural construction of the "superfluous father" contributed to the exodus of fathers from the American homes in the twentieth century.[56] A countercultural script, the "Good Family Man," is needed to restore men back to the family so all family members can flourish.[57] An assessment of Blankenhorn's notion of "good father" is beyond the scope of this study. Yet he is correct to point out that gender-specific analysis is necessary to adequately address the issue of single parenthood and the welfare of children. The family is, after all, not merely the coming together of different minds; it is "an organized network of socioeconomic and reproductive interdependence and support *grounded in biological kinship and marriage*," as defined by Cahill.[58] In other words, family is not a free association of discrete individuals but is a network that grows out of biological relationships. Any sexual ethic or gender construction that ignores biology can, at its best, deal only with the

---

55. Sara McLanahan and Gary Sandefur, *Growing Up with a Single Parent: What Hurts, What Helps,* reprint ed. (Cambridge, MA: Harvard University Press, 1996), 23–38.

56. David Blankenhorn, *Fatherless America: Confronting Our Most Urgent Social Problem* (New York: Basic Books, 1995), 65–69.

57. Ibid., 201–202.

58. Cahill, *Family,* x–xi. My emphasis.

relationship between the couple. It becomes inadequate when children are also considered. It should be noted that heterosexual sexual partners cannot avoid dealing with children unless reliable contraceptives become available. Technology helps remove procreation and biology from our contemporary discussions of sexual relationships. This is another influence that technology brings to late-modern sexual ethics. Technology not only splits the mind from the body, it also separates sex from procreation. Technology encourages us to think that the mind has perfect control over the procreative function of the body. With children out of the picture, we can stop listening to what the body has to say in the relationship between man and woman. This strengthens the assumption that the body is merely an instrument for the enjoyment and flourishing of the mind.

2.4 Sexual Ethics of Thatcher: Coming Together of Bodies

The perfect control of procreative function is also a presupposition in Thatcher's sexual ethic. As discussed above, the centrality of sexual intimacy in human personhood leads him to consider sexual expression as both inevitable and essential. This is demonstrated in his advocacy of cohabitation as betrothal. In modernity, he observes, people marry late due to their desire for more education and economic stability before marriage. The gap between puberty and marriage widens, creating a difficulty as the peak of sexual energy no longer coincides with the time of marriage. The majority of young people, both inside and outside of the church, become sexually active before marriage. Due to pastoral reasons, the church should reconsider the moral status of prenuptial cohabitation so that premarital sexual relationships are not necessarily sinful.[59] Thatcher thinks that sex can hardly be curtailed for young people. In *God, Sex, and Gender: An Introduction*, a book intended for university students, he writes: "I take for granted that all readers, with the exception of one or two saints, and one or two liars, will have had sex before they marry."[60] He simply assumes that

---

59. Adrian Thatcher, *Living Together and Christian Ethics* (New York: Cambridge University Press, 2002), 50–52.
60. Thatcher, *God, Sex, and Gender*, 212.

sexual drive cannot be curtailed and premarital sex is inevitable. The "one or two saints" are not virtuous people to emulate but, similar to the "one or two liars," are aberrant individuals to ignore. If, on the contrary, we assume that sexual drive can be curtailed, the moral ideal of abstinence before marriage need not be revised, even though many fail to live up to this ideal. Sexual abstinence does not necessarily imply an inherent sinfulness of sex or pleasure; it means putting sexual pleasure and intimacy in its proper place. Besides, Christian moral ideals should not be determined by whether sinful people can abide with them; otherwise ethics would fail to inform us of what is good. Thatcher's proposal to relax the moral ideal presupposes that abstinence before marriage is impossible. Another reason that the church needs to revise the morality of cohabitation, contends Thatcher, is to make the church's teaching more palatable to the world. Blanket condemnation on premarital sex and cohabitation in most Christian denominations, he argues, hampers the church from reaching out to those who are cohabitating in defiance of the church's teaching.[61] Legitimating some forms of cohabitation and premarital sex thus increases the church's opportunities to minister to these people. Besides, cohabitation allows the couple to grow in their relationship: "Living together before the ceremony was an opportunity for a couple to acquire skills they would need to support the martial sharing which was soon to be a pledged common life, while the responsibility of the Church remained to provide realistic marriage preparation for couples whatever their living arrangements."[62] No one would object that a couple intending to marry must prepare for their shared lives after marriage. The question is whether sexual activity must be part of this preparation. Thatcher answers in the affirmative: sexual relationship is essential for this preparation, as "effective" preparations must involve "learning by doing."[63] This again reveals that sexual intimacy is an imperative in his thinking. Sexual expression is so important that the traditional church teachings on premarital sex and cohabitation should be revised.

However the emphasis on the necessity of sexual intimacy, Thatcher does not advocate casual sex or promiscuity. Sexual intimacy is foremost an

---

61. Thatcher, *Living Together*, 72.
62. Ibid., 48.
63. Ibid., 248–249.

expression of love as desire; it is not intended to serve the body itself but the mind. Accordingly, sex should only happen between couples who love and commit to each other.[64] The negative account of desire leads to lust and promiscuity and must be avoided, but the positive account of desire brings us into union with what is desired, fulfilling our nature as relational beings.[65] The communion between spouses is analogous to the communion among the divine persons of the Trinity, so marriage can be understood as a form of *perichoresis* – a "dynamic process of making room for another around oneself."[66] He further extends this Trinitarian metaphor of marriage to include children. Children are the outflow of the couple's love, as love is generative. A child is God's gift to the couple, and so is Christ to humanity.[67] The "one-flesh" model of marriage means, first of all, that the couple is brought into "one-flesh" through sexual intercourse. Then the child who comes out of this union also serves as the "bridge" connecting the mother to the father; so the "one-flesh" is also located in the child. The family is "three in one flesh . . . a new union in which all share."[68] Drawing an analogy between the family and the Trinity means that children are of equal dignity as their parents and they must be treated equally in many respects. Besides, children are vulnerable so they deserve the greatest care. Thatcher laments that children have long been neglected in theological discussions, and a "theology of liberation for children" is much needed as a corrective. Jesus's teaching about children offers the foundation of this theology which endorses the rights of all children. If children have rights, others have the duties to protect these rights and the interests of children. These duties, first of all, are laid upon their parents. If their parents fail to provide for them, others should.[69] Thatcher believes that children need families – not just parents – to flourish. The institution of marriage provides a network of support that the couple, by themselves, cannot offer, so families need marriages. Making reference to social studies, Thatcher asserts that lifelong

---

64. Thatcher, *God, Sex, and Gender*, 207.
65. Ibid., 57–74.
66. Thatcher, *Marriage after Modernity*, 228–231.
67. Adrian Thatcher, *Theology and Families* (Malden, MA: Blackwell, 2007), 95–100.
68. Ibid., 106–107.
69. Ibid., 142–165.

marriage is the best family form for both the spouses and their children, and children are best brought up by their biological parents. Therefore, to honor the rights of children, their parents have the duty to marry and form families. This preference for marriage does not mean excluding other forms of family; it assumes that marriage is the "norm" while alternative relationships and family forms should be accepted as long as they demonstrate "marital values" of "deepening love, life-long fidelity, and mutual commitment."[70] Thatcher's "theology of liberation for children" demands that children should be born within the "norm" of marriage that exhibits "marital values."

This "norm" of marriage needed for children, however, creates a tension with the need of sexual intimacy for adults who are not ready to marry. As discussed above, the delayed age of marriage in modernity widens the period between puberty and marriage. Sex before marriage is deemed necessary. But as children must only be born within marriages, no child should be conceived during the period of sexual activity before marriage. In other words, sex is for all couples who love and desire each other while procreation is reserved for married couples. Sexual intimacy is morally acceptable for unmarried couples who love and commit to each other – that is, those who aim at marriage but who are prevented from marrying right away due to their circumstances. This "prenuptial cohabitation" should be welcomed as the couple has already expressed the "marital values" and their relationship has already conformed to the "norm" of marriage.[71] It must be distinguished from "non-nuptial cohabitation" – where the couple has no intention to marry – which is harmful and undesirable.[72] Thatcher proceeds to retrieve the Christian tradition of betrothal, arguing that the "betrothal solution" offers a satisfactory solution to the problem of prevalent premarital sex and cohabitation.[73] The gist of his proposal is that marriage should be a process of growth instead of a one-time event. Betrothal should be added as another ceremony prior to marriage. In the betrothal ceremony the couple confirms their intention to solemnize their marriage in the future.

---

70. Ibid., 115–135.
71. Ibid., 135.
72. Thatcher, *Living Together*, 45.
73. Ibid., 119–207.

Therefore, the betrothal ceremony signifies the *beginning* of marriage and the wedding ceremony becomes a *solemnization* of marriage, where the couple makes "irrevocable consent" to their commitment.[74] Sexual relations would become morally acceptable after betrothal. It must be affirmed with Thatcher that marriage involves a process of growth: personal growth of each partner, relational growth between the partners, procreation of children, and extending the family's love and hospitality to neighbors and strangers. In fact, the process of growth even begins before marriage when the partners first become acquainted with each other. The journey from acquaintance to marriage to family is marked by significant events, and each event has its particular meaning and associated social mores. For instance, consenting to courtship means that the couple is considering whether they will eventually marry each other. Exclusiveness, truthfulness, and the need to spend time together are the usual morality of courtship. Lifelong commitment and cohabitation are not required from a courting couple but become necessary when they marry. The significant events must also follow a particular sequence. Now in most cultures, people usually think that it is good to date and know each other before marriage and to have children after marriage. When children are born, it is best that the couple does not end their relationship. Thatcher also assigns meanings to the various stages and advocates particular sets of ethics to each. For example, he says that sexual intimacy should be reserved for couples who love each other and intend to marry, and children should only be born within the "marriage norm." When marriage is understood as a progressive journey of the relationship, the task of sexual ethics is to make normative claims concerning which conduct is appropriate for which stage of the journey. The "betrothal solution," Thatcher proposes, focuses on the timing of sexual intimacy. It attempts to revise the traditional morality that confines sex to after the wedding by arguing that sex is also appropriate in the betrothal stage. He broadens the definition of marriage to include betrothal, which then comes under the marriage "norm" where sexual intimacy can happen.[75] Thatcher

---

74. Ibid., 73, 217.
75. Ibid., 61.

considers that the "betrothal solution" provides a satisfactory answer for the church to the phenomenon of widespread cohabitation.

A detailed assessment of Thatcher's "betrothal solution" is beyond the scope of this book. I will only focus on how the late-modern mind-body dualism underpins his theory. All appears well in Thatcher's "betrothal solution" and his moving of sex to an earlier stage of marriage. This move assumes that the timing and outcome of each stage of marriage can be controlled at will. In his scheme, a couple can freely decide when to become betrothed and thus to engage in sex, when to wed and thus to solemnize their commitment, and when to have children. It is true that we can decide when to court, engage, and wed. But when to conceive and when not to conceive – if we have sex – have not been strictly under human control until quite recently. That is why traditional morality insists on seeing sex, procreation, and marriage as integrated. Thatcher's "betrothal solution" separates sex from procreation and is predicated upon controlling the very aspect of marriage that has been the most uncontrollable. When he retrieves the betrothal tradition, he recognizes that three options are available concerning betrothal and sex: (1) to prohibit sex until the wedding; (2) to assume marriage as solemnized upon sexual relations, with or without pregnancy; and (3) to perform a marriage for the betrothed couple when the woman is pregnant.[76] The first option, for Thatcher, is unrealistic in modernity and the second option lacks a public wedding ceremony to affirm the couple's "irrevocable consent." For the third option, it appears that he simply assumes that pregnancy would not happen with the use of contraception. He contends that contraception is "an obvious ready answer" to the difficulty of pregnancy during the betrothed stage.[77] It is interesting to note that elsewhere in his work, he does recognize that contraception can fail. He advises women to refrain from having sex with uncommitted partners, using the unreliability of contraception and the moral failure of abortion in his arguments.[78] He also contends that as contraception is unreliable,

---

76. Thatcher, *God, Sex, and Gender*, 246.
77. Ibid., 247.
78. Adrian Thatcher, *The Daily Telegraph Guide to Christian Marriage: And to Getting Married in Church* (London: Continuum, 2003), 55–56.

sexual intercourse should fall under the "norm" of marriage.[79] His caution concerning contraception, however, disappears in his discussions of sex during the betrothal stage. In his extensive discussions on betrothal and cohabitation spanning several books, he never offers a clear indication on how to deal with the possibility of pregnancy during betrothal. The discussion that is closest to this subject reads:

> ... I have suggested that there is a state of life prior to the ceremony of a wedding where sexual relations may begin. Further, these relations may be chaste. It is assumed that contraception will be used, and that straight couples should not have sex unless and until their commitment to one another embraces any children that may result from their love-making.[80]

The last statement suggests that only couples who are ready – in maturity, relational stability, finance, etc. – to have children can have sex. In this way even if the woman conceives, the child would still be born within a relationship that demonstrates "marital values." But this is contradictory to the primary purpose of his "betrothal solution," that is, to allow those who are not ready to solemnize their marriage, those who have reached puberty and need sex but are not ready to affirm "irrevocable consent," to have sex. However, if a couple – consistent with Thatcher's suggestion – is really ready to embrace children when they have sex, it is not clear why they should not wed before having sex. Besides, the statement still does not say explicitly if the betrothed couple must wed in case the woman is pregnant; the case of unintended pregnancy during the betrothal stage is simply ignored. Therefore, Thatcher's "betrothal solution" effectively assumes that pregnancy is impossible when contraception is used. It is predicated upon a perfect control of the procreative function by modern technology. Now technology can free us from bodily limitations, so the mind is free to use the body for the sexual intimacy that the mind desires. In traditional sexual ethics, our bodily nature demands a close connection between sex, procreation, and marriage. Premarital sex is thus considered immoral. Now modern technology splits this connection and the body becomes silent in

---

79. Thatcher, *Living Together*, 28–29.
80. Thatcher, *God, Sex, and Gender*, 247.

our formulation of sexual ethics. Again, the body becomes an instrument for the service of the superior mind. The late-modern mind-body dualism latent in Thatcher's ethics is revealed.

However, we should not be too optimistic about the mind's mastery over our body. The assumption that contraception is entirely effective in avoiding pregnancy is far from true. Statistics show that in the United States, although reliable contraceptive methods have become available since the 1960s, leading to a steady decline of unintended pregnancy in the ensuing years, the decline reversed for poor and less-educated women in the mid-1990s. In 2001, births from unwanted or unplanned pregnancies still made up a significant portion of all births. One out of ten births to women with college educations was unintended and up to four out of ten births for those with only high-school educations were unintended.[81] The "contraceptive revolution" does not eliminate unintended pregnancies. One sociological study reveals that education level has a significant impact on the rate of unintended births; many more unintended children were born to less well-educated mothers, for both white and black populations. Contrary to popular belief, income level or the childbearing desire of the women has little impact on the rate of unintended births. Several reasons for this education-biased rate of unintended births have been proposed: poor accessibility to contraception, economic instability leading to ambivalence about pregnancy, and a low sense of control over one's own behavior.[82] For our discussion, what is relevant is the fact that people with less education are much more prone to unintended pregnancies. If we want to provide stable families for children to flourish, we should argue against Thatcher's "betrothal solution" based on the results of this study. While women are young and generally have less education, it is much more likely for them to become pregnant and give birth to children unintentionally. Thatcher's assumption that contraception always works is empirically wrong, especially for young people. Besides, when we think in terms of contraception and unintended pregnancy, couples preparing for marriage through "learning

---

81. Kelly Musick, Paula England, Sarah Edgington and Nicole Kangas, "Education Differences in Intended and Unintended Fertility," *Social Force* 88, no. 2 (December 2009): 544.

82. Ibid., 559–562.

by doing" ought not to have sexual intercourse. According to Thatcher, the betrothal stage is a period of preparation that involves "trial and error" before the final irrevocable commitment is made. It is assumed that the couple would err during the learning process and make corrections before it is too late. If premarital learning involves sex, they must also learn to use contraception at the same time. Yet they cannot afford to make mistakes in this learning process, otherwise both the couple and the child would be harmed. This is inconsistent with his notion of "learning" which allows the couple to err before things become "irrevocable." One can argue that it is simply unwise to advise people to have sex while assuming that contraception is entirely effective right from the beginning. Thatcher's view on the use of contraception reveals two things. First, he assumes that the mind is much superior to the body. The mind is always rational and can master the body so well that using contraception requires no training and is always effective. Second, he ignores the givenness and limitations of the body. If we take the givenness of the body seriously, it is wise to exclude intimate sexual contact before the irrevocable commitment of marriage is made. In other words, marriage preparation should focus on matters of the mind: fostering mutual love and understanding, improving communication skills, and together planning their future life. It is because the mind is relatively malleable, so any insurmountable problem encountered during the preparation process may indicate that the couple should abandon their intention to marry. Given enough time, the partners should be able to recover from such an unfortunate event. The same is not true for the preparation process that involves sex and the body. Unintended pregnancy resulting from the "learning" process is not as easily rectified, and it may irrevocably harm both partners and the unintended child. There are good reasons why traditional Christian ethics limits sex to within marriage, and these reasons are still applicable today. The lack of gender specificity in Thatcher's sexual ethics further aggravates the situation should unintended pregnancy occur. Biology dictates that it is the woman who bears the child. Any ethic that promotes sex only for the flourishing of the couple is inherently unjust to the woman who must bear a heavier burden should unintended pregnancy occur.[83] The mind-body dualism latent in Thatcher's thinking leads him to a sexual ethic that ultimately jeopardizes the wellbeing of everyone, especially the unintended child and the woman. Again, this shows that Thatcher's sexual ethics, while ignoring the body, fail to reckon with the issue of unintended pregnancy and are inadequate.

2.5 The Gendered Ethics of Farley and Thatcher

Earlier I pointed out the lack of gender specificity in both Thatcher and Farley's sexual ethics; they both assume that gender has no biological basis and can be freely constructed. Looking closer at their views of human personhood reveals that their theories have already been gendered in a foundational way. Arguing from Trinitarian and incarnational theologies, Thatcher concludes that sexual desire is inherent in human nature. He claims that his notion of human personhood is universal, equally shared by men and women:

> The sexuality of women and men drives them out of themselves to seek relationship with others . . . It is that dimension of our being which calls people "to a clearer recognition of their relational nature, of their absolute need to reach out and embrace others to achieve personal fulfilment . . ." Theologically, sexuality is "God's ingenious way to calling us into communion with others." Having a sexuality is part of the meaning of being made in the image of God: we are made for relationship and God's nature is Relationship. The fabric of this relationship, between the divine Persons in the Trinity, and potentially between human persons, is love.[84]

Relationality, love, and sexuality are essentially the same for Thatcher. Compare this with Farley's discussions of sex and love:

---

83. Thatcher likens sex to play: "Play is essential to sex . . . Play however is an activity which we do not have to justify, and its lack of having a serious purpose is central to its definition," (*Liberating Sex*, 39). To conceive of sex as play potentially undermines the procreative function of sex and may be harmful to the woman who bears a heavier burden in case of unintended pregnancy.

84. Thatcher, *Liberating Sex*, 48–49.

> Just about everyone today thinks that sex has something to do with love – somewhere, somehow, for some persons; or at least that this is possible. Sex and sexual desire, for course, cannot be reduced to or equated with sexual love. Moreover, it is always a risk to focus on love in relation to sexuality since it tends to escalate the rhetoric about love in ways that imply that sex, no matter what, is always about love – and about certain forms of love.[85]

Unlike Thatcher, Farley thinks that although sexual desire is related to sexual love, they are not equal. For her, human self-transcendence is through free choice and relationality, which means opening up oneself to others. This opening up is not limited to sexuality. Her notion of love, even sexual love, is also much more diffused than the expression of love as physical union:

> Love, as I understand it, is simultaneously an affective response, an affective way of being in union, and an affective affirmation of what is loved. This applies to love of many different kinds of objects – whether personal or nonpersonal . . . [F]or the sake of simplicity, I am going to use the term "sexual love" to encompass [romantic love or friendship] insofar as they have a sexual dimension – whether only felt or acted upon. These are loves that involve our whole affective self in some way, that engage us deeply, often intensely, sometimes passionately. As I have said before, there are loves like this that do not have as a primary ingredient sexual attraction or an orientation to physical sexual union.[86]

Both Thatcher and Farley consider love and relationality important aspects of human personhood. While Thatcher equates love and relationality with sexuality, Farley tends to suppress the importance of sexual desire and hold a more diffused view of love. While both advocate lifelong commitments, Farley focuses on the end of marriages – how to strengthen existing commitments through exercise of the will, and Thatcher concentrates on

---

85. Farley, *Just Love*, 164.
86. Ibid., 168–170.

the beginning – how lifelong marriages can be created through preparation that involves sexual love. They both argue from their respective views of personhood, assuming that these views are universal across gender. Yet as man and woman, their notions of love and relationality have already been gendered. Impett and Peplau summarize the results of a broad range of research comparing the experiences of men and women and show that there are similarities and differences in their approaches to intimate relationships. Men and women both value emotional-focused over instrumental-focused communication, and both emphasize mutual attraction, dependability, emotional maturity, and pleasing disposition in mate preference.[87] For their differences, women tend to emphasize commitment and are more proactive than men in maintaining their committed relationships. When thinking about sexuality, women tend to link it with commitment and love while men tend to connect it with physical pleasure. Men also show more interest in sex and think about sex more often. In sexual intimacy, men typically take the lead and women usually act as gatekeepers.[88] It must be emphasized that all studies show within-sex variations as well as social and ethnic differences. Yet these tendencies have been found significant across different cultures. It is interesting to observe that Thatcher and Farley's emphases fit quite well with this gendered pattern. While the male theologian, Thatcher, accentuates sexuality, sexual desire, and sexual intimacy, the female ethicist, Farley, underscores relationality and commitment. This observation by no means suggests that Thatcher's ethics is androcentric and Farley's theory is gynocentric; sexuality and commitment are both important for men and women – it is the difference in tendency that distinguishes between the sexes. However, it indicates that sex and gender must be approached from the perspectives of both men and women. Any adequate sexual ethics must consider the experiences and physiologies of male and female, not just the experience of an abstract, asexual person. We remember that both Thatcher and Farley contend that gender has no

---

87. Emily A. Impett and Letitia Anne Peplau, "'His' and 'Her' Relationships? A Review of the Empirical Evidence," in *The Cambridge Handbook of Personal Relationships*, eds. Anita L. Vangelisti and Daniel Perlman (New York: Cambridge University Press, 2006), 275.

88. Ibid., 278–280.

biological basis. But the male's emphasis on sex and female's stress on commitment each have a strong biological basis – this will be further discussed in the next chapter. While both Thatcher and Farley decry any biological basis of gender, their sexual ethics reify this very basis. It is perhaps better to acknowledge the biological basis of gender rather than ignoring it and have it influence us without us knowing it.

2.6 Theological Assessment

A close look at Farley and Thatcher's sexual ethics reveals that the late-modern mind-body dualism undergirds their thinking, leading them to see the body as an instrument for the benefit of the superior mind. Despite the rhetoric of embodiment in their discussions, the body is important only in its functions of gathering experiences and performing tasks for the mind. Subjugation of the body is revealed in the silencing of the body in moral deliberation, in particular in Farley's positing of free choice as the sole resource for keeping marital commitments and in Thatcher's faith in controlling the body using contraception. Disparaging the body also entails a neglect of the biological basis of gender, leading Farley to ignore the importance of motherhood and fatherhood in human flourishing and Thatcher to undermine the injustice done to the woman in the event of unintended pregnancy. What is lacking in their ethics is a robust doctrine of creation that explicates a proper mind-body relationship. Farley constructs her view of human personhood through bodily experience. As discussed above, she attempts to adjudicate between the mind and the body and claims that human beings exist as "embodied spirits" and "inspirited bodies," with no dichotomy or hierarchy between them.[89] While it is the mind that interprets the bodily experiences, her epistemology inevitably leads her to understand the body as an instrument serving the mind. Although she says that the Christian tradition understands that persons are "before God" and affirms the "goodness of creation," these notions have little significance in shaping her view of human personhood.[90] Her view of mind-body relationship is not constructed within the context of God's creation where God is the one

---

89. Farley, *Just Love*, 116.
90. Ibid., 241.

who decides the shape and content of human existence, but is conjectured within a closed system relying solely on human experience with the mind deciding the relationship between the mind and the body. Her exclusion of God from the conversation is further demonstrated by her aversion to employ the notion of *imago Dei* in informing human personhood.[91] To remedy this lacuna in her theory, a doctrine of creation, where God creates the world and determines what is good for human beings, is needed. Thatcher, meanwhile, appears to ground his notion of human personhood on Christian theology. From the doctrine of incarnation, he affirms the importance of the physical and the body. From Trinitarian theology and the *imago Dei*, he argues that human persons share God's triune relationality. His problem, however, lies in his eagerness to equate relationality and sexuality, and his privileging of the mind to control the body. Sexuality governs his notion of relationality so much that even God cannot escape. God's love is interpreted foremost as God's desire for union with human beings, and the Eucharist is God's erotic communion with us. Both human relationship and the body are necessarily sexual; sexual intimacy becomes something good to promote, despite limitations of the body. Sexuality, instead of being a good aspect of God's creation, threatens to usurp God in determining what good is. All relationships are ordered toward sexuality and sexual expression. To remedy this weakness, a doctrine of creation that explicates a proper relationship between God and humanity, and between sexuality and relationality, is needed. Besides, Thatcher resorts to technology to resolve the dilemma between the adults' need for sexual intimacy and the children's need for stable families. His "betrothal solution" undermines the body and separates sex from procreation to the detriment of everyone, especially the unintended child and the mother. These shortcomings necessitate a doctrine of creation that puts sex and procreation in the proper order. In the last part of this chapter, the theologies of Oliver O'Donovan, Gilbert Meilaender, Karl Barth, and John Zizioulas will be used to remedy the weaknesses in Farley and Thatcher's sexual ethics.

---

91. Ibid., 138–142.

2.6.1 O'Donovan and Meilaender: Ordering of Sexual Love and Procreation

Oliver O'Donovan proposes that the doctrine of creation can inform the content of the human moral life. Upon creating the world, he argues, God made an objective order of things which constitutes the basis of human morality. Human actions are considered moral when they conform to this created order. However, our fallenness not only means that we rebel against this moral order but also means that we are unable to understand it correctly. It is through God's revelation in Jesus Christ and his resurrection that the created order is made known. Natural knowledge must be complemented by the knowledge of Christ if we are to understand the moral order.[92] Christ is known foremost in his resurrection, which points both backward to creation and forward to redemption. Christ's resurrection in bodily form brings about the resurrection of humankind and the renewal of all creation. It vindicates not only the raw material of creation but also the order of things that God created. This ordering is both vertically related to God and horizontally among parts of creation. Parts of the world are ordered among one another in a network of relationships, and ethics is to think and decide on these relationships.[93] In the horizontal ordering within the created world, the distinction between two kinds of order – "natural" and "artificial" – is pertinent to our discussions on the relationship between sex and procreation. The "natural" ordering is the order that goes with the natural sequence of things while the "artificial" order arises from human sciences and artifacts and is predicated upon human freedom and judgment. "Natural" ordering implies that sex is ordered to procreation and "artificial" ordering means that human beings can say no to the natural order using technology. Distinguishing these two kinds of ordering does not mean that they must oppose each other or that one is superior to the other. In fact, when human beings are endowed with wisdom and freedom, we are free to adjudicate between these two kinds of order and impose order on what we see fit. Yet our ordering always depends on God's order; the "artificial" ordering must not negate or oppose the "natural" ordering. We

---

92. O'Donovan, *Resurrection and Moral Order*, 17–20.
93. Ibid., 31–35.

are free not because we can create our ordering *ex nihilo*; we are free because we can choose how to respond to an order that has been given:

> ... natural order does not form an impregnable barrier which man [sic] can never choose to breach; it merely establishes the conditions upon which such a breach can be made. . . . human sexual love is ordered . . . to procreation. This is an unchanging principle of order which will continue to be a principle of order even when human beings refuse to procreate. . . . This does not entitle us to say that procreation can never be separated from sexual love. It entitles us to say only that if it is, then sexual love will be frustrated of its natural purposes.[94]

Moral thinking therefore involves a deliberation concerning these two orders: what is the natural order, and how and how much should the artificial order impose on the natural order without negating it. The body tells us that sex is naturally ordered to procreation. Recognizing this natural order allows the body to speak in moral deliberation. Breaching the natural order happens in two ways. First, the use of assisted reproductive technologies tends to free procreation from sex. But as we are not entirely bound to the natural order, we can still decide when and how to use the technology. For instance, Waters suggests that fertility drugs and artificial insemination from the husband may be acceptable. As these technologies only assist the natural process, they do not negate the natural order between sex and procreation. Yet to procreate through *in vitro* fertilization using donated gametes and surrogate motherhood is arguably a negation of the natural order.[95] Our main concern is over the second way of breaching the natural order, that is, the use of contraception where procreation is avoided in sexual acts. Again, not all use of contraception is wrong. We have to decide under what circumstances contraception opposes and negates the natural order. The purpose of contraception is for the couple to enjoy sex while avoiding pregnancy, and to order the birth of children in a timely manner. Contraceptive

---

94. Ibid., 37.
95. Brent Waters, *Reproductive Technology: Towards a Theology of Procreative Stewardship* (Cleveland, OH: Pilgrim, 2001), 49–55.

technologies recognize the link between sex and procreation and attempt to separate them. Therefore, to think about the use of contraception, we have to examine the link between sex for enjoyment and sex for pregnancy, or the unitive and procreative functions of sex. Gilbert Meilaender argues that both procreation and communion between the couple through sex are goods in themselves and so one is not subordinate to the other.[96] Pleasure is not simply a byproduct of sex that aims only at procreation, nor conception merely an accidental outcome of sexual union. As sex serves two goods that are both important, not every act of sexual love must fulfill both. There are instances when sex serves both goods, but there are times when serving only one of them may be adequate. In our freedom we can decide when and how each good is emphasized. We can choose to use contraception to accentuate the unitive purpose of sex and suppress the desire for children, or employ artificial insemination from the husband to temporarily set aside the unitive purpose of sex and elevate the good of procreation. But are these two goods entirely disconnected? Besides the sexual act itself, is there any link between the unitive good and procreative good? Is the expression of love through sex between a couple related to conceiving a child? If no connection is found, then the unitive good of sex would stand on its own and the use of contraception would not be a moral issue. What type, when, and how contraception is used would not be a subject of moral deliberation but would only be a matter of technological mastery.

Meilaender points us in the direction where we can find a connection between the unitive and procreative goods of sex. To counter Augustine's view that the sexual act must be controlled by the rational mind and so procreation is best done without concupiscence, Meilaender argues that passion, not rationality, lies at the center of sexual love. Even when a couple rationally decides to have children, their love making still involves passion and their rational decision to have children is set aside during the sexual act. In essence, sexual love is an expression that is mostly governed by passion, not the calculating mind. It is within this passionate bodily union that a child may result. The child conceived – through passion and not a calculated act – can be said to be a gift and not a product of the mind. If

---

96. Gilbert Meilaender, *The Way That Leads There: Augustinian Reflections on the Christian Life* (Grand Rapids, MI: Eerdmans, 2006), 135.

passion is exorcized from procreation, the child becomes a handiwork of human beings, not a creation of God handed over to parents for caring. The giving of love for each other in unitive sex gives rise to the giving of life in procreative sex, which are linked together by passion.[97] The Augustinian rationalization of sex attempts to elevate rationality and suppress passion, thereby turning procreation into a project of the rational mind. It bears a similarity with the late-modern mind-body dualism that subjugates the body under the superior mind. By naming passion the principle for both sexual love and procreation, Meilaender reminds us that procreation is not a project where the mind decides for the body, but is an intricate collaboration between them. When passion is the principle of procreation, rationality does not make all decisions concerning procreation. There is always something rationally uncontrollable in both sex and procreation, especially when we recognize that we are bodily creatures, not embodied minds. On the one hand, the conception of a child is never a project severed from passionate sex, though some forms of assisted reproductive technology may help with the process. On the other hand, passionate sex can never be severed from the possibility of procreation, though contraception may be used to accentuate the unitive good of sex or to order the birth of children in a timely manner. When a child is conceived despite the use of contraception, it is not a "technical failure" or an "accident," but a recognition that both sex and procreation are beyond our perfect control. The sharing of love between a couple in unitive sex gives rise to the giving of life in procreative sex. This is the natural order embedded in creation. We are free to impose artificial ordering, but any human action ought to respond to this natural order and not to negate it. Waters uses the notion of expanding love to discuss the connection between sexual love and the giving of life. He says that a couple entering marriage discloses an "unfolding and enfolding familial love." When a child is conceived from the marital union, love further unfolds and extends to the child. "We may speak of marital love unfolding into parental love, and a consequent unfolding of a familial love in turn enlarging, enfolding, and transforming the forms of love preceding it."[98] It

---

97. Ibid., 139–140.
98. Waters, *Family in Christian*, 181.

is within the natural ordering of sexual love with procreation that familial love unfolds and extends. Eradicating the possibility of procreation from sexual love negates this unfolding of love, and love between the couple becomes self-serving.[99]

Natural ordering between sex and procreation, therefore, demands that the unitive and procreative goods of sex should not be separated entirely. When a man and woman have sex, they must always expect the conception of a child even if contraception is used, since marital love is naturally ordered to parental love. They should fully prepare themselves for the conception and consider any child as a gift from God for their caring. Thatcher's "betrothal solution" negates this connectedness between sex and procreation during the betrothal stage. An ethic that listens to the body ought to prepare a couple for procreation when they are allowed to have sex. For the benefit of children, sex should remain within the committed relationship of marriage. This sexual morality is not a concession for "technological failure" associated with contraception. Premarital sex should be avoided not only because of the risks of unintended pregnancy. Otherwise the way out is to strive to perfect the technology of contraception and technology would then dictate human morality. To honor children as God's gifts and not projects of our will, to recognize the principle of "passion" not rationality in procreation, and to embrace the possibility of unfolding marital love to parental love, we should be prepared to welcome a child in every act of sexual love. It is for these theological reasons that sex should be confined within the marital covenant. Besides, the natural ordering of sex with procreation means that sexual ethics must be marriage ethics and must also be family ethics. Sexual ethics do not only concern the freedom and relationality of the two persons involved, but also their children and the commitment demanded thereof. Farley's focus on autonomy and relationality in sexual ethics, and her neglect of children in discussing marital commitment, is inadequate. Any sexual ethic that elevates relationality and sexual expressions but ignores procreation is, after all, a disembodied ethic.

---

99. The notion of unfolding love is discussed further in section 5.4.3 below.

2.6.2 Barth: Creation as Limited and Concrete

Both Farley and Thatcher construct their sexual ethics beginning from contemporary experience. Farley questions how the traditional Christian sexual ethics can be relevant to the world in light of recent scientific advancements. Thatcher tries to bridge the church's teaching with the experience of the younger generation. As they rely heavily on human experience in developing their views of personhood, human beings are understood within a closed system consisting of the mind and the body. Inevitably the body becomes an instrument serving the mind, which alone decides what is good for the self. While their ethics are attuned to the late-modern audience, the late-modern mind-body dualism also infuses their thinking. The weakness of their experiential approach can be amended by a doctrine of creation that describes human beings as God's creatures so that God, who is external to human beings, decides the relationship between the mind and the body. A voice external to experience is needed to complement and correct what we learn from experience alone. Karl Barth's notion of divine command offers such a voice to counter the late-modern cultural climate.

Barth might criticize Farley and Thatcher's approach to ethics as shifting the focus from God to human. He argues that theological ethics does not need to reply to human questions; instead, it is a response to the divine command which has already been issued to human beings. God's command is issued in the threefold movement of creation, reconciliation, and redemption. The movement of creation reveals that Christ is the Lord of *nature*, human beings are *creatures* of God, and that the divine command speaks of human's *determination* for God. God determines through creation the good of human beings, and our appropriate response is to obey this command.[100] The good of human beings cannot simply be known inside of human existence and experience but must come from God. Under this scheme, God, rather than the mind, is the final adjudicator between the mind and the body. The body is ordered by God and not according to the person's mind or will. By positing an external authority to human existence, this doctrine of creation can save the body from being subjugated under the mind and can counter the late-modern mind-body dualism. In

---

100. Karl Barth, *Ethics*, trans. Geoffrey W. Bromiley (New York: Seabury, 1981), 45–61.

creating the body, God speaks to us through the body and we must heed this command. Using O'Donovan's language, the body reflects an objective order embedded in God's creation and we should not negate or oppose this order. Therefore, the bodily function of procreation and the link between sex and procreation cannot be ignored in sexual ethics.

Barth further argues that as creatures, human beings are necessarily limited. As the limitation is issued from God, it is good. Human limitation means definition, determination, and affirmation. An unlimited creature is undefined and void; hence, it cannot be good. Limitation is also the basis of differentiation and gives reality to human existence. The primary limitation that human beings face – birth and death – is also good, as only within a limited time span and a specific allotted place can a human person truly live out her life. Consequently, true human freedom is exercised as a response to this divine command of limitation.[101] Viewed from this perspective, bodily limitation can be considered good, and even essential, for human beings to exercise freedom. The task of ethics is not to oppose, overcome, ignore, or even work around bodily limitations; it is to welcome these limitations as necessary for free human response to God the creator. This suggests that we do not need to shy away from facing the limitations associated with children in discussing marital commitments; it is exactly in honoring the limitations posed by the presence of children that a couple freely chooses to make and keep lifelong commitments. The possibility of pregnancy is not a bodily limitation that hinders couples from enjoying sex; it is the very basis for a person to freely choose when and with whom to have sex. Again, the notion of freedom in limitation does not mean that we are always bound by nature. Yet it serves to remind us that our freedom is not from, but is predicated upon, limitations. Without limitations, freedom is reduced to random assertions of will within a boundless and amorphous space, and freedom fails to give meaning to life.

A creature is necessarily limited by time and space; each creature has its own allotted time span and place. Accordingly, human existence is always concrete and particular. Each of us exists as a unique human person called specifically by God; each is to seize this given opportunity and not to

---

101. Barth, *Church Dogmatics Vol. 3.4*, 565–573.

stay aloof or detached, abstracting oneself from one's concrete existence.[102] In the sphere of human fellowship, Barth argues that concrete existence means foremost that a person is either a man or a woman. Man as male and woman as female is a limitation to each, gives reality to each, and is also the basis of differentiation between them. Sexual difference is unique in human fellowship because the distinction is "structural and functional;" other differences in human fellowship such as those between father and son, women of different ages, and persons with different gifts are not "structural and functional." This "structural and functional" difference signifies that a human person never exists as an abstract, neutral being. The concreteness of each person arising from sexual differentiation becomes the norm for all other types of human differentiations.[103] Barth's "structural and functional" indeed means "bodily." The "structural and functional" difference does not negate the fact that both men and women are humans, nor does it entail hierarchy between them. Bodily difference between male and female is simply "there" to demonstrate that no neutral or generic human being exists, and so a person is always concrete and particular. Recognizing the particularity of each person as man or woman is essential for human flourishing. As discussed above, Cahill and Post are correct to argue that human flourishing is predicated upon the concrete experiences of women as mothers and men as fathers. An abstract, asexual person cannot flourish.

Furthermore, the concrete bodily difference between men and women gives rise to the notion of alterity in human fellowship. Bodily difference signifies an observable particularity of a person marked in the body. If a human person is conceived as a mind-body unity, particularity of the body entails particularity of the whole person and each person can be known as an individual who is different from the rest. This preserves individuality and alterity between persons. While investigating the philosophical basis of sexual difference, Roland De Vries writes: "Since the natural and given (the sensate-psychical) is an aspect of a person's distinctiveness, since sexual difference is an aspect of the natural and given, and since one's spiritual being is bound up with the natural and given, then sexual difference is

---

102. Ibid., 575–579.
103. Ibid., 116–118.

vital to a person's distinctiveness."[104] In the same way, only by ignoring the particularity of the body can we understand a human person as an abstract, asexual, or non-gendered being. Once we ignore the body, bodily difference is also ignored, and alterity among persons may be destroyed. The presence of intersex and transgender people does not diminish the force of this argument; they in fact accentuate the importance of sexual distinction based on the body. Therefore, against Farley and Thatcher who think that sexual distinction should be blurred, bodily difference and sexual distinction must be upheld for preserving alterity among people, for viewing a person as concrete and particular, and for understanding the relationships among them. Alterity is essential for community, as it posits that others are not simply repeats of the self so genuine communion is possible. Hans Urs von Balthasar rightly argues that sexual differentiation connects the individual and the community: "For the man/woman relationship can stand as a paradigm of [the] community dimension which characterizes man's [sic] entire nature."[105] A community is made up of concrete and particular individuals. Sexual ethics, which attempts to offer a normative account of the relationship between man and woman, must consider their concrete existence as male or female and uphold the significance of sexual differences.

2.6.3 Zizioulas: Eschatological Transformation of Sexuality

The doctrine of creation also posits a distinction between God, the creator, and humanity, the creature. Although human beings share God's image and likeness through the *imago Dei* and the second person of God takes on human flesh in incarnation, differences between the creator and the creatures must be recognized. O'Donovan says that the vertical ordering between the creator and the creation is "pure teleological," that is, all created things are "ordered to" but never "ordered alongside with" God. It is only within the "horizontal ordering" among created things that "ordered alongside" is found. The whole creation is "for God" and God is the end of all creation.[106] The Orthodox doctrine of *theosis*, while directing the *telos*

---

104. Roland J. De Vries, *Becoming Two in Love: Kierkegaard, Irigaray, and the Ethics of Sexual Difference* (Eugene, OR: Pickwick, 2013), 183.

105. von Balthasar, *Theo-Drama*, Vol II, 365.

106. O'Donovan, *Resurrection and Moral Order*, 32–33.

of human beings toward God, further suggests that salvation is for human beings to "become God." Yet as creatures having a bodily nature and bounded by time and space, human beings can never become God *in toto*. To reconcile the doctrine of *theosis* with the divine-human difference, the Orthodox theologian John Zizioulas distinguishes between the "nature" and "person" modes of human existence. The "nature" mode is materialistic and limited by time and space yet the "person" mode transcends these limitations.[107] Thus, *theosis* is about becoming God in "personhood" and not in "nature."[108] God's personhood, understood from Trinitarian theology, is foremost relational. Closely related to this understanding of personhood are the notions of freedom and love.[109] Human beings are to "become God" by taking on God's relationality, freedom, and love. It is imperative to understand the notion of personhood from God and not from human nature or experience, lest the essence of salvation – *theosis* – cannot be achieved.[110] Our "nature" mode of existence, or the "hypostasis of biological existence," originates from erotic love. It binds human beings to natural necessities and leads to death. The problem with humanity, however, does not arise from biological existence *per se* nor from its ensuing limitations, but from our sinful attempt to become a person *through* our biological existence. Therefore, salvation does not need to destroy our biological existence or eros, but to transform them. Salvation transforms us from "hypostasis of biological existence" to "hypostasis of ecclesial existence" through baptism, giving us a "new birth" into Christ, who is the hypostatic union of divine and human natures. Within the "hypostasis of ecclesial existence" human beings are no longer determined by nature or the laws of biology. The church is a family not of biological kinship or exclusivism. Yet the transformation is also eschatological; the biological and ecclesial modes of existence are in dialectical tension in this age. The ecclesial existence will finally transcend the biological existence in the eschaton, while in this age

---

107. John D. Zizioulas, *Communion and Otherness: Further Studies in Personhood and the Church*, ed. Paul McPartlan (New York: T&T Clark, 2007), 211–213.

108. John D. Zizioulas, *Being as Communion: Studies in Personhood and the Church* (Crestwood, NY: St Vladimirs Seminary Press, 1997), 49–50.

109. Ibid., 40–46.

110. Zizioulas, *Communion and Otherness*, 140–141.

the Eucharist orientates us toward this realization. As such, the ecclesial hypostasis is ascetic, calling for a continual transformation of the body and eros from biological manner to ecclesial manner on this side of the eschaton. Within the community of the body of Christ, relationality, love, and eros should not be reduced to the biological expression of sexuality but should be transformed into the mode of ecclesial existence.[111]

Zizioulas's view of personhood contrasts sharply with Thatcher's. While insisting that personhood must be understood from God, Zizioulas circumscribes sexual desire to the realm of biological existence that pertains only to human beings. Thatcher, on the other hand, understands divine relationality through human experience and assigns erotic desire to both God and human beings. The Eucharist, for Zizioulas, signifies an eschatological movement where human beings can become God. The same sacrament, for Thatcher, is an incarnational movement where God finds erotic union with humanity. While Zizioulas would criticize Thatcher for understanding God through human experience, Thatcher would characterize his ascetic theology as "disembodied." But, as discussed above, Thatcher's sexual ethics is not as "embodied" as it appears to be. Besides, asceticism is not necessarily disembodied. In his study of early Christian asceticism, Peter Brown concludes that sexual renunciation is not only about the mind controlling the body but it is also an attempt to find human freedom amidst bodily limitations.[112] Ascetic practices do not sever the body from the mind. Instead, it reveals "the inextricable interdependence of body and soul" where the body is "allowed to become the discreet mentor of the soul."[113] Sexual renunciation is not always a manifestation of mind-body dualism; instead it can be an attentive listening to the body so that the person can become virtuous. Sexual ethics that advocates for sexual renunciation outside of marriage does not stifle human relationality; instead it can be beneficial in forming virtuous persons.

We can further adjudicate between Zizioulas and Thatcher's views of human personhood using O'Donovan's framework of created order. Moral

---

111. Zizioulas, *Being as Communion*, 50–65.

112. Peter Brown, *The Body and Society: Men, Women, and Sexual Renunciation in Early Christianity*, 20th ann. ed. (New York: Columbia University Press, 2008), 442.

113. Ibid., 236–237.

knowledge from nature, argues O'Donovan, must be complemented by God's revelation in Christ. The created order is vindicated in Christ's resurrection, which points backward to creation and forward to redemption. Redemption is not merely restoration of the original creation; it is a transformation of creation toward its *telos*.[114] In the sphere of human sexuality, the original creation suggests that sexual expression and procreation is the proper *telos* of marriage. Yet redemption points to the transformation of marriage and the extension of marital and familial love to beyond the boundary of marriage and family. Singleness becomes a vocation equal to that of marriage. While marriage is to continue as a witness to God's original creation, singleness now becomes a witness to marriage's eschatological transformation. They are two distinct but equal vocations; people called into each should live their lives according to the way of each.[115] Seen in this light, human sexuality is for expressing marital love and enabling procreation only in the original creation. In the eschaton, sexuality will be transformed. Community will no longer be predicated upon procreation and kinship, and sexual love will be extended and will lose its biological basis. With the in-breaking of the eschaton through Christ's resurrection, sexual intimacy and procreation have become nonessential. Therefore, contrary to Thatcher, relationality does not entail sexual expression. Relational beings – humanity or God – are not bound to express their relationality sexually. Instead, in accordance with Zizioulas, human sexual love will be transformed, losing its biological basis. The doctrine of creation puts sexuality at its proper place: it is an expression of love confined within marriage for the good of procreation. When marriage is transformed, so is sexuality. Sexual intimacy is a good of creation, but it is not essential. This must inform our moral thinking about the relationship between man and woman.

2.7 Conclusions

This chapter examines the sexual ethics of Farley and Thatcher who formulate their theories assuming that bodily differences between men and women are unimportant. Gender, for both, is a construction of the mind

---

114. O'Donovan, *Resurrection and Moral Order*, 55.
115. Ibid., 68–70.

or the culture and is unrelated to biology. As a result, they do not discuss the relationship between man and woman by referring to their differences; man and woman are treated as uniform. This gender-neutral approach leads Farley to ignore the importance of womanhood and manhood in human flourishing and Thatcher to undermine the injustice done to the woman in the event of unintended pregnancy. Furthermore, procreation is neglected from Farley's "just love" and is assumed to be perfectly controlled in Thatcher's "betrothal solution." Although both emphasize mind-body unity and embodiment, the late-modern mind-body dualism in fact undergirds their view of personhood. The mind, which is superior to the body, can use and control the body at will, and the givenness of the body is ignored. Gender is delinked from biology; sex is separated from procreation; and human flourishing is conceived free from bodily limitations. In this chapter, I have explicated how O'Donovan's, Meilaender's, Barth's, and Zizioulas's theologies can counter the weaknesses of Farley and Thatcher's sexual ethics. In summary, when we think about the relationship between man and woman, we must consider their biological differences, acknowledge their concrete existence as male or female, respect limitations of the body, recognize the eschatological transformation of sexuality, and connect sex with procreation, procreation with marriage, and marriage with family.

The main problem with Farley and Thatcher's sexual ethics stems from the late-modern mind-body dualism latent in their thinking. Therefore, we need a notion that recovers the importance of the body and describes a proper relationship between the mind and the body to counter this dualism. Meilaender's depiction of human beings as creatures bearing the *imago Dei* offers such a notion. As we are creatures, he argues, our lives must be understood as a journey through the material and the fleshy bounded by space and time. Yet bearing the *imago Dei*, we are also free, made to transcend the limits of nature. *Duality* captures our condition as creatures standing at the juncture of nature and spirit, body and soul. *Duality* is not *dualism*, where mind and body are split into two opposing entities each trying to dominate the other. In the late-modern technoculture, it is the mind that controls and subjugates the body for its use. *Duality* means that both transcendence and limitation, both freedom and boundedness, and both mind and body characterize human existence. They may come into tension or even conflict; yet human beings must journey through and hold both together, lest the *duality* is torn apart into *dualism*.[116] Meilaender states that a "duality, or polarity . . . holds together in harmonious and creative union two disparate elements – holds them together without obliterating their separateness."[117] He aptly describes our existence within this *duality*:

> We may be free spirits made to transcend all that is finite and to rest in God, but we are just as truly bodies subject to the relentless temporality of human experience . . . We can hardly say that to transcend any of the limits that time, space, and biological necessity place upon us is wrong, for it is precisely this transcending that manifests human freedom. Neither can we assume that freedom is the only essential feature of our being and approve every step beyond old limits simply because such a step manifests the self-transcending power of human freedom.[118]

Duality describes the dynamic interplay within the unity of the human mind and body. O'Donovan's tension between natural and artificial orders, Barth's freedom in limitation, and Zizioulas's eschatological transformation of sexuality are different expressions pointing to this *duality* of human nature. *Duality* offers a way to describe the intricate and often mysterious relationship between the mind and the body. As knowledge of ourselves is always opaque, *duality* defies an exact or universal definition. Yet it must instruct our understanding of human personhood and our construction of sexual ethics, especially when the contemporary technoculture constantly lures us into the trap of dualism.

---

116. Gilbert Meilaender, *The Limits of Love: Some Theological Explorations* (University Park, PA: Pennsylvania State University Press, 1992), 42–44.
117. Ibid., 116.
118. Ibid., 44.

CHAPTER 3

Equal-Regard between Man and Woman

In the previous chapter, I examined the sexual ethics of Margaret Farley and Adrian Thatcher. Underlying their thinking is the assumption that man and woman are essentially the same. I argued that this assumption stems from the late-modern mind-body dualism which posits a superior mind that subjugates the body and uses it as an instrument to obtain experiential input and to carry out decisions for the mind. As the body is disparaged, procreation is neglected from their discussions and the construction of gender is delinked from biology. The coming together of man and woman becomes the coming together of abstract, asexual minds seeking relationships that are free from limitations. The resulting sexual ethics is inadequate for the flourishing of man and woman as concrete and limited creatures. It also neglects the wellbeing of children. As a response to their sexual ethics, I argued from the doctrine of creation that human freedom must be based upon limitations and the givenness of the body. This does not mean that biology alone dictates human sexual expressions; it means that our bodily nature ought to provide the structure upon which sexual mores are deliberated and sexual conducts are expressed. This "natural ordering," in the sphere of sexual ethics, stipulates that sex and procreation are naturally ordered to each other. As sex cannot be severed from procreation, sexual ethics naturally leads to family ethics. The procreative function of human beings, and the biological difference between man and woman, must also be considered.

The Religion, Culture, and Family Project, conducted by a team of scholars under the direction of Don Browning, attempts to address biological differences and procreation in their sexual ethics. In this chapter, I examine the team's concerns, arguments, and recommendations. Their intention is to promote the wellbeing of children as well as the democratization of the family. The ethics of "intact family" and "equal-regard" are proposed to achieve these two goals. However, I argue that these two ethical notions contradict each other. The notion of "equal-regard" is predicated upon a liberal understanding of personhood and family formation. When the family is viewed as a liberal democracy made up of autonomous individuals, man and woman inevitably fall into a dualism where each opposes and conflicts with the other. As a result, stable families cannot be maintained, and the ethics of "intact family" is jeopardized. I propose, based on the notion of God's created order, an alternative narrative to describe the relationship among family members. I contend that God's particular calling upon each person, instead of the notion of equal-regard, should inform family ethics. Furthermore, *duality*, instead of *dualism*, should characterize the relationship between man and woman.

3.1 Critical Familism and Children

Don Browning explains that the Religion, Culture, and Family Project is an attempt to raise a mediating voice in the debate between the progressive and conservative parties on the family issue in the early 1990s. He disagrees with both the progressive solution of celebrating multiple family forms as well as the conservative solution of recovering the traditional family. Instead, he advocates a critical retrieval of the Christian tradition in constructing family ethics. The "intact" two-parent family in the Christian tradition should be retained as it provides the best environment for children to grow up, but the traditional gender role distinction and any lingering patriarchy should be challenged as they lead to inequality for women. Browning calls this "critical familism," a stand that is pro-family and pro-marriage and at the same time critical of the patriarchal traditional.[1] The relationship between man and woman is discussed within this larger framework of marriage and family. The book, *From Culture Wars to Common Ground: Religion and the American Family Debate*, coauthored by five scholars of the

---

1. Browning, *Equality and the Family*, 51–60.

Project, explicates the ethic of critical familism and describes how it comes about by following Browning's method of practical theology. The method involves four "movements": descriptive theology, historical theology, systematic theology, and strategic practical theology.[2] The book first provides a description of the American family in late twentieth century and proposes reasons behind it. Individualism, changing economic patterns, psychological causes, and lingering patriarchy are identified as the four major forces that shape the modern American family, leading to the increasing trends of divorce, out-of-wedlock births, single parenthood, and absent fathers, contributing to the "family crisis" that plagues America. From their discussions, it is notable that they focus on children as the primary victims of this "crisis." Statistics and studies that correlate single parenthood to child poverty, reduced education achievement and career success are cited,[3] but the effects of divorce and family disruption on the couple themselves, their extended families, or the larger community are not mentioned. Poverty is always discussed with respect to the single parent, especially the mother, and not with respect to divorcees who have no children. The absent father is mentioned to highlight the child's need for the care and supervision of the father.[4] When the marriage bond itself is discussed, the focus always turns to the wellbeing of the children. Monogamy is advocated because it "provides a secure environment for dependent infants, protection for the mother during a period of vulnerability [i.e. during pregnancy and immediately after childbirth], increased paternal certainty, [and] the secure grounds for the exercise of kin altruism . . ."[5] These reasons are given not for the marital relationship itself but for the successful rearing of children. Their discussion of marriage permanence is also shaped by their concern for children. They recognize that permanence has always been a good of marriage in the Christian tradition. For instance, Aquinas argued that it offers better care for children, enhances fairness and economic protection for wives, and reflects the unbreakable sacramental nature of the marriage

---

2. Ibid., 38–46.
3. Don S. Browning et al., *From Culture Wars to Common Ground: Religion and the American Family Debate* (Louisville, KY: Westminster John Knox, 1997), 50–58.
4. Ibid., 106–113.
5. Ibid., 279.

bond.⁶ Yet critical familism does not retrieve this tradition of marriage permanence. Instead, a large portion of their constructive ethics is devoted to suggesting ways of relational management that grow out of the notion of equal regard.⁷ The implicit message is that the quality of marital relation has replaced permanence as the ethical principle for the modern Christian marriage. *How* husband and wife live together is much more important than *how long* they remain together. It must be emphasized that the authors do not celebrate the culture of divorce; in fact they say that easy divorce should be avoided as much as possible. But in light of the "reality" of divorce, churches should accept and sustain the divorced and remarried. What is important is to pass along "the idea that divorce is generally not good *for children*."⁸ They suggest that divorce law should be revised, but only for couples who have children. While childless couples may continue to still seek no-fault divorce, extra procedures should be in place for those having children, with an aim to encourage reconciliation. If reconciliation is deemed impossible, financial plans should be drawn up to secure the financial provision for their children until they reach the age of eighteen. If mutual consent cannot be reached between the couple, the court should step in and assign fault and assess damage.⁹ In other words, the ease of divorce should depend on the presence and status of children. The marriage bond must remain strong while children are young, but can be easily dissolved when the parents have no children for whom to care. Again, the permanence of marriage in the Christian tradition is reinterpreted for the sake of children.

Therefore, children are the main concern of critical familism. Browning is explicit about his focus on children, stating that "Mainline churches must recapture their interest in children" and should "put children first" in family ethics.¹⁰ His emphasis on children affects how he retrieves the Christian tradition. Augustine names procreation, fidelity, and permanence as the

---

6. Ibid., 121–122.
7. Ibid., 271–334.
8. Ibid., 318–319. My emphasis.
9. Ibid., 332.
10. Browning, *Equality and the Family*, 57.

three goods of marriage.[11] Critical familism reinterprets these three goods in light of children. Monogamy is good as the stable two-parent family offers the best domestic environment for children to flourish. Marriage "permanence" is retained only for couples who have young children; it ceases to be the norm for all marriages. As a result, permanence is largely qualified – marriages should be "permanent" until children become adults. The good of fidelity becomes the good of spousal relationship that aims at fostering stable family environments for the flourishing of children. Hence, the two goods of fidelity and permanence become instrumental, serving the good of procreation. This contrasts sharply with Farley's and Thatcher's sexual ethics. While Farley and Thatcher emphasize the flourishing of the couple and neglect children, critical familism elevates procreation and encourages good marital relationships for the sake of children. Farley and Thatcher shun bodily limitations; Browning elevates the limitations posed by procreation – children – above other concerns in their sexual ethics. If Farley and Thatcher develop their sexual ethics from their views of personhood – how a person attains fulfillment through sexual relationships, Browning develops critical familism from the social situation of children – how children are to be protected and nurtured through the family. From the perspective of children and procreation, critical familism appears promising in remediating the shortcomings of Farley and Thatcher's sexual ethics.

3.2 Critical Familism and the Democratization of Family

After outlining what contributes to the "family crisis" and its impacts on children, the authors expound two cultural factors that shape the American family: individualism and rational-choice thinking. In American history, individualism gradually shifts people's focus from the collective, extended family to each individual member. The married couple is thought to have obligations to each other and to their children, instead of to the patriarchal head of the extended family. Yet this truncated obligation toward the small

---

11. See Augustine, "The Good of Marriage," in *The Fathers of the Church: Saint Augustine Treatises on Marriage and Other Subjects* (New York: Fathers of the Church, 1955), 9–51.

nuclear family declines further under the cultural climate, leaving individuals to care for themselves only, breaking up the fabric of the family.[12] The other cultural factor, rational-choice thinking, or technical rationality, appears in two forms. One form aims at efficient government control through bureaucracy and the other form encourages economic efficiency through making decisions based on economic patterns. It is the economic form of technical rationality that Americans embrace.[13] Americans tend to make familial decisions based on one's own economic advantages. When women are economically independent, there is no reason for them to stay in unsatisfying marriages. When mothers can raise their children by themselves, single motherhood is no longer problematic. When fathers are not needed economically to raise their children, many choose to leave. The authors contend that it is the combined effect of individualism and rational-choice thinking, together with women entering the paid workforce in the twentieth century and becoming economically independent, that disrupts the American family and harms children.

If individualism, rational-choice thinking, and women's economic independence lead to family disruption and harm children, then we might expect that the family crisis can be averted by countering these trends. Yet it is not what Browning and his team advocate because they think that these trends, though disruptive to the family, are beneficial in some other ways. Economic independence of the women may weaken the marriage bond, yet it brings greater gender equality. Individualism and rational-choice thinking may increase the rates of divorce, out-of-wedlock births, single parenthood, and absent fathers, yet they also bring about a "new *democratization* of families," enhancing mutuality and equality between the couple.[14] The ethical task is not to proscribe individualism or rational-choice thinking but to distinguish the positive and the negative elements within them. The negative elements that disrupt the family should be countered but the positive elements that encourage "democratization of families" should be encouraged.[15] Democratization means, first of all, equal dignity and respect

---

12. Browning et al., *From Culture Wars*, 58–59.
13. Browning, *Marriage and Modernization*, 19.
14. Browning et al., *From Culture Wars*, 65. Original emphasis.
15. Ibid., 60–65.

for each partner. For instance, intimate exchanges of sexuality and affection should be mutual instead of dominated by one partner.[16] Democratization also means equal participation in making decisions. An example is that value formation in the family should be negotiated between the couple, each preserving or reconstructing his or her respective tradition.[17] It also means equal rights and duties. Doing waged work, performing household chores, and taking care of children are all considered rights and duties of each partner, and each should engage in all these activities more or less equally. The authors propose a combined sixty-hour workweek for couples with young children, to be divided between the parents as thirty-thirty or forty-twenty. The father and mother may each have a less-than-full-time paid employment, share household chores and childcare equally. This equal participation would make both father and mother "happier."[18] The democratization of family, brought about by the positive side of individualism and rational-choice thinking, is not only good but is an imperative within and beyond modernity. They state that "In the future, the rhythms and nuances of making love, earning a family income, establishing the values of the family, and exercising parental authority increasingly will be shared equally husband and wife *or the marriage will collapse.*"[19]

The collapse of marriage should be avoided, as marriage must be maintained for the sake of young children. Sociological studies have shown that the best form of family is the intact, two-parent family with both adults having biological connection with their children.[20] The ethical task is to encourage this form of family and avoid marriage disruption. But the promotion of intact family must not undermine the democratization of family. Otherwise marriage will also collapse under the demand for mutuality and equality. Therefore, modernity, with its influence of individualism and rational-choice thinking, is a mixed blessing to the family. On the one hand, it allows the modern marriage to achieve equality through democratization. On the other hand, it threatens to break up families through

---

16. Ibid., 179.
17. Ibid., 66.
18. Ibid., 317.
19. Ibid., 288. My emphasis.
20. Ibid., 71.

inordinate individualism and rational-choice thinking. Married couples must learn to find the "right amount" of individualism and rational-choice thinking. They must ensure successful democratization of family without disintegrating it. The ethic of equal-regard marriage – the main theme of critical familism – has been proposed to help couples navigate this modern terrain. As discussed above, while this notion appears to focus on marital relationships, it is in fact motivated by a concern over the wellbeing of children. Gender relationships in Browning's critical familism must be understood within this context.

3.3 Male Problematic and Family Cohesion

The ethic of critical familism focuses on heterosexual couples with young children who are in the modern western context. It promotes intact, two-parent families for the wellbeing of children while equality between the couple must be maintained. As "good individualism" in modernity means that independence and freedom to choose is good, the ethic should avoid imposing external constraints that coerce the couple to cleave together.[21] The only way, therefore, is to encourage the father and mother to stay according to their own will. An important task is to answer the questions: Why do parents leave their family? How can they be prevented from leaving without resorting to coercion? Statistics from all over the world show that it is the father who increasingly drifts away from his children.[22] The question arises: Why do fathers leave, and how can they be bound to the mother-child dyads? While individualism, rational-choice thinking, and the shifting economic and cultural patterns all contribute to the recent trends of absent fathers, the authors believe that these factors in fact capitalize on an innate tendency for fathers to drift away, causing the modern exodus of fathers from the family. They call this innate tendency the "male problematic," and the notion is developed based on evolutionary psychology. Male and female mammals, the theory argues, have different reproductive strategies. As females can only produce a few offspring, they tend to be selective in choosing sexual partners. Males with superior genes

---

21. Ibid., 65.
22. Browning, *Marriage and Modernization*, 18.

are preferred as partners to copulate. Since males can produce seemingly limitless numbers of offspring, they tend to copulate with many and let the females raise the children on their own. However, the vulnerability and the long periods of dependency of the human infant require the cooperation of both father and mother to raise a child. So evolution pushes the human male to settle down with the female. Women only choose to partner with men who are willing to commit themselves to the women and their children. Men must also settle down with the women to ensure that their offspring can survive, and the human family is formed. But the man is only willing to do so if he is certain that the infant is biologically his so that his genes can successfully perpetuate. His request for "paternal certainty" in turn demands the woman to remain faithful to him, thus giving rise to the human monogamous family. By staying together in stable monogamous relationships, both male and female also benefit from frequent sexual exchanges and mutual assistance for survival. The vulnerability of the human infant, the demand for paternal certainty, the benefit of sexual exchanges, and mutual assistance are the four conditions for the human father to cleave to the family.[23] Despite these natural conditions, the human male, driven by his innate reproductive strategy, is still prone to drifting away from the mother-child dyad. The male problematic must also be overcome through moral and cultural strategies.

The common strategies in human history involve different forms of patriarchy. For instance, the Greco-Roman world in Jesus's time employed an honor-shame ethics, giving honor to the male if he could maintain household order and protect his household – wife, children, slaves – from external molestation. The desire for honor then bound the father with his household. But the honor-shame ethics also created gender inequality and powerful patriarchal structures. The power that the father gained enabled him to control his wife, invest in a limited number of children, while obtaining a wider sexual freedom. These further enticed the father to stay in the family.[24] The man could also gain honor if he could intrude into another man's private world and harass the women in his household. Women,

---

23. Browning et al., *From Culture Wars*, 106–113.
24. Ibid., 141–142.

on the other hand, are expected to exhibit shame, submit themselves to the head of family, and restrict themselves to the private household.[25] Various forms of patriarchy had been effective in overcoming the male problematic in pre-modern societies. Therefore, according to evolutionary psychology, patriarchy is intricately connected with the need to bond the father with the family. It did not stem from the larger physique of the male or an innate power differential between the sexes, but is a strategy developed to enable successful procreation of the human species. In other words, the cultural strategy of patriarchy is a natural consequence of the human procreative structure. But this patriarchal structure, though effective in overcoming the male problematic, is unjust to the women and children and inimical to the ideal of equality. For the democratization of family, Browning and this team argue, an alternative strategy must be developed, and they are taking up this daunting task. The "challenging cultural work," says Browning, is "to combine a love ethic of equal regard between husband and wife with a powerful ethic of paternal care and responsibility."[26]

The alternative strategy, however, need not be conceived anew but can be retrieved from the Christian tradition. Jesus, the authors contend, criticized the oppressive social order of patriarchy and liberated people from it. Equality in Christ, as exemplified in Galatians 3:28, was thought to have social significance. Egalitarianism was practiced in the early Jesus movement, and the honor-shame ethics was replaced by an ethic of peace that emphasized self-giving love of the husband. The newly gained freedom and equality inaugurated a movement toward the intact, equal-regard family. The Jesus movement initiated a new gender ethic that could liberate people from patriarchy. This ethic means that one should "respects the selfhood, the dignity, of the other as seriously as one expects the other to respect or regard one's own selfhood."[27] Equality in Christ should be translated to mean equal respect and equal regard. The equal-regard ethic not only encourages one to pay respect to the other, it also allows one to expect and claim equal respect from the other. As self-sacrifice demands the giving up of oneself without expecting the same from the other, it is incompatible

---

25. Browning, *Marriage and Modernization*, 72.
26. Ibid., 82.
27. Browning et al, *From Culture Wars*, 153.

with the equal-regard ethic. Sacrificial love, especially on the part of the wife, is not the ideal form of love but may only serve as a means to the end of attaining mutuality between the couple. As equal-regard focuses on the mutuality between the couple, practically it requires "intersubjective dialogues" and communicative skills are crucial, especially for the husbands.[28] Counseling and family therapy are good resources to enhance dialogue and foster the ethics of equal-regard within the family.[29] The authors argue that the equal-regard ethic initiated by Jesus "fractured" – but did not eradicate – the honor-shame codes of the Greco-Roman culture in the first century. The same ethic can disrupt the patriarchal family today. In fact, modernity is the most opportune time to implement the equal-regard ethic. Since the second half of the twentieth century, women continued to enter the paid labor force and gained economic independence while individualism exerts its influence. Patriarchy has already been challenged, loosening the soil for the implementation of equal-regard love in the family.[30] National surveys also indicate that people increasingly understand marital love as mutuality rather than self-sacrifice, and the authors interpret the results as a positive sign for the implementation of love as equal-regard.[31] The time is now ripe to rekindle the egalitarian ideal of the early Jesus movement and advocate for the intact, equal-regard family.

According to the authors, the equal-regard ethic of the early Jesus movement did not come to fruition due to pressures from the surrounding culture and a desire for order. It started to recede in the post-Pauline churches, replaced by the language of male headship.[32] The language of headship is not a complete relapse back to Greco-Roman patriarchy, though it falls short of the ideal of equal-regard. In fact, the authors recognize that male headship, together with paternal responsibility and sacrificial love, was advocated to overcome the male problematic. For instance, the exhortation in Ephesians, "Husbands, love our wives, just as Christ loved the church

---

28. Ibid., 106.
29. Ibid., 202–218.
30. Ibid., 152–153.
31. Ibid., 18–21.
32. Ibid., 132–150.

and gave himself up for her," encourages the virtues of male servanthood.³³ This exhortation offers a new male ethic of peace and sacrificial love to counter the honor-shame codes of the time: "Rather than being the agent who guarantees domestic order through challenge and riposte in the public world, the husband is now admonished to imitate the peace of God and the self-giving love of Christ."³⁴ This exhortation to love encourages the husband to be responsible toward his wife as well as his children, though children are not explicitly mentioned.³⁵ As such, the Ephesian household code offers a strategy to overcome the male problematic. Aquinas combines the same Ephesian passage with his naturalistic view of the family to construct an ethic of "love paternalism." A main point of his family ethics is the ideal of permanent and monogamous marriage where the father is also involved in caring for his children. Luther, while countering the Catholic contempt over family life, also emphasizes fathers more than mothers in discharging their parental responsibility.³⁶ Browning and his team, however, are dissatisfied with "love paternalism" as a remedy because these theologies – from Ephesians to Luther – have always been inundated with the language of male responsibility and headship. The language falls short of equality because it is one-sided: husbands are to love their wives and wives are to submit to their husbands, and only husbands are exhorted to treat their wives as themselves but a reciprocal exhortation to the wives is missing. These "unequal" exhortations are devoid of the notion of inter-subjectivity and equal respect. Besides, "love paternalism" falls short of equal-regard as it puts all responsibility and power into the hands of men. It is the man who actively loves and shoulders responsibilities; the woman must passively submit and receive the man's love. As such they have led the later generations to lapse back into patriarchy. Furthermore, "love paternalism" promotes sacrificial love as the superior form of Christian

---

33. Ibid., 60.

34. Ibid., 144.

35. Ibid., 145. It should be noted that Browning et al., do not reference Eph 6:4 ("And, fathers, do not provoke your children to anger, but bring them up in the discipline and instruction of the Lord") in the same household code to argue for an ethic of paternal responsibility. Perhaps the parent-child relationship reflected in this passage is too hierarchical and fails to agree with Browning's ideal of the equal-regard family.

36. Ibid., 123–126.

love. As discussed, the authors consider that self-sacrifice should only be a means to the higher end of mutuality. They argue that the vision offered in the Ephesian household code is only partially successful in countering the Greco-Roman honor-shame codes. It only represents a point within the "trajectory" that aims at full equality, mutuality, and inter-subjectivity.[37] To complete this trajectory, the equal-regard ethic should be advocated so that responsibility and respect is equally shared within the family.

This is what critical familism offers as an ethic to disrupt today's "family crisis." In the end, Browning and his team advocate the ideal of equal-regard alone to address both patriarchy and the male problematic. They seem to believe that if equal-regard is successfully implemented, equality within the family will be achieved while the father, out of regard for the mother-child dyad, will take up his responsibility and remain in the family. But it is doubtful whether the ethic of equal-regard in its opposition to patriarchy – a strategy developed to overcome the male problematic, can successfully replace patriarchy as a new strategy to overcome the notorious problematic. It appears that the tension between equal-regard and the male problematic defies easy resolution. Even Browning himself says later in his career:

> Much of my writing on family has been designed to promote the reconstruction of modern marriage and family in order to enhance both family cohesion and an ethic of equal regard. I have [sic] hoped to do this in spite of the powerful forces of modernization that make these two values of equality and cohesion increasingly difficult to hold together.[38]

A close look at the equal-regard ethic and the male problematic reveals a contradiction between the two notions. John W. Miller observes that the male problematic is a gender-specific issue. Browning's "generalized and degenderized teaching" of equal-regard is inadequate to address the problem.[39] In other words, the inadequacy of the equal-regard ethic arises from its attempt to use a gender-neutral ethic to address a gender-specific issue.

---

37. Ibid., 146–147.
38. Browning, *Equality and the Family*, 347.
39. John W. Miller, "The Problem of Men, Reconsidered," in *Does Christianity Teach Male Headship? The Equal-Regard Marriage and Its Critics*, eds. David Blankenhorn, Don S. Browning, and Mary Stewart Van Leeuwen (Grand Rapids, MI: Eerdmans, 2004), 66.

As discussed, the male problematic arises from the male-female sexual differences and their respective reproductive strategies. The most common cultural strategies to overcome the male problematic have involved different forms of patriarchy. Although these strategies are unjust, yet being gender-specific, they are effective and families cohere well under patriarchal cultures. The "love paternalism" and "male headship" offered in Christian theology is also gender-specific – as revealed in its "one-sided" language – so it is also logically coherent with the male problematic. But the equal-regard ethic, while rejecting any one-sided language, is gender-neutral and is unable to address the problem. Thinking through the logic of the male problematic can reveal why this is so. It is argued that as the male mammal can have unlimited number of offspring by copulating with many females, he has an innate tendency to drift away from the mother-child dyad. Evolutionary psychology identifies four natural conditions for the father to cleave to the mother-child dyad: infant vulnerability, paternal certainty, frequent sexual exchanges, and mutual assistance. These conditions naturally compel and attract the man to stay in the family. Browning adopts a similar strategy and argues that the equal-regard ethic is able to captivate the couple in the family. He contends that equal-regard love encourages one to help one's partner "pursue a range of vital values and goods" such as "food, clothing, housing, pleasant friendships, sexual pleasure, rest, recuperation, and many more."[40] But in modernity these goods are also available outside of the family. With technological advancements and government assistance, the mother no longer needs her husband to raise her children. Mutual assistance is no longer a condition for better livelihood as people can now afford to live alone. In fact, modern people can enjoy freedom, personal control, and self-realization better without the burden of family.[41] Besides, sex is now readily available outside of the marriage bond; a man need not be "tied" to his wife to have sex.[42] Some men even believe

---

40. Browning, *Equality and the Family*, 277.

41. Eric Klinenberg, *Going Solo: The Extraordinary Rise and Surprising Appeal of Living Alone* (New York: Penguin, 2012), 17–18.

42. A survey shows that in 2006–2010, 74.5% of all American men between 15 and 44 had more than one female sexual partner in their lifetime. Among them, 66.8% were reported to have more than three partners and 21.6% had more than 15 partners. Anjani Chandra, Casey E. Copen, and William D. Mosher, "Sexual Behavior, Sexual Attraction,

that sex outside of stable relationships is more adventurous and desirable.[43] While these natural conditions of fatherhood are weakened, even stronger enticements should be offered to men for them to stay with the family. Instead, the equal-regard ethic further undercuts the traditional patriarchal structure that has long been used to entice the man to stay. Equal-regard, as an ethic to counter patriarchy, demands men to take up more parenting responsibilities, relinquish their monopoly on economic and political decisions, and learn communication skills for inter-subjectivity between the couple. In fact, a study has shown that equal role sharing and decision making enhance marital satisfaction for the wives but increase marital tension for husbands.[44] Browning and his team believe that by exercising the gender-neutral equal-regard love within the family, men would gain material and relational goods. But the reality is that they can now obtain these goods without the family. There is little reason why they would "give up" patriarchy, cleave to the mother-child dyad, while gaining no additional advantages. In the end, the equal-regard ethic not only fails to enhance family coherence, it even exacerbates family disruption. Miller, upon seeing that the gender-specific male problematic needs a gender-specific solution, suggests that the affirmation of manhood and fatherhood holds the key to the problem. He argues that an ethic that encourages family cohesion must specify what is required of men and women.[45] Maggie Gallagher offers a similar insight, saying that male headship in the contemporary context does not necessarily mean that the husband is the boss of the family. Instead, "family head" is an honorific title that compensates man for his loss of freedom in binding himself to the family. But it is the woman who really runs the family.[46] Patriarchy, a cultural solution to the male problem-

---

and Sexual Identity in the United States: Data from the 2006–2010," in *International Handbook on the Demography of Sexuality*, vol. 5, ed. Amanda K Baumle (New York: Springer Science + Business Media, 2013), 51.

43. Klinenberg, *Going Solo*, 89.

44. Judith K. Balswick and Jack O. Balswick, "Marriage as a Partnership of Equals," in *Discovering Biblical Equality: Complementarity without Hierarchy*, 2nd ed., ed. Ronald W. Pierce and Rebecca Merrill (Groothuis; Downers Grove, IL: InterVarsity, 2005), 449.

45. John W. Miller, "The Problem of Men, Reconsidered," 66–67.

46. Maggie Gallagher, "Reflections on Headship," in *Does Christianity Teach Male Headship?*, 111–125.

atic, pertains to the "male" and requires a male-specific answer. Miller and Gallagher are suggesting ways to do so.

3.4 Family as a Liberal Democracy

Traditional patriarchy that oppresses women and children must be challenged. Equal dignity among family members must not be subsumed under the desire for family cohesion. The above discussions by no means suggest a recovery of the traditional oppressive patriarchal structures; they only demonstrate that a contradiction underpins family cohesion and the ethic of equal-regard. I contend that the dilemma between male problematic and family cohesion is created from the way that Browning and his team conceive of the family. The way out therefore involves thinking of the family in a different manner. As mentioned above, they identify individualism and rational-choice thinking as the two cultural factors that shape modernity in both good and bad ways. They further reject the bad individualism that disrupts families and retain the good individualism that works against patriarchy, arguing that it encourages the "democratization" of family. The problem, I contend, is not with their analysis of individualism and rational-choice thinking but in their adoption of the modern notion of democracy into the family. According to the German legal scholar Gerhard Leibholz, democracy means that the people is sovereign and constitutes the final authority of a political reality. Although the principle of equality is imminent in every form of democracy, the meaning and expression of equality can vary. As a result, democracy is not necessarily inconsistent with absolutism, monarchism, or even totalitarianism. During the strife against monarchy in western history, democracy found an apt ally in liberalism and thereafter the two notions were inseparable. The notion of equality that flows out from this alliance between democracy and liberalism is characterized by equal involvement of everyone in shaping the will of the state.[47] Despite the blending of the two notions in modernity, democracy and liberalism are fundamentally different: democracy values the community as a whole while liberalism values the "creative freedom of

---

47. Gerhard Leibholz, "The Nature and Various Forms of Democracy," *Social Research* 5, no. 1 (Feb 1938): 84–92.

the individual endowed with reason."[48] In other words, liberalism elevates individual freedom – the freedom of a person to make one's own decisions – above collective freedom – the freedom of the whole people to create a political reality. The marriage of liberalism and democracy leads moderns to assume that the primary aim of democracy is to serve the individuals. Robert Song also contends that at the heart of liberalism lies a concept of the human agent. An individual is thought to be a sovereign chooser, detached from contingencies, and is related to others only through consent. Individual autonomy must also be respected, so any institutional attempt to control or coerce individual decision is an anathema. Another liberal mode of thought is universalism, which leads to the notions of equality of welfare and rejection of discrimination on grounds of class or gender. Individuals are considered identical for public and political purposes. Rationality is usually used as an instrument to settle disputes, to pursue individual goals, and to maximize individual utility.[49] Now it becomes obvious that the "democratization of family" advocated in critical familism is undergirded by this modern notion of liberal democracy. Several similarities are observed between them. First, critical familism aims at challenging patriarchy. Democratization within families means "respect for women and children . . . and the limitation of arbitrary male authority."[50] Invoking the notion of liberal democracy can help dethrone the "monarch" of the family and achieve equality between family members. Second, "democratization of the family" demands mutual exchange of intimacy, equal performance in work and parenting, and equal sharing in values construction.[51] It is an application of the equal-participation principle of liberal democracy in the family. Third, the emphasis on inter-subjectivity and communication skills in critical familism resembles the primacy of reason in negotiation and conflict-resolution in liberal thought. The "democratization of family" that critical familism advocates is in fact an attempt to model the family after the liberal democracy.

---

48. Ibid., 92.

49. Robert Song, *Christianity and Liberal Society* (Oxford: Oxford University Press, 1997), 40–43.

50. Browning et al, *From Culture Wars*, 3.

51. Ibid., 65–66.

While critical familism views the family as a modern liberal democracy, it can hardly resist the notion of individual autonomy from infusing into the family. Song points out that in liberal thought, a person is considered a sovereign chooser who associates with others only through consent.[52] Individuals *choose* to join a family; they are not born or called into one. Families are thought of as agglomerations of discrete individuals, and the association or dissolution of families only depends on the freedom and agreement of their members. As a result, family cohesion relies solely on the free will of its members. Coercion predicated upon power or economic differential, traditional norms, or religious symbols should not be used to bind members to the family. This is why critical familism does not retrieve marriage permanence from the Christian tradition and avoids speaking of marriages as divinely ordained. This is also why Browning assumes that inequality within the family inevitably leads to its "collapse," for a person who joins a democratic association would likely withdraw when inequality is experienced. If family members *choose* to bind together, family cohesion is determined by how attractive the family is. To encourage fathers to stay in the family, Browning toys with the idea that families that practice equal-regard can offer men opportunities to pursue a wide range of premoral goods. On reviewing the Chicago School of Economics' expansion of economic into the family, he suggests that economic incentive and wealth generation can serve as one among many arguments that support the intact, equal-regard family ethic.[53] Similarly, he cites social-science studies to demonstrate that married couples enjoy better health than unmarried people.[54] His intention of referencing these studies is obvious: to construct a narrative that encourages married persons, especially fathers, to stay in the family out of their own will. Resorting to these utilitarian arguments that emphasize the premoral goods of marriage is quite natural for Browning. If the family is understood as a democracy where members freely join for pursuit of their own good, it is the calculation of benefits that governs their decision to stay or to leave.

---

52. Song, *Christianity and Liberal Society*, 40.
53. Browning, *Equality and the Family*, 275–282.
54. Ibid., 298–303.

John Witte, Jr. recounts the history of how marriage, influenced by Enlightenment and utilitarian thoughts, shed its religious, social, and natural dimensions in the last several centuries. By the late twentieth century, only the contractual dimension remained. Now marriage is conceived as a private contract between two adults who are free to enter and exit from their marriage contract without external interference. The parties are only bound to support any young children they have. Yet without the participation of the state, the church, or the civil society, the ever-shortening marriages become destructive, and women and children bear the primary costs.[55] Browning also decries this "contractualism" of marriage, accusing "liberal theology" of accepting this contractual concept, advocating a plurality of family forms while ignoring the "crisis" that results from single-parent families.[56] He claims to separate himself from "liberal theology" by retrieving the Christian tradition of the intact, two-parent family. However, the same liberal thought undergirds his thinking; critical familism, no different from "liberal theology," also assumes that the family is a liberal democracy and marriage a private contract. However, the "intact" family does not chime with the liberal insistence on free consent. If family is a liberal democracy, no fixed form or fixed membership should be imposed. The "intact family," composed of the children's biological father and mother, is an imposition contrary to the liberal ideal. In this respect, the celebration of multiple forms of family proposed by "liberal theology" is in fact a more logical conclusion that results from Browning's "democratization of the family." Brent Waters is correct to observe that "Critical familism is more an attempt to reformulate a Christian understanding of marriage and family in the light of a dominant late liberal ethos than to cast a light of faith upon it."[57] "Liberal" fitfully characterizes the ethos that underlies critical familism.

Browning's attempt to marry the Christian notion of "intact family" with liberalism leads to the contradiction between equal-regard and family cohesion. The rhetoric of Christian family cannot be simply uprooted from

---

55. John Witte Jr., *From Sacrament to Contract: Marriage, Religion, and Law in the Western Tradition*, 2nd ed. (Louisville, KY: Westminster John Knox, 2012), 287–320.

56. Browning, *Equality and the Family*, 105–106.

57. Waters, *Family in Christian*, 241–242.

Christian theology and transplanted into the soil of liberalism. An alternative notion of the family founded upon Christian theology is needed. Before proposing that, I will first explicate several shortcomings associated with seeing the family as a liberal democracy. The first shortcoming arises from the awkward position of the child. The entrance of children into the family poses a tension with the understanding of the family as a liberal democracy. First, children are young and immature. They cannot participate in familial matters as equals to their parents. Second, they are dependent and require extra care which means unequal treatment. This makes the liberal ideal of universalism difficult to implement in the family. Third, as children are vulnerable and need extra care and protection, they often impose great demands on the adults who care for them, thereby curtailing the freedom and autonomy of these caregivers. The adult caregivers, once committed to the care-receivers, cannot simply relate with them out of consent. This obligation on the caregivers undermines the voluntaristic nature of liberal democracy. Browning also recognizes the necessity of this obligation due to children and proposes that biological parents are their best caregivers. This leads him to suggest, against the liberal ideal, that families must not dissolve when children are still young. As a negative measure, divorce should be made more difficult for couples with young children as a discouragement. On the more positive side, the ethic of equal-regard, intersubjective dialogues between partners, combined sixty-hour workweek, counseling and therapies can be used to encourage couples to stay and care for their children. But if there are no children or the children are old enough, the familial association needs not remain intact. This discussion shows that the "natural inequality" between children and parents makes it difficult to adopt the liberal democratic ideal into the family.

However, parental obligation is not totally contradictory to the ideals of liberalism. Universalism in liberal thought entails equal treatment to all, demanding the protection of the rights of the weak and the vulnerable. Witte points out that protecting the rights of children expresses the liberal notion of marriage as a private contract, that the parties must "respect the reliance and expectation interests of their children, who are third-party beneficiaries of their marital or sexual contracts."⁵⁸ Therefore, from the ideal of universalism and equal treatment arises two ethics pertaining to the family: the ethic of equal-regard ensures justice among the adult members, and the ethic of parental duty safeguards the rights of the children. These two ethics do not cohere well in the family, leading to the contradiction between equal-regard and family cohesion in Browning's critical familism. Now we understand the reason behind Browning's emphasis on children. It is not, as mentioned above, the theological notion of procreation that is elevated above marriage fidelity or permanence; it is the liberal notion of protection of rights that motivates critical familism's emphasis on children. Besides, in the liberal framework, the goods of marriage fidelity and permanence become private matters between two consenting adults. These goods need not be retained but can be reinterpreted to protect the rights of children. This analysis shows that critical familism is in fact founded upon liberalism, not Christian theology. Christian theology has little contribution to critical familism. Christian doctrines, such as creation, redemption, or eschatology, do not shed light on the male problematic nor in constructing the notion of equal-regard.

The immaturity of children poses another difficulty in applying the ideal of liberal democracy to the family. Young children cannot participate in familial matters as equals to adults and cannot reciprocate the care and respect given them by their parents. Browning and his team do not think that this prevents us from viewing the family as a liberal democracy or applying the equal-regard ethic to parent-child relationships. Instead, they adopt a "life-cycle perspective" of equal-regard, meaning that "Love as equal regard means different things for different family members at different points in family and individual life cycles."⁵⁹ For instance, the parent-child relationship does not begin as mutual. Parents must give their infant much more than they receive from her. Yet this imbalance is temporary; the parent-child relationship becomes increasingly mutual when the child learns to reciprocate,⁶⁰ and the aim of parenting is to bring children into full equality

---

58. Witte, *From Sacrament to Contract*, 320.
59. Browning et al, *From Culture Wars*, 154.
60. Ibid., 178–179.

and mutuality with their parents.[61] Bonnie Miller-McLemore, a member of Browning's team, further explicates the parent-child relationship using the notion of "transitional hierarchy." Hierarchy between parents and children is necessary as they are in different developmental stages. Children should be given leniency toward their neediness and behavior, and parents should hold more authority in giving them guidance. When children are born, parents enter a period of "transitional renunciation" and they make many sacrifices for them. Being "transitional," the hierarchy must move toward mutuality as children grow up, and self-sacrifice must also be balanced out over the long run.[62] Yet mutuality between parents and children is not merely a distant hope. Browning and his team use Erik Erikson's developmental theory to explicate another aspect of mutuality between them. The theory argues that people at different life stages have different developmental needs. It is obvious that children need their parents to grow up, but the reverse is also true. The development goal of adulthood is generativity, which can be achieved by raising one's own children. Consequently, "children and adult *need each other* to meet these needs."[63] Besides, parents also obtain great pleasure when raising their own children. Enabling their parents to attain generativity and giving them pleasure are the ways that children can reciprocate them.[64] Therefore, the "life-cycle perspective" of equal-regard speaks of two different notions of reciprocity: a temporal notion where the self-giving of parents are to be returned in the future, and a beneficial notion where parents and children both obtain goods from their ongoing relationships. However, both notions fail to live up to Browning's ideal of equal-regard. For the beneficial notion, it is true that childrearing can help parents attain their development goal, but the "regard" between young children and parents can never be truly equal. Miller-McLemore points out that while children can depend on their parents to fulfill most of their needs, the reverse is not true. It is even dangerous for parents to fulfill

---

61. Ibid., 296–297.
62. Bonnie Miller-McLemore, "Sloppy Mutuality: Just Love for Children and Adults," in *Mutuality Matters: Family, Faith, and Just Love*, ed. Herbert Anderson (Lanham, MD: Rowman & Littlefield, 2004), 127–130.
63. Browning et al., *From Culture Wars*, 296. Original emphasis.
64. Ibid., 297.

their personal needs exclusively through raising their children.[65] Parents and young children can benefit each other mutually, yet their relationship is not fully equal or reciprocal.

The temporal notion of reciprocity is even more problematic. If parental self-sacrifice is to be "balanced out over the long run," children must reciprocate their parents when they grow up. Browning avers that "Good parental care should warmly and constantly expect children to grow up and treat both others and parents with equal regard – as ends in themselves deserving respect and the recognition of their human needs."[66] This expectation of equal regard appears praiseworthy until no return can be expected whatsoever from the children, such as in the cases of severely handicapped or dying children. The equal-regard ethic would not advise parents to give continual care to these children. The same ethic, which says that one should always expect the same regard from the other, can also become problematic when a grownup child decides whether she should care for her dying parents who had failed to take care of her when she was young. If she decides to do so, it is out of sacrifice, not equal-regard. Therefore, the temporal notion of equal-regard ethic inevitably breaks down in cases where the future is hopeless or the past is irredeemable. Even in healthy parent-child relationships, it may not be the best to always aim at "balancing out" the sacrifices that parents make. Perhaps the parent-child relationship is simply unlike that between two individuals in a liberal democracy; the care given from parents to children is never expected to be reciprocated in full. A personal experience may illustrate this. When I was in my teenage years, I realized how much my mother, a widow, sacrificed herself trying to raise the three of us. Once I declined her offer to give me a birthday present, telling her that what she had given me was more than enough, and that I had already owed her much. But she insisted on giving me the present and said to me, "Whatever you receive from me, pay it forward to your own children." The parent-child relationship is not simply about two individuals; it is also intergenerational, looking forward to their common

---

65. Miller-McLemore, "Sloppy Mutuality," 130–131.
66. Don S. Browning, "Response," in *The Equal-Regard Family and Its Friendly Critics: Don Browning and the Practical Theological Ethics of the Family*, ed. John Witte Jr., M Christian Green, and Amy Wheeler (Grand Rapids, MI: Eerdmans, 2007), 253.

future. "Paying forward," instead of "paying back," is the essence of familial progeny. Seeing the family as a liberal democracy simply lacks this intergenerational perspective. Even Browning himself never says explicitly that children should take care of their parents when they grow old, although this is the natural conclusion of his equal-regard ethic. Instead, he repeatedly emphasizes that parents must ensure the wellbeing of their children. It is true that children should care for their parents, but it may not be good to do it out of equal-regard. In fact, in Chinese culture, even today, a grownup child is considered disrespectful toward her parents if she regards them as her equals. Besides, the fifth commandment stipulates that everyone shall honor their parents. No reciprocal statement or age specification is given. In fact, the commandment was originally given to adult males and later diffused to the whole assembly of God's people.[67] In other words, honoring one's parents is a lifelong obligation which does not change with one's life-stage. Upon contemplating the virtues associated with this commandment, Yiu Sing Lúcás Chan contends that parents are never merely "friends of their children" and that there is a necessary boundary between them.[68] It is true that the "hierarchy" between parents and children is "transitional," yet it should not be eradicated entirely. Children, no matter how old they are, do not become full equals with their parents as between associates within a liberal democracy. This lingering "inequality" between parents and children does not entail absolute obedience or power differential; it means that children should always respect their parents as those who have given them the gift of life, nourished them, and instructed them when they were young.[69] This aspect of their relationship can never be reciprocated.

Another difficulty of this family concept lies in the relationship between the couple. The equal-regard ethic flows naturally from the liberalism ideal of equality and universalism. As discussed above, the ethic is incompatible with sacrificial love. But Browning and his co-authors recognize that love as self-sacrifice has been central in Christian thought. Instead of expelling

---

[67]. Patrick D. Miller, *The Ten Commandments* (Louisville, KY: Westminster John Knox, 2009), 174–175.

[68]. Yiu Sing Lúcás Chan, *The Ten Commandments and the Beatitudes: Biblical Studies and Ethics for Real Life* (Lanham, MD: Rowman & Littlefield, 2012), 80.

[69]. Ibid., 78.

sacrificial love, they subordinate it to mutuality, arguing that self-sacrifice can only serve as a means to the end of mutuality. Love as equal-regard, they claim, is testified to in the Scripture and should be the ideal form of Christian love.[70] This sparks much debate over what the essence of Christian love is. For instance, Miller-McLemore argues, out of experience, that sacrificial love is not always subservient to mutuality. She observes that love as sacrifice is embedded in nature, especially in the parenting instincts of animals and humans, who do not think about mutuality when they care for their offspring. Besides, enticing fathers to stay with their families involves self-sacrifice, not just equality. Furthermore, the passionless language of equal-regard is often inadequate in day-to-day negotiations between couples; the emotionally-laden language of "sacrificial love" more often serves these real-life practices better.[71] Waters argues that depriving sacrificial love of its inherent value reduces love to a means of self-fulfillment, thereby weakening the familial bonds that the equal-regard ethic aims to strengthen. He avers that the family is not a place for one to negotiate self-fulfillment; it is instead a community where members practice "the sacrificial virtues that give love its greatest breadth and depth."[72] Timothy Jackson engages with the equal-regard ethic through Kierkegaardian theology. He argues that mutuality is predicated upon natural justice and may serve the "political" and "personal" dimensions of marriage well. Yet salvation does not come from natural justice but through Christ, who revealed a divine agapic love that transcends natural justice. Mutual love cannot save the modern family; only the agapic love of Christ can.[73] Based on Søren Kierkegaard's notion of love, Jackson explicates the difference between mutual love and *agape*: the former targets reciprocal justice while the latter is an imitation of Christ in the service of the neighbor. Besides, *agape* must be understood along two dimensions. The vertical dimension is directed to

---

70. Browning et al., *From Culture Wars*, 273–275.

71. Bonnie Miller-McLemore, "Generativity, Self-Sacrifice, and the Ethics of Family Life," in *The Equal-Regard Family and Its Friendly Critics*, 28–30.

72. Waters, *Family in Christian*, 242.

73. Timothy P. Jackson, "Judge William and Professor Browning: A Kierkegaardian Critique of Equal-Regard Marriage and the Democratic Family," in *The Equal-Regard Family and Its Friendly Critics*, eds. John Witte Jr, M. Christian Green and Amy Wheeler (Grand Rapids, MI: Eerdmans), 124.

God, so love is foremost a duty toward God. The horizontal dimension involves unconditional willing of the good of neighbor. Both dimensions are related but the vertical has priority, so neighborly love must be understood in relation to God, not merely in relation to each other. Only when understood as a duty toward God can our love of neighbor be unconditional. Mutuality, instead of being the goal to be desired, is contingent. It is just a byproduct of unconditional love. As mutual love expects response from the beloved, it cannot be unconditional.[74]

The gist of the debate is this question: should a person always expect return from the one she loves, whether a return of respect, love, or action? Browning answers yes while his critics say no. Miller-McLemore observes that parents sometimes act as if they do not expect any return from their children. Waters thinks that expecting return from the beloved reduces love to a means of self-fulfillment. Jackson argues that one should not expect return, though return may come as a byproduct of one's love. When Browning responds to criticisms on love as equal-regard, he clarifies that mutuality does not equate reciprocity. Mutuality is also "unconditional; it is not conditioned . . . by reciprocal return."[75] But he adds, "loving the neighbor as oneself . . . demands that the person exhibiting equal regard *has the right to expect to be treated with equal regard* as well."[76] Effectively Browning is saying that a person should love the other even if the other does not reciprocate, though she "has the right to expect" this reciprocity. I would argue that those who embrace sacrificial love also have this "right" to expect reciprocity. Self-sacrifice is not self-hatred or self-derogation. It does not rejoice in the sacrifice itself but always hopes for restoration, redemption, or vindication. But hope is not necessarily of this world. Gene Outka points out that sacrificial love always has an eschatological reference; human hope does not lie in vindication or reciprocity in this world but in the final triumph of love to be brought in at the *parousia*.[77] This eschatological hope encourages those who embrace sacrificial love to relinquish

---

74. Ibid., 137–142.
75. Browning, "Response," 253.
76. Ibid., 254. My emphasis.
77. Gene Outka, *Agape: An Ethical Analysis* (New Haven, CT: Yale University Press, 1972), 29–30, 172–173.

their "right" to expect reciprocity from the ones they love. Therefore, both mutual love and sacrificial love affirm that the one who loves has the "right" to expect reciprocity. The difference between them is that those who practice mutual love exercise this "right" while those who embrace sacrificial love relinquish it on this side of the eschaton.

By saying that one "*has* the right" to expect reciprocity, Browning seems to allow one to choose either to exercise or relinquish this right (i.e. to choose mutual love or sacrificial love). But this is not the case. His downplaying of sacrificial love, his understanding of the family as a liberal democracy, and his lack of eschatological vision all indicate that his ethic of equal-regard demands one to exercise this right. One does not only "have" the right to expect reciprocity; one should exercise this right. Therefore, contrary to what Browning claims, the ethic of equal-regard and the ethic of reciprocity are not that different after all. In real-life situations, should the beloved fail to honor this right of the lover, the one who loves ought to exercise her right and demand appropriate respect and action from the beloved, and a negotiation process begins. This is why inter-subjectivity dialogue, communication skills, and the therapeutic are important in the ethic of equal-regard: "couples will need . . . to *work out* what is just and equitable in light of the demands of shared housework, their respective skills, personal inclinations, and the needs of children."[78] However, Waters rightly points out that these negotiations do not necessarily promote mutuality; more often they encourage partners to express and strengthen a primary regard for the self. The family then becomes a collection of individuals pursuing their own goods, instead of a community in its own right. Then the individual stories cannot weave into a familial narrative that enfolds into God's creation story, informing and enriching the particular life stories of each member.[79] When the family is seen as a liberal democracy, primacy is given to the individuals who seek self-fulfillment from the association and reciprocity from one another. The language of mutuality is then used to express the idea that individual fulfillment is the main purpose for one to enter into relationships. For instance, Kathlyn Breazeale proposes

---

78. Browning et al., *From Culture Wars*, 318. Original emphasis.
79. Waters, *Family in Christian*, 242–243.

"mutual empowerment" as the paradigm of marriage. Mutuality means that partners should not seek to transform the other into a preconceived image, thereby limiting her possibilities. Instead, through marital intimacy, each should empower the other to "become" toward "greater openness and self-affirmation."[80] In other words, mutuality within marriage is the means to the end of one's own "becoming" and "self-affirmation." Similarly, the language of equality in marriage is often invoked to strengthen one's claim against the other in their negotiation. Joel Anderson advocates equality in the family as it guarantees that "divorce is not available to one spouse on more advantageous terms." He says that if the option to exit from a marriage is equally available to both partners, divorce can be prevented as both voices are backed by an equal "threat of exit" and thus heard equally, and the chance of successful negotiation increases.[81] Effectively, he is arguing that claiming of equal power is necessary for a fair negotiation over the marriage or divorce contract. Another example can be seen in Rhona Mahony's concern over economic inequalities between couples. She contends that men need to do half the work of raising children, otherwise economic equality between the genders cannot be achieved. The key to success is through negotiation over the division of labor at home. Using economics and game theory, she offers practical strategies to women on how to improve their negotiating position to achieve this equality.[82] Mutuality and equality are indeed important in the family; sexual ethics must challenge any destructive inequality and oppression in the familial sphere. But if the family is understood as a liberal democracy, what becomes primary is the protection and exercise of rights of its members. The language that Browning uses – a "right" to expect equal regard – also reveals this ideal. As shown in the above cases, the "rights" approach and the individualistic tendency of liberalism frequently turns desire for mutuality and equality into agonistic negotiations that conceal a self-seeking agenda. Jeremy Waldron

---

80. Kathlyn A. Breazeale, *Mutual Empowerment: A Theology of Marriage, Intimacy, and Redemption* (Minneapolis, MN: Fortress, 2008), 15–18.

81. Joel Anderson, "Is Equality Tearing Families Apart?" in *Mutuality Matters: Family, Faith, and Just Love*, ed. Herbert Anderson (Lanham, MD: Rowman & Littlefield, 2004), 98.

82. Rhona Mahony, *Kidding Ourselves: Breadwinning, Babies, and Bargaining Power* (New York: Basic Books, 1995), 4–6.

also points out that the "rights" language, when used in the family, reduces the good things of marriage – sexual intimacy, fidelity, economic equality, etc. – as a "claim." Such language assumes a querulous and adversarial relationship, ejecting warmth and intimacy from the family. "To stand on one's right is to distance oneself from those to whom the claim is made; it is to announce, so to speak, an opening of hostilities; and it is to acknowledge that other warmer bonds of kinship, affection, and intimacy can no longer hold."[83] This is not to say that familial relationship is only and always based on love and affection; the claiming of rights can be legitimate or even imperative for some instances. But to understand family as a liberal democracy is to assign the protection and claiming of rights as the *modus operandi* of the family. Love and affection becomes contingent and instrumental, only serving the good of equality and equal-regard. This is against the Christian ideal of love as the ethical principle for familial and other relationships. Browning's practical theology of the family, therefore, falls short of this Christian ideal. In the end, although Browning's concern over biology and procreation appears to have remedied the shortcomings of Farley and Thatcher's theories, his ideal of equal-regard jeopardizes the harmonious relationship between man and woman.

3.5 Theological Assessment

Browning contends that the main purpose of his ethics is to promote family cohesion and equal-regard. As discussed above, the crucial task is to solve the male problematic without resorting to patriarchy. The word "problematic" reveals much about his understanding of the family. He perceives human persons as autonomous individuals always seeking freedom and self-benefit. By nature, a person does not bind with others unless compelled by necessity. For instance, the vulnerability of human infants compels them to bind themselves to others in order to survive. Since the mother naturally gives birth, the infant bonds with her first. But as persons are autonomous, all human bindings are inherently problematic. Based on the

---

83. Jeremy Waldron, "When Justice Replaces Affection: The Need for Rights," in *Liberal Rights: Collected Papers, 1981–1991* (Cambridge: Cambridge University Press, 1993), 372–373.

same naturalistic view of human association, the cultural anthropologist Anthony Gittins argues that the mother-child dyad is the "most basic and symbiotic of human relationships."[84] Not only do infants need their mothers, mothers also need their infants for emotional and physical satisfaction. Therefore, the mother-child dyad is born out of mutual necessity and remains strong until the child grows up. On top of this single-parent family, the two-parent family is formed subsequently by adding another member, such as the mother's sibling or her conjugal partner, to this basic unit.[85] It should be noted that this naturalistic view of family formation also assumes that human bonding is precarious. It is the necessity of species perpetuation that demands individuals to bind together for successful childrearing. Based on the same view of family formation, Browning argues for a two-parent family where the biological father is bound to the mother-child dyad. Failure to conform to this best family arrangement results in the two "problematics" that Browning decries: the male and female problematics. The former means an innate tendency for males to drift away from their families, and the latter points to a tendency for the mother to raise her children without the help of the father, thereby harming the welfare of herself and her children.[86] The liberal notion of the human person renders all human bonding precarious. The relationships between man, woman, and their children are intrinsically "problematic." Problems are not contingent, but innate, to the family. This is another reason why Browning finds it difficult to maintain both equal-regard and cohesion in the family.

A proper theological response, I contend, is to test this liberal model of personhood and family formation against the Christian notion of human relationality. O'Donovan's framework of the created order can help formulate such a notion. He argues that morality can be known through an objective created order vindicated in Christ. While natural knowledge can provide us with certain moral principles, God's moral order is only affirmed

---

84. Anthony J. Gittins, "In Search of Goodenough Families: Cultural and Religious Perspectives," in *Mutuality Matters: Family, Faith, and Just Love*, ed. Herbert Anderson (Lanham, MD: Rowman & Littlefield, 2004), 170.

85. Ibid., 170–172.

86. Browning et al., *From Culture Wars*, 106.

in the life, death, resurrection, and exaltation of Christ.[87] In the subject of family formation, natural knowledge offers two conflicting views. On the one hand, the experience of human freedom leads to the liberal view of humans as autonomous individuals always seeking freedom from one another. On the other hand, the need for species perpetuation demands successful rearing of children and in turn requires stable bonding between parents. These two views from natural knowledge lead to different moral principles, resulting in the ethical dilemma that Browning faces. Christian morality, however, should be based on God's created order as vindicated in Christ. But Christ did not simply affirm the original creation; his redemptive work does not merely restore the garden of Eden but also transforms creation toward its fulfillment in the New Jerusalem.[88] In the sphere of marriage and family, both the creation narrative and the eschatological imagery should contribute to the Christian understanding of marriage and human association.

Jesus referred to the creation narrative while discussing with the Pharisees concerning marriage. The Gospels contain two pericopes – Mark 10:2–12 and Matthew 19:3–12 – describing the same event from two different angles. In both texts, the Pharisees started a debate with Jesus concerning divorce. In the Markean pericope, the Pharisees asked Jesus if divorce was lawful and in the Matthean text, divorce was assumed lawful and the ground of divorce was discussed. In both narratives, the Pharisees appealed to the Law of Moses to argue for the legitimacy of divorce. In the ancient Roman world, divorce was common and informal. Infertility, adultery, and a desire to remarry political alliance were the common reasons for divorce.[89] Divorce was also widely considered acceptable among the first-century Jews, as Deuteronomy 24:1 clearly permits it. The subject of contention within Judaism was over on what grounds divorce should be allowed, not over the lawfulness of divorce.[90] However, Jesus responded by correcting

---

87. O'Donovan, *Resurrection and Moral Order*, 16–20.
88. Ibid., 55.
89. Beryl Rawson, "The Roman Family," in *The Family in Ancient Rome: New Perspectives*, ed. Beryl Rawson (Ithaca, NY: Cornell University Press, 1986), 32–33.
90. David Instone-Brewer, *Divorce and Remarriage in the 1ˢᵗ and 21ˢᵗ Century*, Grove Biblical Series, Vol. 19 (Cambridge: Grove Books, 2001), 8–9.

their assumptions. The Mosaic law, Jesus said, did not "command" divorce; it was a concession to those who were hard-hearted. Marriage should not be informed by this law of concession that results from human sinfulness. Instead, the original creation account and the "one-flesh" union between male and female should shape our moral vision concerning marriage.[91] In other words, God's intention in creation provides the basis of marriage morality. Marriage should be permanent as it reflects the "one-flesh" union that God has joined together. A Christian moral vision concerning marriage should not begin with divorce but with the original union between man and woman. Now a similarity can be observed between the Pharisees in the first century and Browning in the twentieth. Both assume that the bond between husband and wife is unstable; both believe in an innate tendency for the husband to leave his wife. The Pharisees accept that the hearts of husbands are hard and Browning presumes that all males have a natural tendency to drift away from their families. As a result, the Pharisees busy themselves with the ground of divorce and Browning tries to protect the children. But Jesus points out that their assumption is wrong. The "one-flesh" union should instead inform our idea of marriage and family formation.

It is upon the same creation account that Barth constructs his theory of sexual differentiation and human fellowship. Observing that "male and female he created them" in Genesis 1:27 immediately follows the phrase "in the image of God he created them," Barth argues that sexual differentiation, or the "duality of man and woman," is the *imago Dei* that a human person bears. The image of God in a human person does not give her intrinsic worth or special abilities; it makes her relational, as the triune God is relational. The relationship between man and woman is the paradigm for all human relationships, either with God or among one another.[92] Therefore, the encounter between man and woman is not confined to the sphere of marriage but can be extended to all other human relationships. Nevertheless, marriage is still the *telos* and at the center of human

---

91. Raymond F. Collins, *Divorce in the New Testament* (Collegeville, MN: Liturgical Press, 1992), 112.

92. Barth, *Church Dogmatics Vol. 3.1*, 184–186.

fellowship.[93] The parent-child relationship, for instance, grows out of this man-woman relationship and is the "second sphere" of human fellowship.[94] This view of human relationality based on sexual difference entails several moral principles that are pertinent to our discussions. First, one should obey God's particular command by affirming one's calling as man or woman so interchanging of vocation must not happen. Yet the particularity of masculinity and femininity is cultural-dependent and cannot be bound to any universal standard.[95] In other words, it is our response to God's calling as man or woman in a particular context, not our own decision in choosing an association that benefits the self that governs our binding with other family members. Second, no individual is self-contained; man is ordered to woman and woman to man. Sexual difference is a polarity where one pole must understand oneself vis-à-vis the other. Third, what is common between man and woman takes precedence over their differences. Oneness in the Lord is the basis of their distinction, and this oneness also directs them to fellowship with each other, forming human communities. Within this fellowship, one must consider the other, question the other, hear and make responsible answer to the other's question.[96] Von Balthasar also constructs his view on man and woman from the creation narratives. From the first creation account, he argues that through the *imago Dei*, human beings take on God's image as father and mother to humanity and as husband to Israel. In other words, a man as father and husband, or a woman as mother and wife, is no mere human undertaking but reflects the symbolic words of God as father, mother, and spouse in the Bible. Creation of the woman from man in the second creation account, according to von Balthasar, suggests that a solitary person cannot attain fulfillment by simply knowing, naming, and mastering over the world. A person is "not good" until one encounters a human counterpart. As the woman is formed out of the man's rib, they are dependent upon each other.[97]

---

93. Barth, *Church Dogmatics Vol. 3.4*, 140.
94. Ibid., 240.
95. Ibid., 149–154.
96. Ibid., 163–167.
97. von Balthasar, *Theo-drama*, 369–372.

Barth and von Balthasar's views of sexual relationship and human fellowship, based on the creation accounts, offer a counter-narrative to that of liberalism. Several implications ensue. First, contrary to liberal thoughts, man and woman are not discrete and autonomous individuals. Instead, they are in original oneness, occupying the opposite poles of a duality and must find fulfillment through human fellowship. Bearing the *imago Dei*, a human person is by nature relational and is dependent on others; life unburdened by human associations is unfulfilling. Second, relationship within family is not predicated upon equal-regard or justice, but informed by the vocation of each person in his or her specific role as husband, wife, father, mother, or child. The biblical images of God as father, mother, and spouse, or the image of Christ as son provide the moral vision pertinent to each particular role. It is not the abstract equal-regard love, but the specific love of the husband, the wife, the father, the mother, and the child that becomes normative in familial relationships. Third, the family is not an expansion of the mother-child dyad for the purpose of species propagation. Instead, it is built upon the husband-wife union with children as extensions of this marital union. Family is not formed by self-benefit or compelled by natural necessities but is a faithful response to God's calling to multiply and be fruitful. It is not because of children that a marriage must remain stable; it is out of a stable and loving spousal relationship that marital love unfolds into parental love.[98]

As Christ's redemptive work brings the original creation towards its fulfillment in the eschaton, the creation narrative must be complemented by the eschatological imagery to give a complete understanding of the Christian family. In his discussions with the Sadducees about conjugal relations in the eschaton, Jesus said, "Those who belong to this age marry and are given in marriage; but those who are considered worthy of a place in that age and in the resurrection from the dead neither marry nor are given in marriage" (Luke 20:34–35, NRSV). The biological conjugal marriage will cease and will be transformed in the eschaton, where the marriage between Christ and the church takes place.[99] This eschatological marriage

---

98. Waters, *Family in Christian*, 181.
99. Rev 19:7–9; 21:2–3; 21:9–11; 22:17.

imagery shows that Christ, the bridegroom, loves the church, his bride.[100] The love within the conjugal marriage is transformed and extended to the whole community of believers,[101] and the church takes on the familial quality as the household of faith.[102] The eschatological transformation of marriage frees the human race from the imperative to procreate on this side of the eschaton. Augustine avers that before Christ came, marriage and procreation was an obligation so that the Savior could be born. But after Christ comes, the formation of God's people no longer depends on biological propagation but through spiritual rebirth.[103] Therefore, singleness and marriage become alternative vocations, subject to a person's particular calling and gift.[104] Now in the age after Christ came, it is not because of natural necessity that a person marries and procreates; it is out of obedience to God's particular calling that she does so.

The eschatological transformation of marriage can shed light on the male problematic that worries Browning. His notion of male problematic, derived from evolutionary psychology, is based on a similarity between humans and other mammals. According to the theory, human beings, similar to other mammals, need to find the best way to propagate. The male problematic arises from the reproductive characteristics of the male mammals, who find it advantageous to copulate with many without investing in their offspring. There are indeed similarities between human beings and animals. The first creation narrative describes the creation of humans and mammals on the same day. Living creatures of the sky and the waters, as well as human beings, are given the command "be fruitful and multiply." The second creation narrative depicts that both animals and humans are fashioned from the dust of the ground. Therefore, it is not remarkable that, being similar to other animals, the human male is also infested with the male problematic. However, a fundamental difference between humans and animals is also suggested in the creation narratives. Barth points out that as only human

---

100. Yohanes Adrie Hartopo, "The Marriage of the Lamb: The Background and Function of the Marriage Imagery in the Book of Revelation" (PhD diss., Westminster Theological Seminary, 2005), 206.

101. O'Donovan, *Resurrection and Moral Order*, 70.

102. Waters, *Family in*, 231.

103. Augustine, "Good of Marriage," 22.

104. Barth, *Church Dogmatics Vol. 3.4*, 143–145.

beings are created in the image of God, we are the only creatures who can hear and obey God.[105] Only we can perform free actions which are not determined by innate, animalistic drives. Helmut Thielicke observes that sex act in animals is completely automatic due to the estrous cycle. Only human beings are exempt from this natural cycle so that we are capable of deliberating and conforming to a sexual ethic. The ability to transcend the animalistic drive gives us the chance to become a human being who is responsible for one's own action.[106] This biological difference between humans and animals in the original creation already suggests that the human males do not necessarily fall under the spell of the male problematic. Besides, the eschatological transformation of marriage further qualifies the innate animalistic drive to propagate. Human hope and *telos*, now fulfilled in Christ, are no longer predicated upon progeny. When the necessity to propagate has been relieved, any decision to marry and procreate becomes a free choice and a free response to God's calling. When human males and females are not compelled to procreate, then the "best strategy to propagate" no longer informs procreation. Instead, procreation is guided by a free and self-giving agapic love aiming at an unfolding and extending of marital love into parental love. Sexual ethics, therefore, should direct our attention toward a discernment of God's calling and receiving the gift of love to live out this calling. A person should discern whether she is called by God to remain single or to marry. If she is called into marriage, further discernment is needed to decide whom she should wed. Besides, marriage does not entail parenthood. Barth is correct to say that parenthood is a "free and . . . optional gift of the goodness of God."[107] A child born to this marriage would then result from a series of careful discernments from singleness through marriage to parenthood. The child is thus a precious gift of God, not out of necessity but in accordance to God's freedom and goodwill. Then the father and mother are to receive the child in gratitude and in awe, nurturing the child as loving and responsible parents. Children are cared for not because they can claim certain rights from their parents but because they originate from and extend the love between their parents.

---

105. Barth, *Church Dogmatics Vol. 3.1*, 178.
106. Thielicke, *Ethics of Sex*, 52–58.
107. Barth, *Church Dogmatics Vol. 3.4*, 266.

Stable bonding between husband and wife becomes a *precondition* of childrearing; it does not become an imperative *after* a child is conceived. Such a moral vision of family formation offers a better alternative to the liberal conception of the family. The sexual ethic that advocates discernment of vocation, obedient response to God's calling, and receiving of the gift of love is also superior to Browning's equal-regard ethic. Instead of claiming rights and expecting reciprocity from each other, family members would invite God, the source of human love, into their family as the head of household. The family would not be a mere agglomeration of individuals each pursuing her own good. Instead, in Waters's words, it would become a place where "the narrative identities of two spouses . . . become the single story of a marriage, . . . the narrative identity of a family becomes the personal stories of parents and children, [and] . . . a familial narrative becomes enfolded into God's story of a vindicated creation."[108]

Browning argues that the greatest achievements of the early Jesus movement in the sphere of family include challenging the patriarchal clan, inaugurating gender egalitarianism, and fracturing the honor and shame codes.[109] These achievements sowed the seeds of the democratization of family which, he suggests, can be brought to fruition in the contemporary world. It is true that the early Christians have influenced the social and political structures of the family. Yet the transformation was not directed toward democracy where power is shared equally among all members. Instead, familial relations were relativized so that people could pledge allegiance to the Kingdom of God.[110] The imperative to marry and procreate was removed so that Christians could serve the Lord better.[111] All were proclaimed equal so that everyone could join the body of Christ through baptism.[112] In other words, people were liberated not to become their own lords but to prostrate under the lordship of Christ. Similarly, in the Christian family, the traditional patriarchal head was replaced by the

---

108. Waters, *Family in Christian*, 243.
109. Browning et al., *From Culture Wars*, 132–147.
110. Matt 10:34–39; Luke 14:26.
111. 1 Cor 7:32–35.
112. Gal 3:28.

headship of Christ.[113] Browning has mistaken this replacement of headship as a democratization of the family. The shortcoming of his critical familism lies in his emphasis on Christ's liberating power while ignoring his lordship. When people are liberated *from* patriarchy but not *for* Christ, they become their own lords. Without the headship of Christ, liberal democracy fills the void and becomes the model for the family. Under the influence of late liberalism, family members are atomized into discrete individuals each claiming their own rights, and equal-regard becomes the only acceptable ethic that governs the relationship between family members. But the result is that family ethics become contradictory and family cohesion is rendered impossible.

3.6 Conclusions

One objective of Browning's critical familism is to enhance family cohesion while promoting its democratization. His liberal understanding of the human person, however, makes stable and loving relationships between family members precarious. In his thinking, successful propagation of the human species requires the mother-child dyad to secure help from the father, who has an innate tendency to drift away. To uphold the ideal of equality, claiming of rights and expectation of reciprocity become the *modus operandi* of the family. Perhaps *dualism* is the word to characterize the relationship between man and woman in critical familism. As mentioned in the previous chapter, *dualism* means that two beings are split into opposing entities which are in frequent conflict, each trying to dominate the other. Union of man and woman under the purview of *dualism* is inherently unstable, and family members would struggle to keep the family intact. This chapter offers an alternative model of human association and family formation based on the framework of God's created order. The creation narrative in Scripture describes man and woman in original union. A solitary human person is "not good," and sexual differentiation – the basis of human fellowship – brings fulfillment to human life. The eschatological transformation of marriage relativizes the imperative to procreate so that marriage and

---

113. 1 Cor 11:3. Paul's letter to Philemon also suggests that Christ's lordship surpasses that of the household head in matters concerning master-slave relationships.

parenthood become vocations. Man and woman are liberated from their animal instincts toward obeying God's calling, whether as singles, spouses, or parents. Children born of such marriages are received and cared for as gifts of God. Sexual differentiation stems from an original oneness so that man and woman are interdependent. Perhaps Meilaender's notion of *duality*, which characterizes the mind-body relationship in the previous chapter, can again provide an imagery for the relationship between man and woman. A "duality, or polarity . . . holds together in harmonious and creative union two disparate elements – holds them together without obliterating their separateness."[114] In Meilaender's thinking, *duality* is undergirded by two necessary elements. First, the two entities must be different so that "individuality is not obliterated or merged into an undifferentiated oneness."[115] Man and woman cannot be reduced to an androgynous or asexual being; each should remain other to the other. Despite their differences, man and woman still belong to the same *duality* and must find a way to harmonious relationship. Otherwise the *duality* is split into *dualism*. Second, man and woman must stand before God. Human beings, he claims, "stand *before* God, hearing the divine address and made for life in harmony with God." This standing before God is also to "stand *beside* each other, addressed by God not in isolation but in the community of male and female."[116] This second element complements the first, preventing the *duality* from falling apart. While pondering the difficulty of keeping marital commitments, Meilaender claims that our earthly commitments must be "drawn into the transforming power of God's love . . . touched and transformed by the Eternal."[117] Human beings are finite and fallen; we cannot remain bound together without God's saving power. Besides, only by standing before God can man and woman live together in harmony. Meilaender believes that mutual submission, crucial to harmonious marital relationship, must ultimately be a submission of both to Christ. It is by committing to marital

---

114. Meilaender, *Limits of Love*, 116.

115. Ibid., 119.

116. Gilbert Meilaender, *Faith and Faithfulness: Basic Themes in Christian Ethics* (Notre Dame, IN: University of Notre Dame Press, 1991), 35. Original emphasis.

117. Gilbert Meilaender, *Things That Count: Essays Moral and Theological* (Wilmington, DE: ISI Books, 2000), 35.

fidelity that a couple can navigate their differences in the seasons of life.[118] God created man and woman from an original oneness. To remain one despite their differences, to uphold the *duality* that characterizes their harmonious relationship, man and woman must stand before God, together and beside each other.

---

118. Ibid., 55–57.

CHAPTER 4

Complementarity between Man and Woman

How can man and woman uphold the *duality* between them? How should they understand and navigate their differences? When man and woman stand before God, what commands are given them regarding their relationship? The conservative brand of American evangelicalism claims that the answers can be found in the complementarian gender ethics that they formulate. They contend that complementarianism is the only gender ethic that is ordained by God, faithful to the Bible, and useful in countering the degenerate secular culture.[1] This chapter offers a summary and an assessment of complementarianism. I argue that although many assumptions that underlie this ethic are valid, its main weaknesses stem from a presumption that gender role is the definitive factor that differentiates the sexes. Besides, complementarianism lacks an eschatological vision; redemption is a nostalgic restoration of the past instead of a hopeful consummation in the future. These weaknesses, together with a neglect of cultural analysis, lead complementarians to universalize one particular cultural expression of gender relationship, rendering the complementarian ethic inadequate and even stifling in other cultures. Finally, I argue that gender ethics should heed the *duality* between the individual and the community, as well as the *duality* between the present age and the future eschaton.

---

1. J. Ligon Duncan and Randy Stinson, "Preface (2006)," in *Recovering Biblical Manhood and Womanhood: A Response to Evangelical Feminism*, eds. John Piper and Wayne Grudem (Wheaton, IL: Crossway, 2006), xi–xii.

4.1 Gender Relationship in Complementarianism

Complementarianism is a gender theory that affirms that man and woman are "equal before God as persons and distinct in their manhood and womanhood."[2] Distinction between the sexes means foremost a divinely ordained male headship in the family and in the church. In both spheres, men should assume authority and leadership while women should submit to men.[3] Advocates of complementarianism believe that church and family are closely tied together, so "male headship in the home and in the church will likely stand or fall together."[4] The issue of male headship in the family is closely linked to the issue of women leadership, ordination, preaching, and teaching in the church. The roots of complementarianism can be traced back to the fundamentalist-mainline battle in America in early twentieth century. Janette Hassey conducts a historical study and reveals that pulpits in evangelical churches were open to woman preachers in late nineteenth to early twentieth century. But since the 1930s when fundamentalists began losing control over many denominations, issues concerning women began to harden within the evangelical circle. The fundamentalists' reaction against the feminist movements in the twentieth century further restricted their view on women. The debate over biblical inerrancy hardened their literalist application of Scripture, thereby reducing their flexibility in interpreting the Bible concerning women in ministry. Gradually women were squeezed out from public ministry.[5] In the 1970s, a "biblical equality movement" began to emerge within the evangelical circle. The movement aims to recover the equality of gender experienced in the early twentieth century by questioning the subordination of women and advocating gender equality in leadership and in role assignment in both the church and the family. Debates began between those who advocate for male headship – the complementarians – and

---

2. The Council on Biblical Manhood and Womanhood, "The Danvers Statement," in *Recovering Biblical Manhood and Womanhood*, 470.

3. Ibid.

4. Wayne A. Grudem, *Evangelical Feminism and Biblical Truth: An Analysis of More Than One Hundred Disputed Questions* (Wheaton, IL: Crossway, 2012), 80.

5. Janette Hassey, "Evangelical Women in Ministry a Century Ago: The 19th the Early 20th Centuries," in *Discovering Biblical Equality*, 46–56.

those who advocate no role distinction – the egalitarians. The association of Christians for Biblical Equality (CBE) was formed by the egalitarians and the Council on Biblical Manhood and Womanhood (CBMW) was founded by the complementarians, both in 1987. In the following year the CBMW published the "Danvers Statement,"[6] affirming their position and naming themselves "complementarians," instead of "traditionalists" or "hierarchicalists" – names which may suggest negative connotations.[7] The CBE responded by issuing the "Statement on Men, Women and Biblical Equality" in 1989.[8] Throughout the past three decades, adherents of both sides have been debating the issue and publishing books and articles to clarify and strengthen their positions, and the debate is unlikely to end in the near future.[9] Complementarianism is therefore formulated in the past several decades within American evangelicalism as a response to the egalitarian movement – or the "evangelical feminism" as they call it.

As the debate is among evangelicals who emphasize the authority of Scripture in moral discernment, biblical interpretation becomes the center of contention. Wayne Grudem, a cofounder of CBMW, contends that the Bible is ultimately at stake in the debate: "the common denominator in [evangelical feminism] is a persistent undermining of the authority of Scripture in our lives."[10] Advocating complementarianism, therefore, is not merely a gender issue but is imperative to protect the Bible from the onslaught of modern liberalism. Scriptural passages are carefully analyzed to argue for a God-ordained order of male headship in the church and the family. The phrase "the head of the woman is man" in 1 Corinthians 11:3 is interpreted to mean that man has permanent authority over woman. A hierarchy between man and woman is established though it is insisted

---

6. The Council on Biblical Manhood and Womanhood, "The Danvers Statement," 471.

7. John Piper and Wayne Grudem, "Preface (1991)," in *Recovering Biblical Manhood and Womanhood*, xv.

8. Ronald W. Pierce, "Contemporary Evangelicals for Gender Equality," in *Discovering Biblical Equality*, 66.

9. Ibid., 58–75.

10. Wayne A. Grudem, *Evangelical Feminism: A New Path to Liberalism?* (Wheaton, IL: Crossway, 2006), 261.

that inferiority of woman is not implied.[11] The exhortation for women to remain silent in the churches in 1 Corinthians 14:34 is interpreted to mean that women should not "enjoy a church-recognized teaching authority over men . . . [or participate in] the careful weighing of prophecies," though they are allowed to utter prophesy that has no guarantee of divine authority.[12] Similarly, the prohibition of woman to teach or to have authority over man in 1 Timothy 2:12, when applied to today's setting, means that women should not preach or teach "Bible and doctrine in the church, in colleges, and in seminaries."[13] Within the family, the household code in Ephesians 5:21–33 establishes the husband's headship and authority over his wife, as Scripture draws a parallel between the headship of the husband over his wife with the headship of Christ over the church. The same household code also admonishes wives to submit to their husbands in all aspects of life.[14] Other "submission" passages in Colossians 3:18, Titus 2:5, and 1 Peter 3:1 also exhort that wives should submit to their husbands.[15] Complementarians aver that this hierarchical interpretation of the household codes has always been attested to throughout church history. Any "egalitarian" interpretation is a novelty, arising from the influence of modern feminism.[16] Male headship and female submission, when applied in the family today, means that the husband is the leader of the family while his wife follows his leadership. However, submission of the wife is out of her submission to Christ; she should not follow her husband into disobeying Christ. Submission does not mean that the wife is less intelligent or capable, or that she must give up independent thought. Instead, she should

---

11. Thomas R. Schreiner, "Head Coverings, Prophecies, and the Trinity: 1 Corinthians 11:2–16," in *Recovering Biblical Manhood and Womanhood*, 130.

12. D. A. Carson, "'Silent in the Churches': On the Role of Women in 1 Corinthians 14:33b–36," in *Recovering Biblical Manhood and Womanhood*, 152–153.

13. Douglas Moo, "What Does It Mean Not to Teach or Have Authority Over Men? 1 Timothy 2:11–15," in *Recovering Biblical Manhood and Womanhood*, 186.

14. George W. Knight III, "Husbands and Wives as Analogues of Christ and the Church: Ephesians 5:21–33 and Colossians 3:18–19," in *Recovering Biblical Manhood and Womanhood*, 170.

15. Wayne Grudem, "The Myth of Mutual Submission as an Interpretation of Ephesians 5:21," in *Biblical Foundations for Manhood and Womanhood*, ed. Wayne Grudem (Wheaton, IL: Crossway, 2002), 221–222.

16. Daniel Doriani, "The Historical Novelty of Egalitarian Interpretations of Ephesians 5:21–22," in *Biblical Foundations for Manhood and Womanhood*, 203–231.

influence and guide him into the ways of Christ. But to honor the husband as the leader, he should be the one who makes final decisions concerning the family. Submission is "an inner quality of gentleness that affirms the leadership of the husband, . . .[honoring] him as leader even when she dissents."[17] This demands her obedience, acknowledging that their relationship is not totally mutual. Although in healthy marriages decisions often come by consensus made after mutual consultation, the wife should honor her husband's leadership by deferring to him as the final decision maker for the whole family. The husband, on the other hand, should not abuse his authority or think of his wife as inferior. He should love and respect her, yet not always give in to her wishes. Since his role as the leader is not optional, he should take up this responsibility and participate actively in family decisions and activities.[18]

Therefore, complementarians equate the notion of headship and submission with the *roles* of leader and follower and the *functions* of leading and following. Alan Padgett observes that the argument of gender *role* difference – instead of *ontological* difference – among traditionalists first appeared in George W. Knight III's book, *The Role Relationship of Men and Women*, published in 1977.[19] In the book, Knight argues that as Galatians 3:28 gives spiritual equality to people of different ethnicity, status, or gender, the assignment of roles to different people would not jeopardize their equality. Role assignment upholds the equality between male and female while expressing their differences. Furthermore, Romans 13:1–7 and 1 Peter 2:13–17 exhort Christians to submit to government authorities, who are authorized by God to rule. This suggests that the assignment of authority that demands submission is not contrary to the intrinsic equality of all. In fact, it is God who assigns authority to establish good orders in human associations.[20] This provides complementarians a scheme to resolve the tension between equal dignity and male headship, as well as a basis to

---

17. Wayne Grudem, "Wives Like Sarah, and the Husbands Who Honor Them: 1 Peter 3:1–7," in *Recovering Biblical Manhood and Womanhood*, 196.

18. Ibid., 200–208.

19. Alan G. Padgett, "The Bible and Gender Troubles: American Evangelicals Debate Scripture and Submission," *Dialog: A Journal of Theology* 47, no. 1 (Spring 2008): 23.

20. George W. Knight III, *The Role Relationship of Men and Women: New Testament Teaching*, rev. ed. (Phillipsburg, NJ: P&R Publishing, 1985), 7–13.

advocate superior male authority. To counter the challenges that accuse them of disparaging the value of women, they always respond by arguing that difference in function, role, or authority does not entail difference in value or worth.[21] In other words, functions, roles, and authority are aspects "external" and unrelated to one's nature or being. Differences in these "externalities" do not jeopardize the "inner" or spiritual equality between man and woman.

The difference between man and woman, however, does not stay at the decision-making function or the leadership role. The essence of the complementarian project is to counter the egalitarian culture, which, complementarians contend, attributes no distinction between man and woman. They argue that the egalitarian ideal necessarily blurs sexual distinctions and undermines God's creation of humanity into male and female. Man and woman then fail to live and work together as God has intended, resulting in the marriage disruptions prevalent in our culture. Feminism is thus the root cause of the modern family crisis. The remedy is to counter the egalitarian culture by emphasizing "the important distinction between masculinity and femininity."[22] Man and woman should embrace "mature manhood and womanhood" by reflecting a masculinity and femininity according to his or her gender. This notion of masculinity and femininity extends beyond simple leadership and obedience. John Piper defines masculinity as "a sense of benevolent responsibility to lead, provide for and protect women in ways appropriate to a man's differing relationships."[23] According to his definition, "to lead" is not limited to decision making but should include the strength to serve and to sacrifice for others, the ability to strengthen and mobilize others, and the willingness to initiate general patterns for others to follow. As the leader, the husband should also initiate sexual relations with his wife and the disciplining of their children. In addition to taking up the role of leadership, the husband should provide for and protect his family. He should be the one shouldering the primary responsibility to provide for his family economically, though exceptions can be

---

21. Grudem, *Evangelical Feminism and Biblical Truth*, 102–108.
22. Duncan and Stinson, "Preface (2006)," x.
23. John Piper, "A Vision of Biblical Complementarity: Manhood and Womanhood Defined according to the Bible," in *Recovering Biblical Manhood and Womanhood*, 36.

made temporarily or in non-ideal situations. Besides, the man instinctively feels that he should protect the woman in the event of danger, rather than the other way around.[24] Being complementary to man, woman should receive the leadership, provision, and protection offered by man. Piper defines femininity as "a freeing disposition to affirm, receive and nurture strength and leadership from worthy men in ways appropriate to a woman's differing relationships."[25] His exposition on femininity is much simpler than that of masculinity: femininity is simply a complement or mirror image of masculinity. Where the man leads, provides, and protects, the woman should obey, receive, and depend. Although he avers that "women are [not] merely recipients in relation to men," men are certainly active in their role while women are passive, according to his definitions.[26] But when the biological dimension is also considered, women take on an active role as mothers, albeit under the leadership of their husbands. George Alan Rekers states that "it is true femininity to conceive and bear a child in marriage" and "to protect the unborn child from outside harm." He observes that the "biologically defined sex role" for women includes bearing a child, giving birth, and breastfeeding.[27] Based on a reading of Genesis 3, Knight argues that in the family, the primary responsibility of the man is breadwinning and for the woman, it is caring for children and the home. It does not mean that mothers should not work outside the home. Yet the final decision about the wife's outside job should still be made by the husband. While the mother is responsible for the direct care of children and the home, she should do so in submission to the leadership of her husband, who has the final responsibility to manage his household well.[28] Therefore, the leadership and submissive roles of man and woman, when fleshed out in the household context, become the ideal masculine roles of breadwinner and

---

24. Ibid., 38–44.
25. Ibid., 46.
26. Ibid., 48–49.
27. George Alan Rekers, "Psychological Foundations for Rearing Masculine Boys and Feminine Girls," in *Recovering Biblical Manhood and Womanhood*, 306–308.
28. George W. Knight III, "The Family and the Church: How Should Biblical Manhood and Womanhood Work Out in Practice?" in *Recovering Biblical Manhood and Womanhood*, 347–351.

protector, and the ideal feminine roles of supporter and caregiver. Grudem summarizes the gender roles in the family as follows:

> There are other differences in roles in addition to headship and submission. Two other aspects of a husband's headship in marriage are the responsibility to *provide for* and to *protect* his wife and family. A corresponding responsibility for the wife is to have primary responsibility to care for *home* and *children*. Each can help the other, but there remains a primary responsibility that is not shared equally.[29]

Embracing these gender role differences, contend the complementarians, reflects God's original design in creating male and female and is the only way to harmonious relationships between man and woman.

4.2 Formulation of "Biblical Manhood and Womanhood"

Complementarians believe that their view of manhood and womanhood is "biblical." Often they claim to uphold the "plain sense of Scripture" when advocating their theory.[30] For instance, Stephen Clark contends that the New Testament teachings on gender roles are clear directives that reflect God's purposes, intended for the whole human race to follow. He thinks that the issue lies not in the interpretation or applicability of Scripture, but in the obedience of its readers.[31] It is true that some plain texts of Scripture, especially the New Testament household codes and "submission" passages, admonish a pattern of headship and submission between man and woman. But to arrive at their theory of gender roles for today, complementarians must bring the scriptural texts forward several steps. Richard Hays argues that the use of Scripture in constructive ethics invariably involves four critical and overlapping operations: the descriptive, the synthetic, the

---

29. Grudem, *Evangelical Feminism and Biblical Truth*, 44. Original emphasis.

30. Claire Smith, *God's Good Design: What the Bible Really Says About Men and Women* (Kingsford, NSW: Matthias Media, 2012), 50.

31. Stephen B. Clark, *Man and Woman in Christ: An Examination of the Roles of Men and Women in Light of Scripture and the Social Sciences* (Ann Arbor, MI: Servant Books, 1980), 562–565.

hermeneutical, and the pragmatic tasks.[32] Therefore, the formation of a "biblical view" is not as straightforward as what the complementarians assume. Using Hays's notion of the "four tasks of ethics," I will assess how complementarians formulate the notion of "biblical manhood and womanhood" based on Scripture.

4.2.1 The Descriptive Task

The first step is the descriptive task. It is exegetical in character, aiming to describe the meaning of the relevant biblical texts in their original contexts. Complementarians devote much effort in this task and most of their writings are exegetical in nature. Careful word studies are frequently conducted, especially for words and phrases crucial to their theory. For instance, much work has been done concerning the word "head" (*kephalē*) that describes man in relationship to woman (1 Cor 11:3 and Eph 5:23). Grudem conducts a survey of 2,336 examples in ancient Greek literature and concludes that the word means "authority over" instead of "source," a meaning that egalitarian interpreters advocate, thereby confirming the interpretation that men have authority over women.[33] Others then reference Grudem's conclusion when constructing their complementarian arguments.[34] However, the meaning of this word may not be as clear and fixed as they assume. Using an approach that allows for a more nuanced definition of the word, Gordon Fee argues that, depending on its immediate context, *kephalē* can take on different meanings. Besides "authority over," it can also mean support, source, or maintenance of life. Then the husband as the *kephalē* of his wife does not necessarily mean that he has authority over her, but can also mean that she depends on him for support and livelihood.[35] Another example concerns the word "glory" (*doxa*) in the phrase "woman is the glory of man" (1 Cor 11:7). Claire Smith contends that the word means that in

---

32. Richard B. Hays, *The Moral Vision of the New Testament: Community, Cross, New Creation* (New York: HarperOne, 1996), 3.

33. Wayne A. Grudem, "Does kephalē ('Head') Mean 'Source' or 'Authority Over' in Greek Literature: A Survey of 2,336 Examples," *Trinity Journal* 6, no. 1 (Spring 1985): 38–59.

34. Smith, *God's Good Design*, 59; Schreiner, "Head Coverings," 127; Knight, "Husbands and Wives," 169.

35. Gordon Fee, "Praying and Prophesying in the Assemblies: 1 Corinthians 11:2–16," in *Discovering Biblical Equality*, 149–155.

"her origins and her purpose, the woman corresponds to the man . . . and that she was made to help him."[36] Thomas Schreiner thinks that "glory" means that the woman was created to honor the man by showing that he is the head and has authority over her.[37] John Frame argues that the phrase further teaches that while man was made to honor God alone, woman was made to honor both God and man. As such, woman should be subordinate to man.[38] According to these three complementarian interpreters, the same word, *doxa*, can mean "purpose," "honoring," or "subordinating." This example shows that they do not necessarily agree with one another about the details of their exegeses, though all of their interpretations support their theory of gender hierarchy. Contrary to their interpretations, Fee contends that *doxa* should mean "origin." The phrase means that the woman "came from man" so he "might be complete and that together they might form humanity."[39] According to this alternative interpretation, not only is gender hierarchy not supported, the woman is even assigned an indispensable position in the man-woman relationship. Detailed assessment of the complementarian exegesis is beyond the scope of this book. Yet these examples show that careful word studies do not necessarily provide a single and non-controversial interpretation. The complementarian exegesis is also influenced by a preconceived ideology of male headship, as interpreters tend to endorse interpretations that support their gender theory.

Furthermore, complementarians hold a particular view of scriptural authority. To respect the authority of Scripture, for them, means that the literal or the "plain sense" of the texts should be obeyed. Hence, their biblical interpretation tends to be literalist. One result of their biblical literalism is that they only advocate gender role distinction in the two spheres of the church and the home; they do not extend their gender theory into the workplace or the society. Grudem believes that as Scripture only commands male headship in these two spheres, male headship is not an imperative in

---

36. Smith, *God's Good Design*, 72.
37. Schreiner, "Head Coverings," 133.
38. John M. Frame, "Men and Women in the Image of God," in *Recovering Biblical Manhood and Womanhood*, 228.
39. Gordon D. Fee, *The First Epistle to the Corinthians* (Grand Rapids, MI: Eerdmans, 1987), 517.

other areas of life, for "[we] should not try to require either more or less than Scripture itself requires."[40]

4.2.2 The Synthetic Task

The second operation is the synthetic task. Hays observes that Scripture often contains a diversity of viewpoints on a single issue, but he believes that some coherence can still be discerned. The synthetic task is to link the different viewpoints together to formulate a coherent message. The task is difficult, as faithful reading of Scripture must allow the tension among different texts to stand. While some interpreters opt to use a single principle to harmonize the texts, Hays thinks that this method should be avoided as it imposes a foreign ideology into Scripture rather than reading the messages from Scripture. He resolves this difficulty by developing a cluster of "focal images" from Scripture itself and then uses these images as lenses to interpret the diverse texts.[41] On the subject of gender relationship, a similar diversity is observed. Paul Jewett notices that the Old Testament assumes that patriarchy is the expressed will of God, and part of the New Testament appears to teach female subordination. But how Jesus treated women, as well as the equality principle reflected elsewhere in Scripture, points to gender equality. He proceeds to resolve this tension by navigating through these diverse texts.[42] However, complementarians do not see the same diversity in Scripture, at least on the subject of gender relationship. Instead of seeing equality in Christ (Gal 3:28) and headship of the husband (Eph 5:22) as contradictory, they argue that as both texts belong to the canon, then "equality and role differences are compatible."[43] Behind this argument is the assumption that the canon is a coherent whole and contradictions within Scripture do not exist. They even make use of the tension apparent in Scripture to justify the tension in their theory. Another example concerns Jesus's treatment of women. Both egalitarians and complementarians recognize that in the gospel narratives, Jesus places high value on women.

---

40. Grudem, *Evangelical Feminism and Biblical Truth*, 393.
41. Hays, *Moral Vision*, 4–5.
42. Paul King Jewett, *Man as Male and Female: A Study in Sexual Relationships from a Theological Point of View* (Grand Rapids, MI: Eerdmans, 1975), 94–105, 129–130, 134–147.
43. Knight, *Role Relationship*, 2.

While egalitarians use this as an argument for gender equality, complementarians instead focus on Jesus's selection of only men as disciples to argue for an all-male church leadership.[44] Again, instead of seeing Jesus's treatment of women and his selection of all-male disciples as inconsistent and requiring further explanations, complementarians do not see such tension. In fact, they use this apparent inconsistency to justify their view that women should be respected yet prohibited from certain roles at the same time. Turning to the Old Testament, the creation of human beings in the first creation narrative (Gen 1:27) is often used by egalitarians to argue for gender equality due to the simultaneous creation of male and female. But complementarians instead suggest that the "man" in the phrase "God created *man (adam)* in his own image" is not a generic term for "humanity." Rather, the text indicates that God prefers to name the human race "man" in distinction from "woman," and male headship is implied.[45] Therefore, both the first and second creation narratives imply male headship: the first through naming of the human race as "man" and the second through primogeniture of the male.

This analysis shows that complementarians hold a homogenous view of Scripture, believing that all texts mirror one another to produce a single message. One result of this approach is that diversity in the Scripture is easily harmonized and doctrines are consistently supported by the whole canon. However, Willard Swartley warns that reading a single message from Scripture is a weakness in biblical interpretation. Assuming diversity in Scripture, he contends, means that the interpreter would encounter messages with which she does not agree. It is through adjudicating among the different messages that her own ideology can be broken, and attentive listening to Scripture becomes possible. On the other hand, seeing Scripture as uttering a homogeneous message leads the interpreter to silence certain messages while accentuating others. The messages that are silenced are often the ones with which she disagrees, so reading Scripture

---

44. James A. Borland, "Women in the Life and Teachings of Jesus," in *Recovering Biblical Manhood and Womanhood*, 120–123.

45. Grudem, *Evangelical Feminism and Biblical Truth*, 34–36.

only serves to strengthen her own preconceived ideology instead of challenging it.[46] The above examples indeed suggest that complementarians often interpret Scripture through a preconceived notion of male headship. The most notable example is their interpretation of *adam* in Genesis 1:27 to mean the specific "man" instead of the generic "humankind," thereby fitting this creation account into the scheme of male headship. This interpretation in turn strengthens their preconceived gender ideology. Perhaps, using Hays's words, they tend to harmonize the diversity of Scripture using a single principle, and the principle is the male headship that they advocate. Besides, by assuming no diversity within Scripture, they can formulate their gender theory using only a few biblical texts, namely, the Old Testament creation narratives, the New Testament "submission" texts, and the household codes.[47] If different parts of the canon all agree with one another, then building gender ethics upon a few passages would not be problematic. If all other canonical texts are bound to mirror and support these few verses, then there is no need to consider the rest of the canon. The synthetic task is rather easy for complementarians; seldom in their writings do they address the diversity within Scripture.

4.2.3 The Hermeneutical Task

The third operation of biblical interpretation is the hermeneutical task, which transfers the scriptural message from its own context to our present situation.[48] Complementarians claim that the biblical texts, in particular the New Testament exhortations concerning the role of women in the church and family, are directly and universally applicable. They assert this claim through two major means: textual and theological. The first means focuses on the biblical text. For instance, they argue that if the scriptural text does not suggest otherwise, the exhortations should be deemed universal. When arguing that women should not teach men in the church based

---

46. Willard M. Swartley, *Slavery, Sabbath, War and Women: Case Issues in Biblical Interpretation* (Scottdale, PA: Herald, 1983), 185–187.

47. For example, in *God's Good Design*, Claire Smith develops her gender theory from the "silence" passages of 1 Tim 2 and 1 Cor 14:26–40, the "head cover" passage of 1 Cor 11:2–16, the household codes of Eph 5:18–33 and 1 Pet 3:1–7, the creation narratives of Gen 1–3, and the "ideal wife" passage of Prov 31.

48. Hays, *Moral Vision*, 5–6.

on 1 Timothy 2:11–15, Douglas Moo contends that as the text does not suggest any particular factors that are related to the prohibition, interpreters should not read them into the text. In other words, as the text does not mention the education level of women or the particular situation of the Ephesian church as reasons behind the prohibition, then we should not use them to argue against its applicability today. It is "a dangerous procedure to import such factors without clear warrant in the text."[49] Claire Smith offers a similar argument. When she discusses the injunction "women should keep silent in the churches" (1 Cor 14:34), she argues against interpreting the text using any historical reconstruction. "To override the plain teaching of the Bible on the basis of a *possible* reconstruction is really taking matters into our own hands."[50] These exhortations should be considered transcultural and universal. Although this interpretation method appears to be "faithful" to the text, it demands the text to be read in isolation from its original context. The text is all there is; any cultural or historical background is irrelevant. But as the biblical writer and the original recipients share the same cultural and historical contexts, there are good reasons why the writer did not need to mention the reasons behind his exhortations. The implicit understanding between them can often be pivotal in understanding the writer's exhortations. Therefore, we can equally argue that ignoring the original contexts may lead to interpretations that are less "faithful" to the text.

Stephen Clark uses another textual approach to argue for the universal validity of scriptural teachings on gender roles. He classifies scriptural materials into four kinds: (1) presentation of facts; (2) description of significant events; (3) instructions; and (4) prophecy. There is a particular interpretation method that corresponds to each. The New Testament teachings on gender roles, he contends, are "instructions" and the correct way to interpret them is for the reader to obey their "intentions." The teaching "contains some *fundamental doctrine* concerning God's intentions for the human race and his purpose for men and women. . . . [It] contains some more or less *clear directives* and a *statement of God's intention*."[51] In other

---

49. Moo, "What Does It Mean?" 193.
50. Smith, *God's Good Design*, 89. Original emphasis.
51. Clark, *Man and Woman*, 564. My emphasis.

words, the texts that are classified as "instructions" in Scripture are timeless doctrines applicable to the whole human race. They are words uttered by God to all human beings, instead of exhortations written by particular persons targeting specific communities. To argue for universal validity of scriptural exhortations, complementarians tend to undermine the cultural and historical factors in their biblical interpretation and elevate particular texts to the level of timeless doctrine. This hermeneutical approach is closely connected with their belief in a single and homogeneous message in Scripture. If scriptural texts are themselves timeless and universal doctrines, then we would not expect to find variations across the canonical texts, and human beings living in disparate historical and cultural environments should all abide with them.

Complementarians also give theological reasons to support the applicability of gender role distinction today. As gender role distinction is the corollary of male headship, a transcultural ethic of gender role difference requires a permanent and universal view of male headship. They appeal to the doctrine of creation to establish this argument, claiming that male headship has already been embedded within God's original creation. From the second creation narrative, Bruce Ware contends that the order by which Adam and Eve were created has significant theological meaning. While Adam was created first from the dust of the ground, he was created in an "unmediated fashion." Eve was created second from Adam's rib, so she was created in a "mediated fashion." This difference in order and material of creation has theological implications, showing us that the woman's life and nature is derived from that of the man's.[52] When the primogeniture of male is read in conjunction with 1 Corinthians 11:7 ("the man is the image and glory of God, and the woman the glory of the man"), Ware considers that "Woman *with* man is created in the image of God, but woman *through* man has her true human nature and hence her glory."[53] The nature of woman, though equal to man, is totally dependent on man. This establishes a theological priority of male over female. Raymond Ortlund also argues that as the woman was created as the man's "helper," they are in some sense

---

52. Bruce A. Ware, "Male and Female Complementarity and the Image of God," in *Biblical Foundations for Manhood and Womanhood*, 82–83.
53. Ibid., 86. Original emphasis.

"unequal" as this aspect of their relationship is non-reversible: the woman was made to "help" the man and not vice versa. The woman, he says, was made "*from* the man (her equality) and *for* the man (her inequality)."[54] As the woman is made for the man as his helper, she should submit herself under his leadership. Both Ware and Ortlund appeal to the first two chapters of Genesis to establish their arguments. Since these narratives describe the human situation before the fall, they argue that male headship is not a result of sin but is embedded in God's original creation and constitutes the very nature of male and female. Instead of challenging male headship as a condition of the fallen world, they aver that we should emphasis it to recover the goodness of God's created order. However, other interpreters have suggested alternative interpretations of the same texts. Upon considering parallel ideas between the Old Testament and other Ancient Near East literature, Richard Hess argues that the sequential creation of male and female in Genesis 2 serves only to "demonstrate the need they have for each other, not to justify an implicit hierarchy."[55] Leon Kass even argues that the narratives suggest a higher status of woman and a dependency of man on woman. He says that while the man was created from dust, a lower form of material, the woman was created from living flesh. While the man, missing a rib, always desires to fill this void through the woman, the woman is from the beginning complete and whole by herself.[56]

Despite these alternative interpretations, complementarians insist that male headship is part of God's original creation. Men bear a divinely ordained authority that requires the subordination of women. But they also assert that male and female are created equal, both bearing the image of God. A tension between headship and equality then ensues from these two assertions: how can two persons, one having greater authority and requiring submission from the other, be equal? As discussed above, Knight offers an answer to this question. He examines three pairs of "role relationships": master and slave, government and citizens, man and woman.

---

54. Raymond C. Ortlund, Jr., "Male-Female Equality and Male Headship: Genesis 1–3," in *Recovering Biblical Manhood and Womanhood*, 102. Original Emphasis.

55. Richard S. Hess, "Equality With and Without Innocence: Genesis 1–3," in *Discovering Biblical Equality*, 84.

56. Leon Kass, *The Beginning of Wisdom: Reading Genesis* (New York: Free Press, 2003), 101.

These role relationships, he argues, are not only compatible with spiritual equality but are further regulated in Scripture. Although certain human institutions, such as slavery, are not ordained by God, the essence of its role relationships is. The relationship between master and slave can readily be translated to that between employer and employees today. As the employer-employee and government-citizen role relationships are necessary for the good order of society, the role difference between man and woman should also be maintained for the same purpose.[57] It is true that role relationships are often necessary and are not incompatible with equality of being among persons. However, the role relationship of man and woman in complementarianism is fundamentally different from that of the other two pairs. The roles of masters, slaves, government officials and citizens are not necessarily connected to a person's being. They are functional and temporary, changeable in one's life time and contingent upon one's particular situation. But according to complementarians, the roles of man to lead and woman to submit are necessarily and permanently connected to one's being as male or female. It is true that certain roles are necessarily connected to one's sex as man or woman. For example, only men can be fathers, and only women can be mothers and child-bearers. But one's sexual identity does not entail these roles. Not all men would become fathers or women mothers. One may cease to retain one's role as father or mother in one's lifetime, and certainly in the eschaton. In other words, the roles of fathers, mothers, or child-bearers, though necessarily sex-linked, are nonetheless contingent and temporary; these roles do not define what a person is. But complementarianism posits that the roles to lead and submit are necessarily and permanently linked to one's sex. Rebecca Merrill Groothuis argues that equality and role difference is only compatible in functional subordination, which is temporary and related to one's ability. But if one's role is necessarily linked to one's nature, then the difference in role necessarily implies difference in nature. Permanent and necessary role assignment entails a merger between a person's role and her being. Therefore, any insistence on

---

57. Knight, *Role Relationship*, 7–15.

female role submission entails that her being is also submissive, and ontological equality between the sexes cannot be logically sustained.[58]

In response to this challenge, complementarians appeal to Trinitarian theology. The relationship of the husband to his wife, argues Grudem, is parallel to the relationship of the Father to the Son within the Godhead. This parallel shows us three things. First, as the Father and Son are ontologically equal yet have different roles, husband and wife are ontologically equal but have different roles. Second, as the Father has authority over the Son and the Son submits to the Father, the husband also has authority over his wife and she should submit to him. Third, this subordination of the Son is eternal, woven in the very fabric of the Trinitarian relationship.[59] In other words, the submission of the Son to the Father is not temporary, limited to his lifetime on earth, but is pre-existent and eternal. Grudem claims that this view of eternal subordination of the Son is both attested to in Scripture and endorsed by the church throughout history.[60] He then concludes: "the idea of headship and submission existed *before Creation*. It began in the relationship between the Father and Son in the Trinity. . . . It has *always existed* in the eternal nature of God Himself."[61] This provides a strong theological basis for the theory of male headship. Now headship and submission is not only an aspect of God's creation; it is an outflow of God's very own nature. The doctrine of eternal subordination of the Son is used by complementarians to defend themselves against the challenge of logical inconsistency between permanent subordination and ontological equality. Yet the doctrine itself does not resolve the logical inconsistency. Complementarians simply use the doctrine to dismiss the challenge. For instance, Claire Smith appeals to this Trinitarian theology in responding to the challenge. She says, "There is an assumption [held by the egalitarians] that you cannot have differentiation and hierarchy without also having inferiority and superiority of dignity or worth. But you can. . . . All three persons of the Godhead share in the same divine being and nature,

---

58. Rebecca Merrill Groothuis, "'Equality in Being, Unequal in Role,' Exploring the Logic of Woman's Subordination," in *Discovering Biblical Equality*, 314–322.

59. Grudem, *Evangelical Feminism and Biblical Truth*, 45–47.

60. Ibid., 405–422.

61. Ibid., 47. Original emphasis.

yet there is an asymmetry within the divine relationships."[62] The logical inconsistency need not be addressed through logic. It can be dismissed by pointing out that within the Godhead both subordination and equality exist together, thus these two notions cannot possibly be logically inconsistent. This argument is similar to the argument that the complementarians use to harmonize Scripture and synthesize a single biblical message. As discussed above, instead of seeing gender equality and the submission and silencing of women in Scripture as contradictory, they argue that since Scripture endorses both, we can have both in our gender theory. They use the tension within Scripture to justify the tension in their theory. By the same token, they use the doctrine of the eternal subordination of the Son to justify the contradiction in their theory. But this does not solve the logical inconsistency between equality and subordination; the inconsistency is simply moved into the doctrine itself.

Moving the logical inconsistency into the doctrine, however, has adverse ramifications. Kevin Giles contends that the doctrine of eternal subordination of the Son equates immanent Trinity with economic Trinity, thus disallowing God to be more than what God has revealed to us.[63] In other words, it reads back the temporal role subordination of the Son into the immanent or eternal Trinity.[64] Besides, he argues what the eternal role subordination of the Son implies is that the Son is ontologically subordinate.[65] Therefore, the doctrine can be likened as a form of the Arian heresy. Giles conducts a historical survey of Trinitarian theologies and observes that subordinationism has been condemned by the creeds and rejected by all major theologians. Complementarians adamantly protest this charge of heresy, asserting repeatedly that eternal subordination of the Son has been testified in the writings of many orthodox theologians and should not be deemed heretical. Grudem further claims that to affirm the subordination of the Son is in fact the only way to uphold the Trinitarian doctrine. For the Trinity to stand, he argues, difference among the three persons must

---

62. Smith, *God's Good Design*, 61.

63. Kevin Giles, *The Trinity and Subordinationism: The Doctrine of God and the Contemporary Gender Debate* (Downers Grove, IL: InterVarsity, 2002), 28.

64. Ibid., 84.

65. Ibid., 85.

be maintained, lest the Trinity collapses into monism. "The differences in authority among Father, Son, and Holy Spirit are the only interpersonal differences that the Bible indicates exist eternally among the members of the Godhead. . . . If we did not have such differences . . ., then we would not know of any differences at all, and it would be unclear whether there *are* any differences among the persons of the Trinity."[66] Similarly, Ware opines that difference in authority is what distinguishes the three persons. Authority and submission "marks the relationship of the Son to the Father from eternity past to eternity future."[67] However, Giles contends that it is the eternal *begetting* of the Son, instead of the eternal *subordination* of the Son, that grounds the differentiation between the Father and the Son in the Godhead. To speak of the Son as "begotten" of the Father affirms their same nature, explicates their difference, and avoids implying that the Son is a creature of the Father.[68] It is in this spirit that the Nicene Creed states that Christ is "eternally begotten of the Father" but is "of one being with the Father." Authority difference or subordination has never been the basis of differentiation between the divine persons in the church's formulation of the Trinity.[69] While Grudem posits authority as the only locus of interpersonal differentiation, he rejects the doctrine of the eternal *begetting* of the Son, suggesting that the language of "eternal begetting of the Son" should not be retained in modern theological formulations.[70] Rejecting this doctrine is perhaps his attempt to ameliorate his Trinitarian theology from appearing too subordinationalist; perhaps affirming both eternal *subordination* and eternal *begetting* in his Trinitarian theology would make it too difficult for him to fend off the charge of Arianism. He opts to drop the doctrine of eternal *begetting* of the Son and retain the doctrine of eternal *subordination* in order to support his gender theory. By rejecting the language of *begetting* he isolates himself even further from the creeds,

---

66. Grudem, *Evangelical Feminism and Biblical Truth*, 433. Original emphasis.

67. Bruce A. Ware, *Father, Son, and Holy Spirit: Relationships, Roles, and Relevance* (Wheaton, IL: Crossway, 2005), 98.

68. Kevin Giles, *The Eternal Generation of the Son: Maintaining Orthodoxy in Trinitarian Theology* (Downers Grove, IL: IVP Academic, 2012), 258–259.

69. Ibid., 148–150.

70. Wayne A. Grudem, *Systematic Theology: An Introduction to Biblical Doctrine* (Leicester, England: IVP, 1994), 1234.

the church tradition, and orthodoxy. In the end, although venturing into Trinitarian theology appears to have supported his complementarian theory, it creates other more serious theological problems. Giles opines that complementarians err in their eagerness to use doctrine to strengthen their gender theory: "In their concern to more securely ground their teaching on the male-female relationship, they have embraced an old error that undermines the most fundamental truth of all – the Christian doctrine of God."[71]

This analysis shows that caution must be exercised in using Trinitarian theology to construct gender theory. The Father and the Son in the Godhead are in many ways different from man and woman in the world. Relationship within the Godhead is tripolar, more akin to a community than the bipolar relationship between man and woman. The Father and the Son are in eternal relationship. They are unbounded by necessity and are totally free. Man and woman, however, are limited creatures. Their relationship is predicated upon temporality and informed by their existence as bodily beings. Besides, the relationship between two "masculine" divine persons is at odd with the gendered relationship between man and woman. The only link that complementarians draw between divine and human relationality is the notion of headship. But they have ignored the most important aspects of Trinitarian relationality – love and freedom.[72] While complementarians capitalize on the phrase "the head of Christ is God" (1 Cor 11:3) to emphasize the subordination of the Son under the Father,[73] they overlook the many scriptural passages that testify to the love between them. Giles contends that headship and submission are so important in their theory that they read hierarchical and role relationships between human beings back into the Trinitarian relationships. Their endorsement of the eternal subordination of the Son and their use of the modern concepts such as "role" to describe the divine persons reveal such tendency. As such, they have made the mistake of construing God from human understanding.[74]

---

71. Giles, *Trinity and Subordinationism*, 109.

72. John Zizioulas argues that Trinitarian theology can inform us the notion of personhood, in particular relationality, freedom, and love between persons. See section 2.6.3 above.

73. Grudem, *Evangelical Feminism and Biblical Truth*, 45.

74. Giles, *Trinity and Subordinationism*, 109–112.

Instead of allowing divine relationality to inform human relationality, their understanding of the divine Father-Son relationship reflects their understanding of the human man-woman relationship. Furthermore, as I will argue below, their understanding of the human man-woman relationship stems from their own particular culture. Once they read this particular cultural understanding into doctrine, the particular then claims universality.

4.2.4 The Pragmatic Task

The fourth and final task of biblical interpretation, according to Hays, is the pragmatic task. It aims to embody the Scripture's moral vision developed in the previous three tasks in the Christian community.[75] In the first task of describing the scriptural texts through exegesis, complementarians establish that "head" in Scripture means "authority over" and man should have headship over woman. In the second task of synthesis, they argue that the whole canon supports one single moral vision concerning gender relationship: male headship and female submission. In the third task of hermeneutics, this moral vision is claimed to be transcultural, applicable in all ages and among all cultures. In this fourth task of embodying the gender ethics in Christian community, the notions of headship and submission take on meanings that can be readily applied in the contemporary context. "Headship" implies "leadership" and decision making while "submission" means obeying and following the decisions that the leaders make. As discussed above, complementarians do not stop at the roles of the man as leader and the woman as follower. The complementarian project aims to counter the egalitarian culture, which, they think, is powered by liberalism. The egalitarian culture produces "evangelical feminism," which attempts first to deny anything masculine, then to destroy the image of God as Father, and finally to approve homosexuality.[76] To counter the egalitarian culture, masculinity and femininity should be accentuated. Men and women should model themselves after the ideal of "mature manhood and womanhood." Men should lead, provide for, and protect women and their family. Women should obey and support their husband, nurture and care for their children. Practically, the husband should be the "primary

---

75. Hays, *Moral Vision*, 7.
76. Grudem, *Evangelical Feminism*, 223–249.

breadwinner" and the wife should be the "primary one to care for the children and the home."⁷⁷ This results in a gender division of labor in the family: the husband should work outside for income to support the family while the wife should stay home to care for the children and the household. Yet the husband should still maintain leadership in the home through giving directions to his wife in her household management.

This ethics of gender and familial relationships attempt to apply the moral vision of male headship and female submission in today's world. Economic and cultural background of the modern industrial world is implicit in this ethic. For instance, it is assumed that material needs of the family are met through someone employed in waged work outside of the home. The household is assumed to be a place of consumption, made up of the nuclear family consisting of only the couple and their children. A clear public-private division is also assumed between "outside" and "inside" of the family. The private family is thought to be a safe haven, provided and protected by the husband from outside, cared for and managed by the wife inside. Within the confines of the family, children are nurtured and instructed. In the pragmatic task of biblical interpretation, complementarians seldom discuss the cultural background of the contemporary family or the differences between the world of the Bible and our world. But Allen Verhey points out that Scripture is "strange" to us; the scriptural world is often remote and alien to us. We should not simply identify the canonical texts with "timeless truth dropped from heaven or repeat without qualification as Christian counsel today."⁷⁸ Complementarians are making this mistake. When Knight describes the ideal roles of man and woman by quoting Scripture, nowhere does he discuss the cultural gap that separates the world of Scripture and today's world. For instance, he equates "toiling in the fields" (Gen 3:17–19) in the ancient agricultural world with working outside of home in today's context.⁷⁹ When equating the two, he focuses on only one common aspect of the activities: to feed one's family. As the text associates Adam with "toiling in the fields," Knight conjectures that

---

77. Knight, "Family and the Church," 348–350.

78. Allen Verhey, *Remembering Jesus: Christian Community, Scripture, and the Moral Life* (Grand Rapids, MI: Eerdmans, 2002), 51.

79. Knight, "Family and the Church," 347.

breadwinning is the "primary calling" of man. Since "breadwinning" today is usually done through employment outside of the home, man should direct himself "outside" of his family. This establishes the inside-outside gender division of labor. However, archeological studies reveal that in ancient Israel (c. 1200–1000 BCE), families usually owned small plots of fields and vineyards to grow their own food. Women also participated heavily in agricultural activities.[80] "Breadwinning" was not done outside of the home and was not just the responsibility of men. When this cultural background is considered, Genesis 3:17–19 should not be interpreted to support an inside-outside, homemaking-breadwinning gender division of labor. The text only serves to describe the hardship that befalls humanity after they sin, not to prescribe a gender division of labor. It is obvious that Knight is reading back into Scripture a preconceived notion of gender relationship manifested in his own cultural context. When an interpreter ignores the cultural gap between the biblical world and today's world, when she applies scriptural texts without qualifications, she inevitably reads her own culture back into Scripture.

Complementarians claim to be faithful to the Bible and obey the "plain sense" of Scripture. However, what they advocate is not as faithful to the Bible as it appears. In fact, only part of their gender ethics has direct scriptural warrant. In *Recovering Biblical Manhood and Womanhood*, a major publication coauthored by twenty-two complementarian advocates, all twelve chapters in the theoretical section "exegetical and theological studies" are about headship, submission, authority, and leadership. The conclusion of these chapters is that man and woman are equal in being but unequal in authority. Hence, man should lead and woman should submit to his leadership. Male headship and female submission is the only moral vision that concerns gender relationship explicated in Scripture. But in the "application and implications" section of the book, the roles of man as provider and protector, as well as woman as caregiver and childbearer, are added. While describing the "vision of biblical complementarity," Piper lists "to lead, *provide for* and *protect* women" as the three major

---

80. Jennie R. Ebeling, *Women's Lives in Biblical Times* (New York: T&T Clark, 2010), 33–36.

responsibilities of men.[81] The imperative to "provide and protect" is not directly commanded in Scripture, despite his claim that the "vision" is "defined according to the Bible." If complementarians are indeed faithful to the "plain sense" of Scripture and do not "try to require more than what Scripture requires," then they should not require men to provide for and protect women. Men only need to be leaders to make decisions and women only need to obey. Then a husband can decide to send his wife to work outside while he stays home to care for their children. As long as he makes the decision, Scripture is obeyed. However, this role division is unacceptable to complementarians. Piper says that "any role reversal at these basic levels of childcare and breadwinning labor will be contrary to the original intention of God, and contrary to the way he made us as male and female for our ordained roles."[82] This claim does not have biblical basis, at least not formulated in the "exegetical and theological studies" section of the book. Nonetheless, he suggests an exegetical justification for the husband's imperative to provide, but only in a footnote. There he argues that naming the man "head" of his wife implies that he should provide for her.[83] This is an interesting suggestion as this interpretation requires the word "head" to take on the meaning of "source" or "nourishment," an interpretation that complementarians themselves adamantly reject.[84] This example demonstrates that their biblical interpretation is indeed strongly influenced by their complementarian presuppositions. Giles is correct, then, to say that complementarians read their own ideology back into Scripture, instead of formulating a theory from Scripture.[85]

What is the gender ideology that complementarians read back into Scripture? How does it come about? Anthropologists point out that the phenomenon of gender categories is universal. In all known cultures, men and women are conceived as two distinct varieties; each has its corresponding activities, attitudes, values, objects, symbols, and expectations. Yet how

---

81. Piper, "Vision of Biblical Complementarity," 36. My emphasis.
82. Ibid., 43.
83. Piper, "Vision of Biblical Complementarity," 43, n15.
84. "... the evidence for the meaning "source" is far weaker, and it is fair to say that the meaning has not yet been established." Wayne Grudem, "The Meaning of *Kephalē* ('Head'): A Response to Recent Studies," in *Recovering Biblical Manhood and Womanhood*, 467.
85. Giles, *Trinity and Subordinationism*, 193.

gender is categorized depends on the particular historical and political circumstances. Gender role division is observed in all cultures, but the exact shape of the division varies from society to society.[86] We can expect that the form of gender role division that complementarians advocate is linked to their particular social and historical contexts. Rosemary Radford Ruether traces the historical development of the western family from its Greco-Roman roots and suggests that changes in gender relationships in history coincided with changes in economic patterns. She argues that the modern form of gender division of labor began with the rise of cities and the guild system in medieval Europe. When the guilds started to exclude women from their trades, women increasingly assumed unskilled and unpaid work. While husbands became master craftsmen, their wives supported them in the household shops. A skilled versus non-skilled gender division of labor began to develop.[87] In the eighteenth and nineteenth centuries, in both Europe and America, the household gradually lost its productive functions. The "family production economy," where the needs of the family are produced inside the household, was replaced by the "family wage economy," where family members accept outside works to support the family. For the working-class families, all members, except the very young and the infirmed, must work to support the family.[88] At the same time, the Victorian family was hailed as the model for all to emulate. It promoted an ideal picture of husbands working away from home to earn wages while wives stayed home to care for the household and the children. All other family arrangements were deemed deviant. "The ability of the male 'breadwinner' to support a full-time housewife was the mark of middle-class success. . . . The women who worked – that is, left the home for a paying job – was seen as nonnormative. Such work was allowable for young women or 'spinsters,' but it was regarded as selfish and destructive to family life for married women with children."[89] Ruether further argues that a notion of masculinity and femininity arose from this breadwinner-homemaker ideal:

---

86. Graham, *Making the Difference*, 59–74.

87. Rosemary Radford Ruether, *Christianity and the Making of the Modern Family* (Boston, MA: Beacon, 2000), 63–66.

88. Ibid., 87–89.

89. Ibid., 102.

A polarized dualism of masculinity and femininity evolved in Victorian thought, shaped by the separated spheres of home and work, of woman as nurturer and man as worker. The woman was to be sexually pure, physically delicate, emotional, dependent, and loving, in contrast to the man, who was sexually virile, physically strong, aggressive, dominant, and rational. Men and women were socialized to model themselves after these opposites, interdependent ideals as their true "natures."[90]

Ruether's study demonstrates that the complementarian gender ethic is very similar to the Victorian middle-class gender ideal. The breadwinner-homemaker gender division of labor, the leadership and submission between the couple, the masculinity-femininity polarity, and the linking of gender roles to nature are all common themes between them. As discussed at the beginning of this chapter, complementarianism was formulated in the past several decades in response to the egalitarian movement within American evangelism. It appears that complementarianism is a recovery of the Victorian family ideal packaged with careful exegesis and theological arguments. What complementarians read back into Scripture is in fact the Victorian notion of family.

Ruether's study also reveals that the family and gender relationships are always adapting to the changing economic and political circumstances. It is true that God instituted marriage and family so there are certain forms and *teloi* of these institutions that lie beyond human decision. For instance, Augustine explicates the form and *telos* of marriage through his "three goods of marriage" – procreation, fidelity, permanence.[91] The manner in which we express these three goods in real life varies according to our own circumstances. Gender role division, and even headship and submission, are expressions aiming to serve certain goods of marriage in particular cultural contexts. As discussed in chapter 3, male headship has been advocated as a cultural strategy to attract fathers to stay in the family, thereby serving

---

90. Ibid., 103.
91. See Augustine, "Good of Marriage," 9–51.

the goods of marriage permanence and procreation.[92] The New Testament household codes are also exhortations targeted to a specific community of a particular culture to serve the goods of marriage. Elevating these particular exhortations to the level of transcultural truth is to confuse the *telos* of marriage with its expressions.[93] While complementarians ignore the importance of culture in their theory, they also fail to acknowledge that both Scripture and they themselves are embedded in culture. This leads them first to conflate their own cultural expression with that contained in Scripture, then to claim this conflated expression as universal and imperative. Neglecting cultural analysis also renders them unable to critique their own culture. As discussed, the "mature manhood and womanhood" they advocate assumes a society characterized by a public-private split and an inside-outside dichotomy. The nuclear family is also assumed to be the basic household unit. Their gender theory simply accepts this cultural background without examining whether it conforms to the Christian moral vision. Besides, their lack of cultural analysis prevents them from recognizing the similarity between their gender theory and the Victorian family model, which arose two centuries ago in a very different social environment. As Ruether points out, the model was idealized and failed to reflect the real family life, even for middle-class families of the eighteenth and nineteenth centuries.[94] Furthermore, the breadwinning-homemaking model has become increasingly difficult to achieve in the past several decades. The rising living and education costs and the widening gap between the rich and the poor increasingly demand both the husband and the wife work in order to support their family.[95] This results in a drastic increase of dual-earner families in America from the 1960s to 1990s.[96] The same trend is observed in other parts of the world. For instance, the proportion of dual-earner families in

---

92. See section 3.3.

93. It does not mean that the household codes, being culturally embedded, have no relevancy today. In fact, they express an important redemptive message that can continue to inform familial relationships on this side of the eschaton. See chapter 6 for further discussions.

94. Ruether, *Christianity and the Making*, 84.

95. Ibid., 190–205.

96. Linda J. Waite and Mark Nielsen, "The Rise of the Dual-Earner Family, 1963–1997," in *Working Families: The Transformation of the American Home*, eds. Rosanna Hertz and Nancy L. Marshall (Berkeley, CA: University of California Press, 2001), 35.

Canada rose from four out of ten in mid-1970s to seven out of ten in the late 1990s.[97] In Hong Kong, the percentage of dual-earner families among high-income households increased by 48 percent from 1996 to 2006.[98] While adhering to the Victorian family model, complementarianism is unable to address this global economic trend. It is perhaps only feasible for a small, wealthy population where the husband can earn enough to support the whole household. If complementarians wish to promote the breadwinner-homemaker model as the universal ideal, they must address how the current social-economic trend can be reversed. Otherwise, the male-breadwinner model would castigate husbands who fail to support their families alone as not attaining "mature manhood." This would also imply that "masculinity" is in fact predicated upon one's income level. However, such economic discussion is absent from the vast collection of complementarian writings. On the other hand, assigning women as the primary caretaker of the family puts extra burden on working women. Studies show that in the 1990s, women still performed three-quarters of the housework, although seven out of ten households were dual-earner families.[99] When women are compelled to work and contribute financially to the family, it is reasonable to expect men to share more domestic chores and childcare responsibilities. The "responsible male headship" of complementarianism seems to support this ethic, but its rhetoric of the woman as the primary homemaker makes men reluctant to take on more household and childcare responsibilities. Insisting on this role assignment would likely deteriorate the relationship between modern couples. Therefore, when complementarians insist on universalizing a fixed set of gender roles, their ethics fails to adapt to the changing world. Perhaps this is anticipated from their assignment of role

---

97. Katherine Marshall, "The family Work Week," *Perspectives on Labour and Income* 21, no. 2 (Summer 2009): 21–29. Cited 8 August 2014. Online: http://search.proquest.com/docview/213987360?accountid=12861.

98. Hong Kong Legislative Council Subcommittee to Study the Subject of Combating Poverty, "Household Income Distribution in Hong Kong," LC Paper no. CB(2)2385/06-07(03), 3. Cited 8 August 2014. Online: http://www.legco.gov.hk/yr04-05/english/hc/sub_com/hs51/papers/hs510710cb2-2385-3-e.pdf.

99. Waite and Nielsen, "Rise of the Dual-Earner Family," 31; Scott Coltrane and Michele Adams, "Men's Family Work: Child-centered Fathering and the Sharing of Domestic Labor," in *Working Families: The Transformation of the American Home*, eds. Rosanna Hertz and Nancy L. Marshall (Berkeley, CA: University of California Press, 2001), 82.

as the definitive factor that distinguishes between man and woman. Role is directly linked to function, which varies according to specific situations. As situation changes, so should functions and roles. The task of Christian ethics is to transcribe the moral vision of Scripture into specific decisions, conducts and roles according to the changing situations. When the moral vision of Scripture is reduced to a set of fixed roles, the vision becomes solidified, failing to inform people who live in the changing world.

4.3 Theological Assessment

This analysis shows that the complementarian gender theory is not as faithful to Scripture as its advocates claim it to be. It is not divinely ordained and is heavily influenced by a particular culture. However, we should not abandon this theory just yet, for many of its underlying assumptions are correct. First, complementarianism affirms the importance of the body and sexual distinction. Unlike Farley who undermines the body and sees marriage as the coming together of two asexual minds, complementarians spell out an ethic of sexual difference that is firmly rooted in the body. Second, unlike Thatcher, who splits sex from procreation, complementarians affirm that marriage is inseparable from parenthood and procreation. Third, unlike Browning who sees the family as a liberal democracy, complementarians believe that marriage is instituted by God and should reflect God's good created order. Fourth, the notion of vocation, instead of free choice, governs the familial association: husbands and wives should live out their callings before God. Therefore, we are tempted to think that if the main weaknesses of complementarianism can be remedied, it may still be promising to offer a satisfactory Christian gender ethics. Before advocating an improved version of complementarianism, we should conduct a theological assessment of the theory. The most crucial theological claim of complementarianism is that male headship and female submission is the Christian moral vision that informs gender relationship. Our theological investigation should evaluate the truthfulness of this claim.

Although complementarians usually appeal to the New Testament epistles to construct their ethics of male headship and female submission, they often refer to the creation narratives for theological support. One important question they have to answer is: how are the New Testament instructions on the silencing of women, headship of husbands, and submission of wives timeless and universally valid? They answer the question by claiming that these instructions are based on a created order reflected in Genesis 1–3. As discussed above, they contend that headship and submission is not a result of human sinfulness but is inherent in God's creation and even embedded within the Trinity. The authority for man to lead and the imperative for women to be subordinate are ingrained in their very nature. Then the problem with gender relationship is not sexual hierarchy *per se*, but the corruption of it. Sin distorts this hierarchy, turning male headship into domination or passivity, and women into usurpers or doormats.[100] Christ's redemption restores the original created order. Headship and submission "is the beauty of the original relationship between Adam and Eve that the New Testament is restoring in our new creation in Christ."[101] Although complementarians use the language of created order, this creation order only points backward toward the original creation. However, O'Donovan is correct to argue that equating the created order with the original creation is inadequate. As sin corrupts our understanding of the created order, he contends, correct understanding of this order must be through God's revelation in the resurrection of Christ.[102] Yet Christ's redemptive work in his resurrection does not only point backward to the original creation but also forward toward its fulfillment. Redemption is not merely restoration; it does not put humanity back to the garden of Eden as Adam and Eve. Instead, redemption brings creation to its fulfillment in the New Jerusalem, where the human community becomes the bride of Christ.[103] Christian ethics do not only speak of a nostalgic return to the original creation but also of a hopeful fulfillment in the eschaton. The eschatological transformation of marriage and family, discussed in the previous chapters, should also inform the Christian moral vision concerning gender roles and relationships. Jesus teaches that those in the resurrection will "neither marry nor are given in marriage" (Luke 20:35). As discussed in chapter 2, this eschatological vision implies that sexual love will lose its biological basis, biological kinship

---

100. Grudem, *Evangelical Feminism and Biblical Truth*, 43.
101. Ibid., 110.
102. O'Donovan, *Resurrection and Moral Order*, 19.
103. Ibid., 53–57.

will be replaced by spiritual kinship, and the natural family will be replaced by the household of God. The in-breaking of Christ's resurrection relativizes the imperative to procreate on this side of the eschaton, and singleness becomes an equal vocation to that of marriage.[104] In chapter 3, I argued that as marriage and procreation are no longer mandatory, any decision to marry and procreate becomes a free choice, subject to God's calling on each particular person.[105] The question becomes: What is the eschatological vision concerning the relationship between man and woman, and how does this vision inform us today?

Jesus teaches that there will be no marriage between persons in the eschaton. For our purposes, we must decide if sexual distinctions will remain. I contend that human beings will continue to exist as man and woman due to the following reasons. First, the affirmation of bodily resurrection means that each person will continue to exist as a concrete and particular creature. Since alterity and human fellowship is predicated upon sexual difference in the body, this difference must continue in order that alterity between persons can be preserved.[106] Second, Barth argues from Genesis 1:27 that sexual distinction in humanity reflects the *imago Dei*. Human existence as male and female in the original creation is not contingent but is grounded in God's triune nature.[107] Christ's redemption does not negate God's original creation but brings about its fulfillment. The existence of human beings as man or woman will not be obliterated; the full purpose of sexual distinction will instead be manifested in the eschaton. On the contrary, eliminating sexual distinction in the resurrection means that God's original creation is flawed and requires correction. It is a negation of the "good" that God pronounces toward the universe in the creation narratives. Third, Augustine is correct in his reading of Jesus's teaching concerning "neither marry nor are given in marriage." Jesus does not say that there will be "neither male

---

104. See section 2.6.3.

105. See section 3.5.

106. See section 2.6.2.

107. Barth, *Church Dogmatics Vol. 3.1*, 182–187. Note that it is the analogy of relationship between persons that sexual distinction finds parallel with the Trinity, not the hierarchical difference for which complementarians argue.

nor female" in the resurrection; only "marriage" will cease.[108] As only men "marry" and only women are "given in marriage," Jesus's teaching actually assumes the continued presence of men and women in the resurrection, just that they will not marry.[109] The continued presence of sexual distinction in the eschaton also affirms the argument I made in chapter 2, that sexual difference is essential to a human person and is therefore significant in sexual ethics.[110]

Since complementarians emphasize the differences between male and female, they would also agree that sexual distinction will remain in the eschaton. Their gender theory does not stop at underscoring sexual difference but also names the content of this sexual distinction in terms of authority difference. They appeal to God's original creation, as interpreted by their reading of Genesis 1–3, to support this view. But will this authority difference remain in the eschaton? When marriage and the resulting roles of husband and wife discontinue in the resurrection, will male headship and female submission, or men as leaders and women as followers, linger? The created order, for complementarians, is only related to the garden of Eden and not to the New Jerusalem. Nowhere in their writing do they discuss eschatology or explicitly answer these questions. Yet their theology entails the view that male headship and female submission will remain in the resurrection. First, they contend that Christ's redemption is a restoration of the garden of Eden. The eschaton, for them, is a reenactment of the original creation with its intrinsic order of male headship and female submission. Second, they argue for the subordination of women through the doctrine of eternal subordination of the Son. As the Son submits to the Father in eternity, women also submit to men in eternity. Third, as the church is

---

108. Besides, St Paul's saying "neither male nor female" in Gal 3:28 does not suggest an eschatological negation of sexual distinction. It only negates the division of humanity based on gender. See Judith M. Gundry-Wolf, "Christ and Gender: A Study of Difference and Equality in Gal 3,28," in *Jesus Christus Als Die Mitte der Schrift: Studien Zur Hermeneutik Des Evangeliums,* eds. Christof Landmesser, Hans-Joachim Eckstein, and Hermann Lichtenberger (Berlin: W. de Gruyter, 1997), 476.

109. Augustine, *City of God, Book 22.17,* trans. Henry Scowcroft Bettenson (London: Penguin, 1984), 1058.

110. See section 2.3. For further discussion on the significance of sexual difference, see Christopher Chenault Roberts, *Creation and Covenant: The Significance of Sexual Difference in and for the Moral Theology of Marriage* (New York: T&T Clark, 2007).

an eschatological community, the church today should be a reflection of what will happen in the eschaton.[111] By insisting on male leadership in the church, complementarians also project that males will continue to be leaders over females in the age to come. Fourth, as they advocate male headship and female submission as the moral vision that informs gender relationship today, this ideal is the *telos* of human relationality which will be fully realized in the eschaton. Therefore, complementarians are claiming that in the resurrection, though the earthly husbands and wives will become brothers and sisters in God's household, half the population of New Jerusalem will continue to head over the other half.

The heart of the issue, I contend, is to distinguish what will continue and what will cease in the resurrection. As God's creation will be brought to fulfillment in the eschaton, things that remain in the resurrection are eternal and can inform us of the *telos* of human existence. In other words, they go to the very nature of our being. In the resurrection, we will continue to be bodily human persons, bearing the *imago Dei*, having communion with fellow human beings, relating to and obeying the triune God, and existing as male or female. On this side of the eschaton, we should also regard these aspects of our existence as essential to human personhood. Marriage will cease in the eschaton, together with procreation and the related familial roles such as husband, wife, father, and mother. All will become brothers and sisters, not related by blood but by the Spirit through baptism. In this vein, Jana Marguerite Bennett is correct to say that "water is thicker than blood" under the purview of the eschaton.[112] The cessation of marriage in the eschaton suggests that today, not all need to marry, to procreate, or to become a parent. Even if one does marry and become a parent, her status as a wife and mother may not last for life. In other words, the aspects that will cease to be in the eschaton do not define who we are; they only pertain to the temporary and contingent functions we perform before the *parousia*. Our question then becomes: will the roles of man as leader and woman as follower remain in the eschaton? As discussed above, complementarians

---

111. Stanley J. Grenz and Denise Muir Kjesbo, *Women in the Church: A Biblical Theology of Women in Ministry* (Downers Grove, IL: InterVarsity, 1995), 175–176.

112. Jana Marguerite Bennett, *Water Is Thicker than Blood: An Augustinian Theology of Marriage and Singleness* (Oxford: Oxford University Press, 2008), 31.

say yes to this question. Three difficulties arise from this view. First, when we speak of the roles of man and woman, usually the roles of husband and wife, father and mother, or perhaps breadwinner and homemaker would come to mind. All these roles will cease in the eschaton. It is very curious that only the roles of leader and follower will remain. It is incoherent to say that this particular role difference lingers while all others cease. Second, roles are related to functions. To argue that the sexual roles will remain in the eschaton is to assign eternal functions to persons. It also means that the performance of functions goes to defining the very nature of our being. In Christian thought, it is the question "who we are," not "what we do," that defines personhood. Third, the hierarchical image of sisters subordinating themselves under the headship of brothers does not fit the scriptural depiction of the eschatological community. Instead, equal yet different members belonging to the same body is the image that Scripture provides. In other words, the relationship between members of Christ's body, instead of male headship and female submission, is what informs our gender relationship. Regarding this third argument, further discussions are given as follows.

In St John's vision of the eschaton, New Jerusalem is the new covenantal community. The heavenly city is also depicted as the bride of Christ.[113] This marriage imagery affirms that Christ loves and redeems his people, who should be faithful to him and clothe themselves with righteous deeds.[114] Using the same imagery, St Paul likens the Corinthian church to a "chaste virgin to Christ," urging Christians to remain loyal to Christ.[115] Richard Batey argues that the imagery of marriage between Christ and church had been well known among the early churches in Asia Minor. The imagery was further elaborated in the Ephesian household code, where the head-body metaphor was added to describe the marriage relationship: "The church is not only the Bride of Christ; the church is also the Body of Christ."[116] Therefore, the New Testament describes Christ as the husband who loves the church and the head which connects to the community. The imagery of the body is further used to describe the relationship among members of

---

113. Rev 21:1–27.
114. Hartopo, "Marriage of the Lamb," 156, 171–172.
115. 2 Cor 11:2–3.
116. Richard A. Batey, *New Testament Nuptial Imagery* (Leiden: E. J. Brill, 1971), 65.

the community. Raymond Collins observes that St Paul invokes the image of the body to urge unity within the church. By saying that the different members of the body all belong to the one body of Christ, unity among Christians is stressed.[117] Anthony Thiselton notes that in St Paul's view, the Spirit bestows gifts to each individual so that each can perform specific tasks for the good of the whole community.[118] Every member of the community receives her particular gifts from the same Spirit, so no one should boast about the relative importance of the various gifts. St Paul uses the image of the body to explain the relationship between "one and many" in the church. The "one" points to spiritual equality so distinction should not be based on race, class, or gender. The "many" corresponds to the various spiritual gifts, which are given by the Spirit for the purpose of building up the church community.[119] Stanley Grenz also contends that when the body is used to describe the eschatological community, the old way of structuring interpersonal relationships through social distinctions should be replaced by equality in Christ.[120] While contemplating Augustine's thoughts, Bennett argues that both "marriage and virginity point toward humanity's eschatological future, but they do so because of their relationship with the Body of Christ as a whole."[121] Therefore, the image of different members belonging to the same body describes how individuals relate to one another in the eschatological community. The body of Christ provides the image for this eschatological community, in which persons are the eyes, ears, hands, and feet of the same body. Unlike the complementarian assumption, male headship and female submission is not the image that depicts the relationship within the eschatological community; the body of Christ is. Difference in spiritual gifts, not authority, becomes the basis of differentiation among persons. Besides, St Paul says that these spiritual gifts are temporary, for gifts such as prophesies, tongues, and knowledge will

---

117. Raymond F. Collins, *The Many Faces of the Church: A Study in New Testament Ecclesiology* (New York: Crossroad, 2003), 41–3.

118. Anthony C. Thiselton, *The Holy Spirit: In Biblical Teaching, through the Centuries, and Today* (Grand Rapids, MI: Eerdmans, 2013), 71.

119. Collins, *Many Faces of the Church*, 37–40.

120. Grenz and Kjesbo, *Women in the Church*, 176.

121. Bennett, *Water Is Thicker*, 131.

cease.[122] They are instrumental, given for the sake of building up the body of Christ. Similarly, one's familial vocation on this side of the eschaton is temporary and contingent. Marriage and singleness are simply "states of life." What is eternal is our membership in the household of God.[123] Unlike one's sexual distinction as male or female, one's vocation and the related spiritual gifts, roles, and functions are temporary; they will not be carried over into the resurrection.

Therefore, contrary to what complementarians claim, fixed functions and roles will not be found in the eschaton. They do not inform the essence of human existence and are contingent on this side of the eschaton. Any hierarchy between the sexes or attribution of authority to the male is a contingent human response to the created world, not a manifestation of the God's original creation or the *telos* of human existence. Male headship is simply a human device, and depending on how it is expressed, can be either rightful or sinful. Contrary to the complementarians, male headship is not an order ordained by God. Also contrary to the egalitarians who insist on the sinfulness of male headship,[124] I contend that male headship can be one benign gender conception constructed in response to the reality of sexual difference. For instance, my discussions in chapter 3 suggest that male headship can arise as a cultural strategy to compensate for the "paternal uncertainty" that befalls fathers.[125] Although male headship is prone to corruption and easily degenerates into male dominance in the fallen world, it is not necessarily sinful. Now that male headship and female submission is contingent, it is not necessary to reify the difference between man and woman. The role to lead or to follow is like marriage and procreation, contingent in our world today and subject to God's particular calling. We do not need to insist on these roles to affirm sexual distinction. Sexual difference is foremost and essentially known through a person's bodily existence as male or female, and derivatively manifested through gender construction based on the bodily sexual difference. Robert Scruton's view on gender, as discussed in chapter 2, can help us explicate the relationship between sex

---

122. 1 Cor 13:8.
123. Bennett, *Water Is Thicker*, 128.
124. Hess, "Equality With and Without Innocence," 94–95.
125. See section 3.3.

and gender.[126] He argues that gender, though a cultural construct, is based on biological sexual difference. Gender is constituted from both our understanding of sexual difference and our response to this understanding. This "understanding" and "response" is culturally dependent, so the *conception* of gender varies from culture to culture. Yet as sexual difference is universal, the *concept* of gender is transcultural. In other words, each culture has its own notions of masculinity and femininity. The notions are based on both biological sexual difference – which is universal – and the culture's unique historical and political circumstances. We should expect to find similarities as well as differences among the different conceptions of gender. As long as the *concept* of gender is reflected in a culture, sexual difference is affirmed. "Manhood" and "womanhood" defined by complementarians is nothing but one conception of gender arising from a particular context. The mistake of complementarianism is not so much about the content of their gender theory, but their claim of universality of their own gender conception.

Although the conception of gender is culturally dependent, it is not morally neutral. For instance, a culture that derogates women is morally wrong and should be challenged. A sexual ethic that denounces monogamy or marital fidelity should also be criticized. Christian theology can help construct a gender conception that is faithful to Scripture and congenial to human flourishing. It should consider the cultural situation of each particular community. While Scripture offers a single moral vision concerning gender relationship, this moral vision should be contextualized in the many different cultures.[127] Contextualization of the "one" Christian message into the "many" cultures is also attested to in scriptural narratives. When the early Christians received the Spirit on the day of the Pentecost, they spoke in different languages each intelligible to a specific people. The one Spirit gave them the gift to speak in many languages, yet the many languages all utter one message: the wonders of God.[128] Similar to the "one" body and the "many" members within the Christian community, the gift of the Spirit is again the link between the "one" message and the "many" cultures. Therefore, any concrete ethical exhortation given to a community

---

126. See section 2.2.
127. This single moral vision will be explicated in chapter 5 below.
128. Acts 2:1–11.

should be founded upon one moral vision, with the guidance of the Spirit, attuned to the community's historical and political circumstances. The New Testament household codes are such particular exhortations and should be interpreted this way. In the same token, anyone attempting to make use of these household codes or the biblical notion of male headship should also recognize their cultural embeddedness and contextualize them within one's own community. For instance, when examining how C. S. Lewis and Thielicke support male headship in marriage, Meilaender observes that while Lewis appeals to the character traits that give men the advantage in dealing with the society at large, Thielicke invokes the Christian tradition in his argument. What is common between them is their attempt to encourage marriage permanence in their contemporary culture through the notion of male headship.[129] John Stackhouse, Jr. offers another example of contextualization. In an attempt to find a way out of the complementarian-egalitarian debate, he advocates the notion of "holy pragmatism," meaning that gender is only a "pragmatic" issue subordinate to the more important agenda of evangelism.[130] "Holy pragmatism" calls egalitarians to grant concessions to cultures that embrace patriarchy,[131] and complementarians to relax their limitations on women's roles in egalitarian cultures,[132] both for the purpose of facilitating evangelism. Gender ethics can respond to the cultural environment in a flexible manner. To assess Lewis, Thielicke, and Stackhouse's arguments is beyond the scope of this book. I want to note, though, that they give examples of how one takes into account cultural background when constructing gender ethics. Male headship and female submission, as a human response to the created reality, need not be condemned across the board. Yet as it is only one particular way of response, it should not claim universality either.

Considering specific cultural contexts, however, does not mean that functions and roles are unimportant or can be arbitrarily assigned. In fact, some gender roles are tied to biological sexual difference. For instance, only

---

129. Meilaender, *Things That Count*, 44–57.

130. John G. Stackhouse Jr., *Finally Feminist: A Pragmatic Christian Understanding of Gender* (Grand Rapids, MI: Baker, 2005), 38–39.

131. Ibid., 40–41.

132. Ibid., 56.

women can bear and nurse children. Men are on average physically stronger. It is reasonable, because of this, for wives to stay home and care for their children while husbands provide for and protect them, at least initially after their children are born. When we are on this side of the eschaton where marriage still has not ceased, gender role assignments related to our bodily characteristics are often necessary and can even be good in bringing out God's intention for married couples. Barth contends that God gives us our calling in and through our reality as human creatures and each as particular man or woman.[133] It is in our particular "psycho-physical existence" that we receive our vocations and the corresponding roles.[134] As discussed in chapter 2, our bodily structure provides the material limitations upon which we can live out our true freedom. One's identity as a man or a woman, together with the corresponding bodily structure, should be embraced and not overstepped.[135] The spiritual gifts bestowed on each member of Christ's body also do not negate but complement one's bodily structure, as Michael Welker correctly argues, "The Spirit of God is not a force that erodes, squelches, impairs, and deforms life *in* the flesh. Rather, the Spirit of God is a power that liberates life *in* the flesh from the power of sin."[136] Furthermore, the Spirit bestows gifts to each individual so that each can perform particular tasks for the good of the whole community.[137] In the familial context, when God calls a person to be a mother, the Spirit gives her the corresponding gifts to perform the specific tasks as a mother. The same is true for the calling of a father. As a result, the assigning of gender roles that reflect and respect our biological differences – but not necessarily determined by them – is often necessary. Seen in this light, complementarianism and its gender role assignment can be a viable sexual ethics for couples in a certain cultural and economic context. The breadwinning-homemaking outside-inside paradigm can still be a reference for couples navigating in the modern world. What must be avoided

---

133. Barth, *Ethics*, 178–183.
134. Barth, *Church Dogmatics Vol. 3.4*, 608–610.
135. See section 2.6.2.
136. Michael Welker, *God the Spirit*, trans. John F. Hoffmeyer (Minneapolis, MN: Fortress, 1994), 262. Original emphasis.
137. Thiselton, *Holy Spirit*, 71.

is the universalizing of this paradigm, the solidifying of role assignment, or the hailing of male headship as the moral vision for gender relationships.

Our theological assessment concludes that male headship and female submission is not part of the original created order and should not be the moral vision that informs gender relationships. This conclusion also alleviates other difficulties in the complementarian theory. Giles points out that if male headship belongs to the created order, then it should be applicable in all spheres of life, not only in the home and the church.[138] Advocating male headship in all spheres of life would in fact help further the complementarian agenda, which is to counter the egalitarian culture and the undermining of sexual distinction. Contrary to their view of the created order, they limit the scope of application to within the home and the church, resulting in an inconsistency in their theory. If male headship is delinked from the created order, a community can choose to advocate this gender relationship in certain spheres and not others, depending on the actual circumstances. Another problem with the view of eternal sexual role difference is that a person cannot be complete without his or her "complement." The meaning of "complement" is very specific: men, as leaders, need to lead women; whereas women, as followers, need to submit to men. It is in this specific leading-following relationship that a person's gendered nature can be fulfilled. The single person presents a difficulty. How can a single person live out this imperative to lead or to submit? Ware answers this question by admonishing singles to join a "mixed group" in a local church and involve themselves with the "authority structure" of that church. It is through leading or following in the church group that one's need of "complementary" can be fulfilled.[139] This recommendation effectively suggests singles to join church groups for self-serving purposes. Other group members become instruments to fulfill one's own need. Note that this "need of complementarity" is not the same as the need for the opposite sex to understand oneself.[140] While the *presence* and *understanding* of the opposite sex is needed

---

138. Giles, *Trinity and Subordinationism*, 176.

139. Ware, "Male and Female Complementary," 91–92.

140. For example, Barth says, ". . . there is no such thing as a self-contained and self-sufficient male life or female life. . . . It is always in relationship to their opposite that man and woman are what they are in themselves." *Church Dogmatics Vol. 3.4*, 163.

for us to understand our own sexuality, complementarianism requires the *engagement* with others in *gender-specific roles*. One's counterpart becomes an instrument to utilize, not an "other" to behold. The same can happen in marriage relationships. One's spouse can become an instrument for one to fulfill his or her imperative to engage in an "authority structure," thereby achieving "mature manhood or womanhood." When roles and functions are deemed essential in constituting personhood, persons inevitably become instruments. By severing the link between these roles and the created order, the problem is solved. A third problem with the view of eternal gender role is related to the person Jesus. Barth professes that we can only understand the nature of humanity through the person Jesus, who reveals an uncorrupted vision of humanity through his sinless life. Jesus is also fully divine, so we must acquire our understanding by keeping to his human nature.[141] Jesus, in his concrete human nature, is a man. If we assign different and eternal roles to man and woman, Jesus can only reveal knowledge to us about man and not woman. Then we have no way to know the role of women or have a theological basis of femininity. Perhaps this is why, in complementarianism, femininity is simply a mirror image of masculinity. Besides, Jesus failed to live up to the standard of "mature manhood" by never marrying or having a family to support. Perhaps this is also why complementarians do not appeal to Jesus as a model of mature manhood. These problems can be solved by disconnecting gender roles from the created order. Then gender role is simply an outflow of one's sexual identity, instead of an imperative to be achieved. Jesus, as a concrete person, is also allowed to manifest his own manhood in his particular circumstances according to his specific calling.

4.4 Conclusions

One aim of the complementarian project coincides with the purpose of this book: to formulate a Christian gender ethics that responds to the challenges posed by contemporary culture. Many of their presuppositions are

---

141. Karl Barth, *Church Dogmatics Vol. 3.2, The Doctrine of* Creation, eds. G. W. Bromiley and T. F. Torrance, trans. H. Knight, G. W. Bromiley, J. K. S. Reid, and R. H. Fuller (Peabody, MA: Hendrickson, 2010), 41–44.

also correct. They rightly uphold the importance of sexual difference, link between sex and procreation, and vocation in family association. They err in making *role* the definitive factor that differentiates the sexes. Focusing on *role* reduces man and woman to their instrumental functions, and elevates one particular set of behaviors to the level of eternal truth. When ethics is constructed starting from behavioral rules, doctrines and hermeneutics must be twisted around the rules. This has apparently happened in the formulation of complementarianism in which male headship and female submission is designated as the moral vision that governs gender relationships. Our analysis shows that this should not be the case. An alternative moral vision is needed. We have suggested that the body of Christ is the image that depicts the eschatological community. What is the moral vision that informs gender and familial relationships within this community? This question will be answered in the next chapter.

Besides, claiming a set of gender behaviors as transcultural and universal overlooks the reality of economic and political changes. While the complementarian gender ethics may be suitable in certain cultures, the same set of rules becomes stifling in others. When we formulate gender ethics, we must consider our own cultural environment. Gender is a human construction based on the reality of sexual difference as well as our understanding of this difference. As human understanding is bound up with culture, so is gender. However, it does not mean that Christian ethics should simply follow the ideology of the world. If constructing an ethical theory is like constructing a building, we must first lay a solid foundation – the Christian moral vision – then construct the superstructure – particular moral exhortations – to suit the needs of its inhabitants. A "one-size-fits-all" building is usually not a good building to live in. Furthermore, the image of the body of Christ reminds us that each member of the body possesses different gifts and so gender roles and functions are never rigid and unchangeable. Although an ethical theory developed for a particular culture should be useful for all persons within that culture, it must not dictate how individuals decide on their specific familial roles and functions. A person's gender and familial roles must be decided through careful discernment considering the Christian moral vision, the economic and political circumstance of her society, the gender conception of her culture, the specific situation of her family, as well as the gifts she receives from the Spirit. In this regard, the notion of *duality* is again applicable. We must heed the *duality* between the individual and the community in our assignment of gender and familial roles: the culture and gender conception of the community and the situation and gifts of the individual must both be considered.

For the subject of gender relationships, the picture is further complicated by an eschatological vision that depicts the *telos* of human existence. This *telos* does not need to be fully realized in the present age. While marriage and procreation will cease in the resurrection, they still remain on this side of the eschaton, bearing witness to the original creation. Consequently, not all need to remain single nor should biological kinship be broken immediately. Nevertheless, we are now situated in between the two ages. Christian gender ethics must therefore heed another *duality*: between the present age and the future eschaton. Meilaender describes this duality as follows:

> Christians find themselves living in two realms, in this age and the coming age that is already also here — and both are God's. We live as children, parents, spouses, workers, citizens; yet, unless we wish to sever entirely the two realms of the one God's activity, we must affirm that it is faithfulness to which we are called in the worldly spheres of life and faithfulness in which they train us.[142]

We now live *in* this age, but we are not *of* this age. Relationship between man and woman in the natural family happens only *in* this age, yet the moral vision that informs this relationship is not *of* this age. It is through Christ, who straddles both ages, that we can know the way between man and woman.

---

142. Meilaender, *Faith and Faithfulness*, 116.

CHAPTER 5

Love between Man and Woman

5.1 A Retrospective

In the previous chapters, I conversed with three different schools of thought on the subject of gender and family. Each school addresses a specific issue and formulates distinctive ethical notions through retrieving different facets of the Christian tradition. While all of them offer valuable insights into the relationship between man and woman, my analysis shows that each is founded upon certain faulty assumptions, rendering the resulting gender ethics inadequate. I argued that O'Donovan's moral theology – in particular his notion of moral order vindicated through the life, death, resurrection, and exaltation of Christ – can remedy these shortfalls. I also used Meilaender's notion of *duality* to characterize the different aspects of human existence that are pertinent for constructing a gender ethics that is theologically robust. The salient arguments and conclusions of the previous chapters are recapitulated as follows.

Both Farley and Thatcher address the issue of marital permanence. Farley contemplates on the difficulty of keeping personal commitments and suggests that sustaining love between the couple is the key to marriage permanence; it is the spiritual bonding between the two minds that enables marriages to last. She says that love is not entirely beyond a person's control but can be directed by the mind. How a person interprets her experience with her partner becomes important in maintaining marital stability. In her scheme, the body is indispensable, but only as an instrument for gathering experience and carrying out actions for the mind, which is the locus of personal fulfillment. Farley's thinking is influenced by late-modern mind-body dualism that subjugates the body under the superior mind. This results in her theory neglecting sexual difference and procreation, jeopardizing the welfare of children and overlooking the importance of manhood and womanhood in the flourishing of men and women as concrete persons. Thatcher, on the other hand, focuses on the beginning of marriage and advocates a betrothal stage before the solemnization of marriage so that couples can learn to live together before things become irrevocable. As the body is important, he thinks that love between persons must involve erotic bodily union. The betrothal stage should then include sex as an expression of love but must avoid pregnancy to avoid any "irrevocable" situation. This demands the splitting of sex from procreation using modern technology. This split reveals the same late-modern mind-body dualism latent in his thinking: when contraception is assumed to be perfectly effective, the body is again subjugated under the controlling mind. But as the natural connection between sex and procreation cannot be entirely severed, Thatcher's sexual ethics is potentially harmful to all parties involved in case of unintended pregnancy. The shortcomings of Farley and Thatcher's theories can be remedied by recovering the importance of the body, perceiving it not merely as an instrument that serves the mind but as an essential aspect of human existence. What the body reveals – the link between sex and procreation, the physiological and psychological differences between the sexes, the material limitations, etc. – must be heeded in constructing gender ethics. Our examination of their sexual ethics points us to what is internal to a human person: the relationship between the mind and the body. Meilaender's notion of *duality* – holding together in harmonious and creative union of two disparate elements without obliterating their separateness – should characterize the relationship between the mind and the body in our formulation of gender ethics.

Browning and his team address the issue of equality in the family. To uphold equality between the couple means that traditional patriarchy must be challenged and replaced by the ethic of "equal-regard." Equality is also the goal of the parent-child relationship. Although this ideal cannot be fully achieved when children are still young and cannot reciprocate, it gives rights to children so they must be protected and nurtured. Browning and his team contend that their parents should be the ones who honor the rights of their children and shoulder the duties of parenting. Their family ethics, which they name "critical familism," is a promotion of the two-parent "intact" family within which the ideal of "equal-regard" is nurtured and practiced. By focusing on the welfare of children, critical familism fills the void of Farley and Thatcher's theories. By using evolutionary psychology to explain the conditions of paternal investment, the importance of biology and the body is acknowledged. However, critical familism fails to resolve the contradiction between equal-regard and family coherence; paternal investment needed for the flourishing of children is logically incoherent with the notion of equal-regard, which encourages family members to claim rights against one another. I contend that this difficulty arises from Browning's understanding of the family as a liberal democracy where members are free to enter or exit out of consent and motivated by self-benefit. This notion of family association assumes that members are discrete individuals prone to drifting apart. To resolve this problem, the Christian notion of family association – where man and woman are in original, "one-flesh" union and children are the offspring of this union – should instead inform how we conceive of the family. Our examination of critical familism points us to what lies between human persons: the relationship between man and woman. The notion of *duality*, again, is useful in characterizing the relationship between man and woman: they are distinct persons, equal in dignity, yet interdependent and in original union. Meilaender argues that to maintain the *duality* between man and woman, they must stand side by side and before God. The family is formed by God calling each member into it, not through a conglomeration of individuals out of consent or self-benefit. Christian family ethics, in other words, becomes the hearing of and response to God's calling.

Complementarianism is claimed to be the gender ethic rooted in God's calling upon men and women. Based on a literalist interpretation of Scripture, complementarians say that male headship and female submission is embedded within God's created order and should govern the relationship between man and woman. The issue that they address is the blurring of sexual distinction brought about by modern feminism, and they believe that affirming gender distinction holds the key to the problem. They advocate a complementary view of masculinity and femininity, where men should be leaders, protectors, and providers, while women should be followers, supporters, and caregivers. This results in a gender division of labor where men should seek paid employment outside while women should stay home to care for the household and the children. Appealing to a universal moral vision of male headship and female submission, complementarians believe that these fixed gender roles are transcultural and should be implemented by all married couples in all cultures. While complementarianism heeds the bodily distinction between man and woman, attends to the welfare of children, and hearkens God's calling on each family member, its weakness stems from a lack of eschatology and the equating of the redeemed created order with the original creation. As the eschatological transformation of the family is ignored, any transformation of gender relationships and roles is disallowed. Gender relationship then solidifies into one particular gender role expression, which happens to be the Victorian family ideal that complementarians advocate. This inflexible gender role assignment renders the complementarian gender theory stifling in many cultures. The remedy, I argued, is to replace the image of male headship with the eschatological image of the body of Christ in apprehending the familial association. According to this latter image, family members are not, as complementarians suggest, occupants of a hierarchical structure which lasts into eternity. Instead, husband, wife, and children are members of the one body headed by Christ, each receiving gifts freely bestowed by the Spirit to fulfill her familial roles. Therefore, gender roles, though important in the proper functioning of families, are by no means fixed and transcultural. They can adapt to the particular cultural and economic situation in which a couple lives. Our examination of complementarianism points us to what lies beyond the familial association: the relationship between the family members and the concrete economic and cultural circumstances, and between what they are today and what they will become in the eschaton. The notion of *duality* can again describe these aspects of human existence.

5.2 Dualities of Human Existence as Framework of Gender Relationship

"Ethics . . . was not some 'aspect' of life, but rather inclusive of all that constituted a person's life."[1] Hauerwas's reminder rings true for our analysis of the different gender theories. Each of my conversation partners focuses on one specific gender issue so each can help us address certain dimensions of life. But as ethics is inclusive of all aspects of a person's life, each of their analyses is in itself incomplete. However, it does not mean that a "complete" gender ethic can be constructed by simply combining all of their theories. In fact, to formulate a "complete" ethic that addresses all issues for all persons is simply impossible, as demonstrated by the mistake of the complementarians who claim universal applicability of one particular gender expression. Verhey says that moral decision is not made by "some generic 'reasonable person' but a particular person, bound by ties of loyalty to other particular persons, related by history and by covenant to concrete communities, burdened by specific grievances inflicted or endured, sustained by and identified with others."[2] The task of ethics, I contend, is to provide a *framework* and a *moral vision* to assist particular persons in their own moral discernment. The *framework* marks the boundaries where moral conducts should not transgress, and the *moral vision* provides the *telos* toward which moral actions should be directed. The *framework* for gender ethics is discussed in this section while the *moral vision* will be developed in the next.

The four *dualities* of human existence described above, I contend, can offer such a *framework* for gender ethics. In other words, moral decisions about gender relationships and familial roles should be made within the space encircled within the "boundaries" marked by the *dualities* of mind and body, man and woman, individual and community, and present and future. Otherwise, certain essential aspect of human nature or relationality is transgressed. While detailed discussions on these "boundaries" have

---

1. Stanley Hauerwas, "How 'Christian Ethics' Came to Be," in *The Hauerwas Reader*, eds. John Berkman and Michael G. Cartwright (Durham, NC: Duke University Press, 2001), 38–39.
2. Verhey, *Remembering Jesus*, 4.

been offered in the previous chapters, their salient features are repeated as follows.

First, upholding the *mind-body duality* suggests that both the mind and the body should be respected. While the mind is free and can decide what the body should do, bodily structures and functions are not arbitrary and should not be treated as mere technological artifacts. Biological differences between the sexes should be an important aspect of human nature and sex should always be in some way connected to procreation. Human freedom is not an escape from bodily limitations but is realized through respecting and engaging with these limitations. On the other hand, biology should not be the sole determinant of gender, lest the mind and human freedom is disparaged. One's familial roles should not be dictated by biology and sex. Besides, the unitive function of sex should not be subsumed under the procreative function, and familial associations should not be predicated upon bloodline alone. This implies that both the biological and social dimensions of the family should be held in balance.

Second, to uphold the *man-woman duality* means that each person is distinct yet all persons arise from an original oneness. On the one hand, it is not good for man or woman to be alone. Relationality is an essential aspect of human nature and communion with others is indispensable for both single and married persons. The family, among other communities, offers such a place for human communion. As the family enables human communion, it is in itself good and should not be considered merely an instrument for other purposes such as the successful upbringing of children[3] or the promotion of a particular lifestyle and social norm.[4] On the other hand, respecting the individuality of persons means that each person is in a sense complete. One need not depend on others to complete one's human nature. It is not necessary to engage with the opposite sex to achieve one's gendered personhood,[5] nor must a person marry to become a "complete"

---

3. As implied in Browning's critical familism.

4. For instance, Nancy Cott argues that the United States government has been using family laws to encourage a particular form of family that supports the American political ideals. While her analysis may be correct, the main purpose of the family is still the communion of persons within, not the promotion of a political ideal. The latter must not trump the former. See Cott, *Public Vows*, 2–3.

5. As implied in the complementarianism gender theory.

person.⁶ Although a man must understand himself vis-à-vis the woman and vice versa, one sex is not simply a mirror image of the other.⁷ This would destroy otherness between man and woman, for in the mirror-image conception of gender, Francis Watson avers, "the image of the other [only] serves the image of the narcissistic self and has no identity of its own outside that necessary service."⁸

Third, upholding the *duality* between *the individual and the community* means, on the one hand, that the normative gender conception of a couple's community always offers a good starting point for them to construct their own gender relationship. For instance, the breadwinning-homemaking model, in certain economic circumstances, may still be the best arrangement for families with young children. In cultures where men still earn more than women, it may be more sensible to follow the norm and have the husband earn wages outside while the wife stays home to care for the household and children.⁹ But gender role assignment would look much different for families where both husband and wife must work to support the family. The split of housework and childcare in this case should be much more equal between the husband and the wife. On the other hand, the "individual" side of the duality suggests that the exact gender conception and role arrangement should also depend on the particular gifts bestowed on each. While mothers naturally form stronger bonds with their infants due to gestation and nursing, some fathers are particularly gifted in the caring and nurturing of children. Gender role arrangement for any particular couple should consider all these factors.

Fourth, the *duality* between *the present and the future*, or between this side and the other side of the eschaton, reminds us that marriage will ultimately be transformed. The imperative to marry has been relieved and

---

6. The community-based, gender-segregated monasteries where celibates live together therefore constitute a viable communal arrangement for human flourishing.

7. For instance, femininity described by the complementarian advocate John Piper is effectively the mirror image of his notion of masculinity. See "Vision of Biblical Complementarity," 31–59.

8. Francis Watson, *Agape, Eros, Gender: Towards a Pauline Sexual Ethic* (Cambridge: Cambridge University Press, 2000), 4.

9. It does not mean that seeking wage equality between genders is unimportant as a social justice issue. This example only points out that gender construction and gender role arrangement for a couple should heed their concrete cultural and economic situation.

singleness has become an equal and alternative witness alongside marriage in the Christian church. One's role as husband, wife, father, or mother is now a matter of vocation, subject to God's particular calling. Familial roles and the bond of kinship are not permanent; they are subordinate to the spiritual bond of baptism shared by all members in God's household.[10] As the natural household is oriented toward God's universal household in Christ, family members should not close in upon themselves. Strangers should be welcomed through the practice of hospitality.[11] The "present" side of the duality reminds us that marriage still bears witness to the original creation. "The married must still live in the ways of marriage," avers O'Donovan.[12] Procreation, fidelity, and permanence should continue to be the goods of marriage. The eschatological transformation of marriage, though rendering these goods nonessential, does not obliterate them from marriages today.

5.3 Christ's Love as Moral Vision of Gender Relationship

Gender ethics should be formulated within the *framework* bordered by these four dualities of human existence. The *framework* outlines the shape of the created order where human beings are placed: mind and body, man and woman, individual and community, present and future. Within the space bounded by these dualities, a *moral vision* that informs the affiliation of man and woman is needed. Based on O'Donovan's notion of the created order, I contend that *love* is this moral vision. The moral order embedded in God's creation, argues O'Donovan, is vindicated in the life, death, resurrection and exaltation of Christ. Christ's redemption gives us knowledge about God's moral order. This moral order does not stay as some objective knowledge external to us. Through Christ's redemption and the transforming power of the Spirit, the objective moral order becomes the subjective moral order of the moral agent, who no longer abides with the moral order as an external law but embraces it through sharing Christ's authority over

---

10. Bennett, *Water Is Thicker*, 132–134.
11. Ibid., 163.
12. O'Donovan, *Resurrection and Moral Order*, 70.

the created order. This shifting of moral order – from objective to subjective – allows the moral agent to assume a proper place within the creation and respond to God's moral order in freedom and not under compulsion. This Christian freedom is characterized by the notion "love."[13] O'Donovan writes, "Love is the overall shape of Christian ethics, the form of the human participation in created order."[14] Barth further links love and freedom with the notion of obedience, saying that,

> as [a person] . . . receives . . . the freedom to [love God], he inescapably discovers that in this freedom, which is the freedom to give himself to God in return, he has no option but to place himself under the will and Word and command and order of God as he hears it, and therefore to be obedient. Obedience is the required action of love.[15]

Seen in this light, we can argue that love allows us to act freely in obedience to the moral order, that is, to act within the boundaries drawn by the dualities that characterize human existence. But for love to abide with the moral order, it is not any kind of love. O'Donovan continues, ". . . the love that the Spirit enables is the same love as that which was historically realized in the humanity of Christ. It was the mark of love within Christ's Lordship."[16] In other words, as Christ vindicates God's created order and he also acts out of love, his love conforms to God's moral order. *It is Christ's love that informs our gender ethics, enabling us to abide with God's moral order and to heed the dualities that characterize human existence as created by God.* This statement roots the goodness of our moral acts in both Christ and God's creation. John Webster's summary of Barth's view of ethics succinctly depicts this: "Christian moral theology is essentially an assertion that good

---

13. Ibid., 22–25.
14. Ibid., 25.
15. Karl Barth, *Church Dogmatics Vol. 4.2, The Doctrine of Reconciliation*, eds. G. W. Bromiley and T. F. Torrance, trans. G. W. Bromiley (Peabody, MA: Hendrickson, 2010), 800.
16. O'Donovan, *Resurrection and Moral Order*, 26.

human action is action which is most in accord with the way the world is constituted in Jesus Christ."[17]

In chapter 4, I argued that eschatology is important to our moral thinking in a way that what remains in the eschaton informs the *telos* of our existence. In the resurrection we will continue to be bodily human persons, bearing the *imago Dei*, having communion with fellow human beings, worshipping and obeying the triune God, and existing as male or female. On this side of the eschaton we should also regard these aspects of our existence essential to human personhood. But as marriage will cease in the resurrection, natural marriage, biological kinship, and familial roles are contingent on this side of the eschaton. These things do not define who we are. Eschatology then offers us a direction toward which we should aim our moral thinking and conducts. I further argued that the body of Christ is the image that depicts the eschatological community. We should act by envisioning one another as different members of the same body. But what is the moral vision that governs the relationship between the different members? Under the purview of the eschaton, the moral vision that informs these relationships is, again, love. As discussed in chapter 4, roles, functions, and spiritual gifts will cease in the resurrection. The performance of any function, the adoption of any role, or the possession of any spiritual gift should not govern how we relate to one another. But St Paul claims that what never ceases, is love.[18] Love remains in the eschaton. Therefore, love informs the *telos* of all human relationships, today and in eternity. This offers another reason why love should be the moral vision for gender and familial relationships.

In his commentary on St John's exhortations concerning love (1 John 4:7–12), John Painter observes that St John is addressing four issues about love. First, love must be defined by God's action, which, in the pericope, refers to God's sending his Son to save the world. Second, the source of love is God, so human love is always a response to God's initiating love. Third, human love is prone to corruption, needing continual correction by God's command. Fourth, God's love to us is both a gift and a command. When

---

17. John B. Webster, *Barth's Ethics of Reconciliation* (Cambridge: Cambridge University Press, 1995), 219.

18. 1 Cor 13:8.

we receive God's love, we are at the same time commanded to share this gift. The word *kathōs* in Jesus's exhortation – "Just as (*kathōs*) I have loved you, you also should love one another" (John 13:34) – has two meanings: "because" and "in the same way." Christ loves us so that we may love one another in the same way as he loves us.[19] Painter's reading of St John can help us understand the love that should inform our gender ethics. It is God, not human beings, who defines what love is. This love is foremost revealed in Christ's acts of love for us. Love between man and woman owes its existence to God and needs God to preserve it against corruption. Christ's love for us should be received and shared between husband and wife, parents and children, and those inside and outside of the family. Upon receiving Christ's love, we respond by loving one another with this same love of Christ. Love in Christian thoughts always has two dimensions: a vertical dimension between God and humanity and a horizontal dimension among human beings. These two dimensions are closely related to each other. Barth argues that as a person lives in concrete human relationships, her love for God takes the form and dimension of love for her neighbor, who is also concrete. As God's love for humanity is shown in the history of salvation, and as the history of salvation is both a history of God and humanity and a history among persons in God's community, love of God and love of neighbor correspond to each other: "The connexion [between persons in God's community] is their mutual love; the love of each for his neighbor. It is their love for one another because they are those who together are loved by God and love Him in return. . . . The awakening to mutual love succeeds instantaneously the awakening to love for God."[20]

Not only does our love for God entail our love for neighbor, mutual love between neighbors also corresponds to God's love through the notion of witness. Barth sees Christians as witnesses to one another. A witness is a person who imparts information to the other, information which would otherwise be inaccessible to the other. To say that Christians are witnesses to one another means that in their communion, mutual impartation of information – or mutual proclamation – is expected. In God's community,

---

19. John Painter, *1, 2, and 3 John*, Sacra Pagina Series Vol. 18 (Collegeville, MN: Liturgical Press, 2002), 270.
20. Barth, *Church Dogmatics Vol. 4.2*, 810.

what is mutually proclaimed is the concrete love of God to each person. This proclamation takes the form of concrete human action. Through mutual witnessing in God's community, God's love for us is expressed in our loving action to one another. Besides, a witness imparts information that she does not create; what she witnesses is something external to her. As a witness of God's love, a person only loves her neighbor through a reflection of and a response to God's love for her. This reflection of God's love cannot replace God's love itself; the proclaimer of God's love is never herself God. Without receiving God's love, she cannot know or practice Christian love. This mutual and witnessing love forms the basis of Christian communal life and links God's love with human love. Embraced by the Christian community, the mutual love among God's people further bears witness to God's love in the world. The love command – love of God and love of neighbor – becomes the witness that buttresses the mission of the church to the world. Love as a command means that it is a Christian duty. One's act of love is not conditional upon the response of one's neighbor. Barth's notion of mutual love is different from Browning's equal-regard love which is predicated upon reciprocity. For Barth, Christians are compelled by God's love to love the others. Love within the Christian community is mutual not because mutuality *per se* is required or aimed at, but because love is an essential character for all Christians. By witnessing God's love, a Christian reminds her fellow Christians of their own obligation to love. It is through this witnessing love that God's love is revealed in the world today. As Christ is the only person in history who has faithfully and perfectly witnessed God's love, we are to learn to love through him.[21]

This notion of mutual and witnessing love among Christians, I contend, is how the moral vision of Christ's love should be embraced in the family. Practicing love in the family is not foremost for the benefit of its individual members, or for the stability of spousal relationship, or even for the wellbeing of children. Love is first of all received from God through the redemptive work of Christ. Then it is shared with one another as a response to this redemptive love. Subsequently, the mutual love practiced among Christians bears witness to God's love for the world. Embracing mutual

---

21. Ibid., 812–824.

and witnessing love does not mean that individual fulfillment, spousal relationship, or the flourishing of children is unimportant. The notion of mutual and witnessing love suggests that the primary aim of love should not remain on the human level. Mutual and witnessing love can perhaps explicate Meilaender's idea that man and woman should stand alongside each other and before God. To help couples weather the seasons of life, he avers, love between man and woman must be "touched and transformed by the Eternal."[22] Otherwise the fallen human nature invariably renders any human bonding precarious. But when we receive and share God's love in the family, individual fulfillment, marriage stability, and the flourishing of children would likely follow.

5.4 The Moral Vision

How can we understand and bear witness to God's love? Earlier I claimed that God's love is revealed in the life, death, resurrection, and exaltation of Christ. But it appears that the narrative of Christ's life itself can give us little direct information concerning love between man and woman within the family, for Christ remained single throughout his life. Here O'Donovan's observations about Christian love can give us some hints on how to proceed. He observes that the Christian descriptions of love often invoke the notion of "wisdom," which is "the intellectual apprehension of the order of things which discloses how each being stands in relation to each other."[23] Therefore, it is through human wisdom that we can begin to ponder and appreciate how Christ's love can inform our understanding of familial love. For this reason, we should not leave our conversation partners behind just yet, as they have provided valuable insights into the forms of love between man and woman and within the family. By gleaning the wisdom of our conversation partners, we can begin to formulate a notion of familial love that is congruous with Christ's love. This is the task of the remainder of this chapter.

---

22. Meilaender, *Things That Count*, 35.
23. O'Donovan, *Resurrection and Moral Order*, 26.

5.4.1 From Just Love to Friendship

The wisdom that Farley offers is that marital commitment is, at least in part, predicated upon the presence and experience of love between the couple. This love, in her discussions, is "primarily the kind we find in romantic love or in friendship."[24] She begins by addressing romantic love, which pertains to one's affection and passion and is often not grounded in prior knowledge between lovers. Romantic love is usually fleeting and, on its own, fails to support long-term commitments. The institution of marriage can no longer stabilize romantic love today so an alternative must be proposed to foster long-term commitments. She resorts to free will and free action in her proposal. Love is more than mere feelings but is something we do. What is "done" in love include affirming, uniting with, and responding to the lovableness of the beloved. Love, as an action, can be directed through exercising of our free choice into conformance with certain frameworks.[25] She proposes, in the sphere of sexual love, the framework of "just love," which includes seven guidelines: to do no harm, free consent, mutuality, equality, commitment, fruitfulness, and social justice.[26] Long-term commitment is possible through diverting our attention from emotion, which is intractable, to choice, which can be controlled by our will. Farley's "directing" of love is actually an attempt to supplement romantic love with friendship. In *Friendship: A Study of Theological Ethics*, Meilaender observes that friendship is particular and preferential love that arises under four conditions. First, physical proximity between two persons is needed to develop friendship. Second, the compatibility between them – such as age and intellect – plays a part. Third, their shared interests and values draw them closer. The fourth and most important factor is that they make favorable judgment on each other's character.[27] Within marriage, the first three conditions of proximity, compatibility, and shared interests and values have already been established between the couple. The fourth and most important factor – favorable judgment – is the one that Farley

---

24. Farley, *Personal Commitments*, 30.
25. Ibid., 30–46.
26. Farley, *Just Love*, 215–232.
27. Gilbert Meilaender, *Friendship: A Study in Theological Ethics* (Notre Dame, IN: University of Notre Dame Press, 1981), 28.

advocates. Her proposal to "direct" love from emotion to free choice so that spouses can make favorable judgment on each other is effectively a way to foster friendship between them. In other words, the key to long-term commitment, for Farley, is the promotion and maintenance of friendship between the couple.

It is in fact reasonable for Farley to appeal to friendship to secure the conjugal bond. Our discussions in chapter 2 show that her thinking is infected by the late-modern mind-body dualism that elevates the mind above the body. The coming together of man and woman in marriage, for her, is effectively the coming together of asexual minds. Friendship, as Diogenes Allen points out, does not have a sexual element nor does it involve the rearing and nurturing of children. Thus friendship is an "unphysical" love.[28] It is exactly this "unphysical" nature of friendship that fits Farley's notion of marriage. Besides, Farley's emphasis on friendship also reveals her attempt to render her ethics intelligible and persuasive to the late-modern culture.[29] In *Haven in a Heartless World*, Christopher Lasch recounts how the western family shed its various functions in the past several centuries. The industrial revolution shifted the productive function of the family to the factories and offices outside of the home. The rise of social sciences changed parenting from a skill innate to fathers and mothers to a science that must be studied and taught by the professionals. Gradually, schools and the social welfare system replaced parents as the primary educators of children, and the state took over the responsibility of childrearing from the family. The only function left for the family is the provision of a safe haven against the outside heartless world. The family is reduced from an institution of production and procreation to a place for the conjugal couple to enjoy companionship.[30] When Farley attempts to render her sexual ethics persuasive in this cultural context where companionship is the only *raison d'être* for marriage, friendship becomes the only guiding principle for marriages. However, Lasch argues that family is an integrated system: "some of the

---

28. Diogenes Allen, *Love: Christian Romance, Marriage, Friendship* (Eugene, OR: Wipf & Stock, 2006), 37.

29. Farley, *Just Love*, xii.

30. Christopher Lasch, *Haven in a Heartless World: The Family Besieged* (New York: W. W. Norton & Co., 1995).

family's functions [cannot] be surrendered without weakening the others."[31] While Farley accepts the reduction of the family to companionship and equates love with friendship, her notion of love becomes inadequate for the family. Within the family, though friendship is an important form of love, it should not be the only form.

Later, we will discuss other forms of love that are also important to the family. But at the moment we can affirm Farley's wisdom that friendship is, nonetheless, a crucial aspect of marital love. Our task is to construct a notion of friendship that is congruent with Christ's love. Otherwise, we fail to witness God's love when we advocate friendship between man and woman. The problem we immediately face is that friendship, as commonly understood, is preferential, reciprocal, and mutable. These properties appear incompatible with Christ's love.[32] Edward Collins Vacek believes otherwise. He argues that friendship is an important aspect of Christian love, though the notion of friendship must be understood not from human perspectives but from God's love for us. He identifies three kinds of love in Christian thought: loving for the sake of the beloved (*agape*), for the sake of the self (*eros*), and for the sake of the relationship between them (*philia* or friendship).[33] Instead of pitting these three against one another, he argues that all are needed. He even demonstrates that God's love encompasses all three kinds and so Christians should also practice them all, otherwise our love is deficient.[34] For our purposes, we will focus on his argument about friendship. He defines friendship as a love that does not focus on the lover or the beloved but the relationship between them. Fostering mutuality – the sharing and communion between persons – is the *telos* of friendship. Focusing on the relationship between persons means that the identity and situation of each person is unimportant to friendship. Therefore, contrary

---

31. Ibid., 130.

32. Meilaender, *Friendship*, 3. Besides preference, reciprocity, and mutability, Meilaender also discusses why civil friendship and the notion of vocation may be incompatible with Christian love. However, civil friendship concerns the political sphere and the notion of vocation only pertains to work and not the family. These two aspects of friendships are not discussed here.

33. Edward Collins Vacek, *Love, Human and Divine: The Heart of Christian Ethics* (Washington, DC: Georgetown University Press, 1994), 157–158.

34. Ibid., 308–312.

to Aristotle, friendship is not predicated upon equality between persons.[35] In his reading of the Johannine corpus, Vacek observes that mutuality between the Father and the Son is further extended to that between Jesus and his disciples. We can become friends with Jesus and even God, though we do not share equality with God.[36] Christ's redemptive work, argues Vacek, does not only save us from damnation but allows us to respond to God's love. God's grace enables us to "accept God's loving participation in our lives . . . [and] to cooperate with God in loving the world."[37] Our friendship or mutuality with God does not mean that God is in need in any way. But it does mean that by freely offering ourselves to God, "God gains a friend – a paltry, measly, almost insignificant, often traitorous friend, but a friend nonetheless."[38] Although God does not need our love, he would still wish to gain our hearts. In fact, God would be happy if we repent and love him in our freedom.[39] Hence, mutuality between friends means a possibility of communion and response between persons, though this communion is not compelled by an inner necessity of either side. He defines mutuality as "a form of sharing life through interaction of free persons who communicate themselves to one another in a way that is progressively involving."[40] It is the sharing, interaction, and communication that are important in friendship. The communion between friends would in turn deepen their friendship over time, and this also characterizes our relationship with God. Finally, Vacek argues that God shows preference for and establishes special relationships with Israel and with the person Jesus.[41] The preferential aspect of friendship is not incompatible with Christian love, as long as it is balanced by agape love.[42] To summarize, Vacek's notion of friendship focuses on the relationship and interaction between persons, deemphasizes

---

35. Aristotle, *Nicomachean Ethics*, VIII.5, trans. Joe Sachs (Newbury, MA: Focus Pub./R. Pullins, 2002), 1158a.
36. Edward Collins Vacek, *Love, Human and Divine: The Heart of Christian Ethics* (Washington, DC: Georgetown University Press, 1994), 319–320.
37. Ibid., 321.
38. Ibid., 323.
39. Luke 15:7, 10.
40. Vacek, *Love, Human and Divine*, 287.
41. Ibid., 307.
42. Ibid., 308.

the situation and self-fulfillment of the lovers, and approves of preferential relationships.

Vacek's arguments can provide a model of friendship as an aspect of Christ's love. The three commonly perceived properties of friendship – preference, reciprocity, and mutability – can be transformed into notions compatible with God's love. I now examine how his notion of friendship can inform the relationships within the family by addressing these three properties. First, Vacek argues that God shows preference for Israel, thus God's love is partial. God's partiality toward Israel is not immoral; in fact it is important to demonstrate God's freedom in his election. Besides, this partiality also entails God's special demand from Israel and his special retribution toward them.[43] In other words, preferential love is a natural consequence of God's freedom in his encounter with the world. Unequal treatment does not negate equal dignity among persons. It simply reflects the nature of special relationships between God and humanity: when God shows partiality to a person, he demands more from her. The same partiality is observed in Jesus, who elected the twelve disciples, developed a close relationship with them, and placed special demands on them. This understanding of preferential love is compatible with Christ's love. Meilaender also justifies the practice of preferential love with another argument which is, again, based on God's freedom in election. As creatures, he argues, human beings are bound in time and space. God, in his freedom, calls a person into her concrete circumstances, surrounds her with concrete and particular neighbors, and assigns her to a particular family. Her duty is to love those within her reach, instead of usurping her limitations and attempt to love all.[44] Consequently, special relationship and preferential love are not incompatible with Christian love; they are in fact the result of our recognition of our creatureliness and limitations. This is especially pertinent to our discussions. When we accept our roles in the family as God's calling,[45] we should respond to this calling by faithfully attending to the demands arising from these special relationships. Preferential treatment of family members therefore becomes a fitful response to God's particular calling on us.

---

43. Ibid., 307.
44. Meilaender, *Friendship*, 19–21.
45. See section 3.5.

Besides, Vacek observes that special relationship implies special demand. It is reasonable for one to expect more from her own family than from outsiders, and for her family to expect more from her than from strangers. This brings us to reciprocity, the second characteristic of friendship. For Vacek, friends do not necessarily have to be equal and thus friendship does not entail equalization between them. The interaction and communication between friends should not be understood as mere exchange of benefits. Equality of treatment or reciprocity is not required. It is true that persons in special relationship expect more from each other, yet communion between friends must be expressed out of freedom. As such, mutuality does not demand reciprocity, though the former looks forward to the latter. In usual cases of friendship, the sharing and mutual participation between friends results in reciprocity. But reciprocity is only a *result*, not a *precondition*, of friendship. Friendship can be sustained without reciprocity. Now friendship is not predicated upon reciprocity or the intrinsic goodness of the friends; it can be enduring.[46] When friendship is understood as mutuality, the primary concern is what lies between friends, not the behavior of each person. When a friend fails us, we can remain faithful toward the bond of friendship that informs our relationship, trusting that one day our friend will turn back and mutuality is restored. Friendship itself need not be mutable, though the actual interaction and communication between friends may vary over time. Again, this notion of immutability and fidelity is pertinent to the family. Faithfulness between the married couple is not predicated upon the partners, lest the unfaithfulness of a partner entails the dissolution of the marriage. Instead, fidelity is determined by what lies between them, that is, the marriage covenant. It is toward the marriage covenant that each spouse pledges his or her fidelity, not the faithfulness or behavior of the other. This same notion of covenant is revealed in God's covenantal relationship with humanity. Victor Hamilton says that "covenant, in the biblical sense, is not a contract or an agreement between two parties, but something that is imposed, an obligation."[47] In God's covenantal relationship with humanity, God is obligated not by any agreement

---

46. Vacek, *Love, Human and Divine*, 287.
47. Victor P. Hamilton, *The Book of Genesis* (Grand Rapids, MI: Eerdmans, 1990), 438.

or response from human beings, but by the covenant itself. In the same token, relationships among family members are informed by the bond of kinship, not by the behavior of each family member. Just because a person is my father, mother, son, or daughter, I am obligated to treat him or her as such. How he or she treats me does not negate the bond of kinship between us. It is not until the transformation of marriage and kinship in the resurrection that I can be released from these familial bonds. According to Waters, it is the covenant, not contract, which undergirds familial relationships: "A covenant requires an ordering of internal and external goods binding individual together by its imposed terms. . . . [It] confirms and embodies the given nature, structure, and *telos* of an association or social sphere . . . [and] guides the will of those in covenant."[48] In other words, friendship, as an aspect of Christ's love, is not simply a voluntary agreement between persons but entails obligations on each party.

Vacek's notion of friendship is pertinent to the relationships between married couples. Similar to Farley, who advocates that couples should make favorable judgments on each other, Vacek emphasizes free interaction and communication between them. Besides, both believe that the marital relationship can be deepened over time through cultivating friendship between the couple. But Vacek's notion of friendship offers remedies to the shortcomings of Farley's sexual ethics. Unlike Farley who demands equality in her notion of "just love,"[49] Vacek does not consider equality imperative between couples. This releases the couple from the imperative to reciprocate, though Vacek insists that the special relationship between them places extra burden on them, expecting them to treat each other better than outsiders. When married couples are released from the *quid pro quo* mode of exchange, they can express their love for each other in freedom. Furthermore, Vacek's notion of friendship also differs from Farley's in a way that he sees friendship as a covenant instead of a contract. Unlike what Farley assumes, marital permanence is not predicated upon favorable judgments between the couple but is based on an external covenant which obligates them to the marriage itself. When marital commitment is based

---

48. Waters, *Family in Christian*, 176.
49. Farley, *Just Love*, 223.

on one's judgment upon her spouse's action, the behavior of her spouse still has a strong grip on the marriage. Fidelity is ensured only when the basis of commitment is removed from the couple themselves and placed on the marriage covenant itself.

Earlier I argued that friendship alone is inadequate for marital relationships and must be supplemented by other forms of love. One such form of love can be inferred from recognizing what friendship lacks. The psychologist Caryl Rusbult conducted an investigation on why couples remain committed in their intimate relationships and identified three major factors. First, greater satisfaction obtained from the relationship leads to greater commitment. Second, the larger the investment already put into the relationship, the less likely a person withdraws from it. This "investment" includes time, emotional effort, self-disclosure, mutual friends, shared memories and material possessions. Third, the poorer the alternatives to the existing relationship, the less likely the relationship is to end. In other words, people are not likely to leave unless an attractive alternative comes along.[50] Among the three factors of satisfaction, investment, and alternatives, Farley only discusses how relational satisfaction can be enhanced through fostering friendship between the couple. But this psychological study shows that commitment requires more than relational satisfaction and the two other factors – "investment" and "alternatives" – can point us to what friendship lacks. Familial relationships involve heavy "investments" in both physical and spiritual dimensions. Elizabeth Zarelli Turner rightly points out that it is the sharing of the body in sexual acts – the "one flesh union" – that distinguishes married partners from friends.[51] Unlike friends, family members intimately share their living space, food, materials, and even genes and bodies. Divorces entail material changes such as separation of living space, finance and property settlement and redistribution, and possibly child custody adjustments. None of these is necessary when friendship ends. A person's emotional investment into her family is also

---

50. Caryl E. Rusbult, "A Longitudinal Test of the Investment Model: The Development (and Deterioration) of Satisfaction and Commitment in Heterosexual Involvements," *Journal of Personality and Social Psychology* 45, no. 1 (July 1983): 101–117.

51. Elizabeth Zarelli Turner, "Love, Marriage, and Friendship," in *Men and Women: Sexual Ethics in Turbulent Times*, ed. Philip Turner (Cambridge, MA: Cowley, 1989), 172–173.

heavy. Another psychological study reveals that death of spouse, divorce, death of close family member, and marital separation are the four most stressful life changes that a person experiences.[52] A person's material and emotional investment into her family is much heavier than into her friends. The third factor that affects a person's degree of marital commitment is the availability of alternatives. Contrary to popular belief, a person's relationship with her family simply has no alternatives at all. We are born into our family and cannot choose our father, mother, sibling, or relatives. We can decide whether to have children but cannot dictate who would become our children. The most we can do is to disown our family members. Yet disowning them does not mean that they can be freely replaced. Although people commonly believe that they can choose their partners, things are not as simple as they appear. It is true that we can choose our spouse before marriage. But once chosen, the marriage immediately engraves on us a permanent mark which even divorce cannot wipe away, for divorce cannot negate the existence or the lingering effect of the previous marriage.[53] A divorce changes a person into a divorcee, who is not the same as a person who has never before been married.

This analysis shows that on top of friendship, heavy investment and the unavailability of alternatives are the other characteristics of familial relationships. A notion of love is needed that recognizes these two features of the family. I contend that Christ's incarnational love offers such notion. T. F. Torrance avers that Christ's incarnation demonstrates his "*compassionate* and *sympathetic* solidarity" with humanity.[54] Theology upholds the full humanity of Christ and affirms that "God had . . . actually come all the way to man, that he had . . . really *got a foothold in our creaturely world*, as it were, within the time series in which we are."[55] Christ's incarnation affirms God's physical and emotional investment in humanity. The doctrine of Christ's dual nature affirms that God is imbricated with the material

---

52. Mark A. Miller and Richard H. Rahe, "Life Changes Scaling for the 1990s," *Journal of Psychosomatic Research* 43, no. 3 (1997): 279–292.

53. Oliver O'Donovan, *Marriage and Permanence*, Grove Booklet on Ethics, vol. 26 (Bramcote: Grove Books, 1978), 10.

54. Thomas F. Torrance, *Incarnation: The Person and Life of Christ*, ed. Robert T. Walker (Downers Grove, IL: IVP Academic, 2008), 137. My emphasis.

55. Ibid., 185. My emphasis.

realm and would not withdraw. Some kenotic Christologies even imply that God's very being is changed in Christ's incarnation.[56] We can say that God's "investment" into humanity through Christ's incarnation forecloses other "alternatives": once Christ incarnates, there is no turning back, even for God. The incarnation is God's participation in the material reality in solidarity with humanity. It also reveals God's love for humanity through Christ.[57] Bringing Christ's incarnational love into family ethics can supplement the inadequacy of friendship.

5.4.2 From Equal-Regard Love to Incarnational Love

Next we turn to the wisdom that Browning and his team offer. As discussed in chapter 3, their two main concerns are gender equality and the wellbeing of children. As their interest in children is prompted by the liberal ideal of protection of rights, both issues in fact stem from a liberal concern over equality within the family. The only ethics they advocate is love as equal-regard. This notion of love, they argue, is applicable to both husband-wife and parent-child relationships. Equal-regard love can resist male domination between the couple. Hopefully, it can also enhance the wellbeing of children by encouraging parents to stay together and nurture their children into persons who embrace the equal-regard love ethics. I have shown that critical familism and the equal-regard love ethics is undergirded by a concept of the family as a liberal democracy where members are free to join and withdraw. When individual freedom and equality are stressed, family members do not cohere well, and contradiction between equal-regard and family cohesion ensues. Nevertheless, Browning does offer important insights into familial relationships. He is correct to point out that children need extra care to grow up and flourish, though he errs in assuming that children can be treated as equals with their parents so the same notion of equal-regard love is applicable for both. His advocacy of equal-regard love also leads him to discourage the practice of sacrificial love in the family. Sharing the same concern with some feminist theologians, he argues that promoting self-sacrifice would lead to its abuse, relegating women into

---

56. Graham A. Cole, *The God Who Became Human: A Biblical Theology of Incarnation* (Downers Grove, IL: InterVarsity, 2013), 145.

57. Thomas F. Torrance, *Incarnation: The Person and Life of Christ*, ed. by Robert T. Walker (Downers Grove, IL: IVP Academic, 2008), 112.

the role of sacrificial worker and perpetuating gender inequality. But he does not abandon the notion of self-sacrifice completely. Instead he argues that sacrificial love, if invoked, should only serve to promote equal-regard love. Self-sacrifice should be instrumental and transitory for achieving the higher ideal of equal-regard.[58] Browning discusses two kinds of love: equal-regard and sacrificial. While being suspicious of self-sacrifice, he subsumes it under equal-regard. However, I also showed that the equal-regard love that he advocates is inadequate. The argument I now put forward is that Christ's incarnational love can both remedy the weaknesses of equal-regard love and alleviate Browning's concern over sacrificial love.

A notion of incarnational love is needed to develop this argument. Christ's incarnation, argues Jürgen Moltmann, is necessary to demonstrate God's love for the created world. As love pertains to God's very own nature, love is not contingent upon human sinfulness. Christ's incarnation does not only serve the function of sacrificial atonement but has been premeditated before the creation so that God's love for the world can be revealed. Christ's kenotic movement, his self-emptying and self-limiting, is not an *ad hoc* measure to deal with sin but is necessary to demonstrate God's love for the creation.[59] Moltmann argues that in Christ's incarnation, he does not simply enter into finitude; he also shares and adopts the same God-forsaken situation with humanity. The completion and perfection of God's love is realized in Christ's kenosis on the cross.[60] Self-emptying, self-limiting, and self-sacrifice are aspects of God's love which shows God's solidarity with humanity. Starting with this notion of the incarnation, I now formulate my arguments through a comparison between equal-regard, sacrificial, and incarnational love.

First, I will compare equal-regard love and incarnational love. The *telos* of equal-regard love is equality. As discussed in chapter 3, equal-regard love seeks reciprocity and equal treatment; any unbalanced relationship or self-sacrifice is only transitory and instrumental in bringing out the ultimate equality of treatment between persons. That is why childcare, housework

---

58. Browning et al., *From Culture Wars*, 127.

59. Jürgen Moltmann, *The Trinity and the Kingdom: The Doctrine of God* (San Francisco, CA: Harper & Row, 1981), 114–118.

60. Ibid., 119.

and waged work should be shared between husband and wife, and beneficence between parents and children should be balanced out on the long run. Undergirded by the ideals of liberalism, equal-regard love assumes an intrinsic equality between individuals and aims to realize this equality in actual life. Christ's incarnation, suggests Torrance, reveals God desire for solidarity with humanity.[61] The *telos* of incarnational love is solidarity, not equality, between persons. The lover seeks to identify with the beloved by taking on the material reality of the beloved. This is illustrated by Christ's kenosis, where he takes on human flesh to identify with humanity. Incarnational love is not predicated upon an intrinsic equality between persons, especially at the beginning of their relationships. It must be emphasized that the notion of incarnational love by no means implies unequal dignity among human persons.[62] It does mean that the contingent, material characteristics of each individual are different – even unequal – and these differences are recognized as important. Incarnational love encourages one to love others through identifying with them in regard to their material differences. As such, incarnational love tends to equalize the differences between persons, though achieving equality is only an attendant feature and is not a goal in itself. In case the material differences cannot be completely equalized, incarnational love still encourages persons to continue seeking solidarity with each other. Precisely because incarnational love recognizes the importance of material differences, it is especially pertinent to relationships between "stronger" and "weaker" persons, such as those between parents and children. However, solidarity is not simply achieved through the "lowering" of the strong to the level of the weak, though this may be the impression we have when we only focus on Christ's kenotic movement. Christ's incarnation is not only kenosis. Athanasius's famous words, "God assumed humanity that we might become God," point to

---

61. Torrance, *Incarnation*, 137.

62. The assumption of unequal dignity must be avoided when we appeal to the model of incarnational love. For instance, John Hick says that the doctrine of incarnation has led to a "Christian superior-complex" among the western nations and resulted in their anti-Semitism and colonial aggression. But he admits that the fallen human nature, not the doctrine itself, is to be blamed. See *The Metaphor of God Incarnate: Christology in a Pluralistic Age*, 2nd ed. (Louisville, KY: Westminster John Knox, 2006), 80–88.

another important aspect of incarnational love.[63] Christ does not come to the world merely to take on the God-forsaken reality of humanity; he redeems us and enables us to live out the *telos* of being humans, that is, to reflect God's image and likeness. The solidarity that incarnational love aims at is not satisfied with a simple identification between human persons. Solidarity between persons is ultimately solidarity with Christ, for God grafts us into the body of Christ through Christ's redemptive work. We are saved as we become members of the body of Christ, who embodies the fullness of both humanity and deity. To practice incarnational love is to identify with others with an aim to bring all into communion and likeness of Christ so all can share in God's abundant life. Permissive love that allows the beloved to remain immature or fallen, or erotic love that drags the lover down to the lowliness of the beloved, is not Christ's incarnational love. Incarnational love does not allow others to remain in debased conditions but empowers them to grow into maturity. The empowerment of incarnational love is not dominating or coercive, precisely because the one who loves first lowers herself into solidarity with the beloved. For this reason, Anna Mercedes believes that Christ's encounter with us is not "power over" us, but a self-emptying "power for" us. This "power for" does not seek reciprocity but the empowerment of and solidarity with the beloved. A person leans toward the other in self-giving, while the subjectivity of both the lover and the beloved is maintained.[64] It is the "power for" aspect of Christ's incarnational love that encourages the strong to empower and seek solidarity with the weak.

Now we turn to the differences between incarnational love and sacrificial love. The first thing to recognize is that incarnational love frequently requires self-sacrifice, as seeking solidarity with others entails "lowering" of the self, especially for the "strong" one in the relationship. A definition of sacrificial love is now needed. Sacrificial love aims at the benefit of the other; any act of self-sacrifice is directed toward the good of the others. Sacrificial love is not self-denial, which celebrates the acts of suffering and martyrdom

---

63. Athanasius, *The Incarnation of the Word of God*, s54, trans. a Religious of CSMW (New York: MacMillan, 1946), 93.

64. Anna Mercedes, *Power for Feminism and Christ's Self-Giving* (New York: T&T Clark, 2011), 69–70, 134–135.

in themselves. Perhaps Garth Hallett's notions of "self-subordination" and "self-forgetfulness" in his categorization of Christian neighbor-love fitfully describe what sacrificial love looks like. He defines "self-subordination" as "[giving] consideration to one's own benefit . . . only on the condition that maximum benefit of others is first assured." "Self-forgetfulness," on the other hand, means "a person should consider his or her own benefit only in relation to others; it should not be given any independent weight."[65] Both definitions point to the *telos* of sacrificial love, that is, the other's benefit. To practice sacrificial love means that the benefit of the other always trumps the benefit of the self. This demand placed on the self leads to two different evaluations of sacrificial love. One evaluation assumes that self-giving entails damage to the self: the lover often gives up so much that the wellbeing of the self is easily overlooked. This is the meaning that feminists assume when they oppose the promotion of self-sacrifice in Christian ethics.[66] For the same reason, Browning subsumes sacrificial love under equal-regard love. In chapter 3, I argued that this evaluation of sacrificial love lacks an eschatological dimension: if this life is all there is, self-giving without return entails injustice.[67] The other evaluation of sacrificial love, however, is more positive. Not only does it incorporate an eschatological dimension into the acts of love, it also understands self-giving through Christ's incarnation. In his incarnation, Christ gives up his freedom from material limitations and even his life on the cross. Paradoxically Christ's taking on human flesh is also a *realization* of God's freedom. The incarnation, says Barth, shows that God is not limited to be just God but "can cross the boundary between Himself and us"[68] yet "at the same time is and remains what He is, the true and eternal God."[69] God's freedom for humanity is revealed in the

---

65. Garth L. Hallett, *Christian Neighbor-Love: An Assessment of Six Rival Versions* (Washington, DC: Georgetown University Press, 1989), 5.

66. Catherine Keller, "Scoop Up the Water and the Moon Is in Your Hands: On Feminist Theology and Dynamic Self-Emptying," in *The Emptying God: A Buddhist-Jewish-Christian Conversation,* eds. John B. Cobb, Jr. and Christopher Ives (Maryknoll, NY: Orbis, 1990), 105.

67. See section 3.4.

68. Karl Barth, *Church Dogmatics Vol. 1.2, The Doctrine of the Word of God,* eds. G. W. Bromiley and T. F. Torrance, trans. G. T. Thomson and Harold Knight (Peabody, MA: Hendrickson, 2010), 31.

69. Ibid., 37.

very act of Christ's self-limitation. Similarly, Christ's giving up of his life on the cross is not a purely tragic event. In fact, St John equates Christ's crucifixion with the moment of his glorification.[70] This is the paradox of self-giving in Christ's incarnation. Moltmann expresses, "God's limitations inwardly are de-limitations outwards. God is nowhere greater than in his humiliation. God is nowhere more glorious than in his impotence. God is nowhere more divine than when he becomes man."[71] The act of self-sacrifice, viewed from this perspective, can paradoxically bring fulfillment to the self. In fact, a person often realizes her freedom and lives life to the fullest through self-limitation and self-giving for the benefit of others. It has almost become a cliché to mention figures like Mother Teresa to illustrate this. Self-fulfillment through self-giving also happens in the family. We are reminded of Cahill's argument that to become a mother, despite the sacrifices associated with motherhood, is in fact "an avenue of fulfillment and flourishing for women."[72] Sacrificial love, when envisaged through Christ's incarnation, is not self-impairment. Contrary to Browning, acts of self-sacrifice need not be transitory or instrumental, just as Christ's kenosis is foremost an expression of God's love and is not simply instrumental for the salvation of the world.

There is one further reason why the notion of incarnational love can ameliorate the "self-damaging" charge against sacrificial love. Critics of sacrificial love worry that promoting self-giving would deteriorate the well-being of those who are already "weak," such as demanding women who already have no economic power to give up more of themselves for sake of their families. Incarnational love does not advocate self-sacrifice alone but promotes solidarity between persons. It demands the "strong" to lower themselves for the sake of the "weak," and not the other way around. It does not mean that only the "strong" need to practice incarnational love, for seeking solidarity involves all persons in the relationship. It means that the specific tasks of each person would be different: the "strong" should lower themselves and cater for the needs of the "weak" and the "weak"

---

70. John 12:23. See J. Ramsey Michaels, *The Gospel of John* (Grand Rapids, MI: Eerdmans, 2010), 688.

71. Moltmann, *Trinity and the Kingdom*, 119.

72. Cahill, *Sex, Gender, and Christian Ethics*, 89.

should strive to mature and become strong so all persons are transformed in the relationship. Incarnational love can thus avoid exploitation of the weak by the strong. Furthermore, the *telos* of incarnational love suggests how persons in loving relationships should be transformed, for solidarity is not only between persons but is ultimately with Christ. A direction is given for all persons in the relationship: all are to become like Christ. The practice of incarnational love, therefore, is also an invitation of Christ into the relationship. The one who gives is to emulate Christ in his giving, and the one who receives is to mature into the likeness of Christ.

Despite the similarities between sacrificial love and incarnational love, a major difference between them is that sacrificial love assumes a conflicting relationship between the lover and the beloved while incarnational love does not. Gene Outka argues that self-sacrifice arises from an environment of limited resources where conflicting demands between persons necessitate the giving in or giving up of certain parties. Sacrificial love, which is unilateral, entails sustained suffering of the lover and is not sustainable. This view leads him to consider that mutual love, as the more sustainable form of love, should be the *telos* of human relationship.[73] Influenced by Outka, Browning elevates equal-regard above self-sacrifice in his family ethics.[74] Incarnational love also assumes the situation of limited resources yet it does not assume that conflict and competition are bound to happen. Instead, it suggests how people in solidarity should share lives in light of the limited resources by taking into consideration the material differences between them. As the *telos* of incarnational love is solidarity, the sharing of life, not avoidance of suffering, becomes the main concern. When people live in solidarity with one another, they rejoice and suffer together, depending on the concrete circumstances that surround them. Christ's body is again a fitful image of this community: "God has so arranged the body, giving the greater honor to the inferior member, that there may be no dissension within the body, but the members may have the same care for one another. If one member suffers, all suffer together with it; if one member is honored, all rejoice together with it" (1 Cor 12:24b–26 NRSV).

---

73. Outka, *Agape*, 24–44.
74. Browning, *Equality and the Family*, 84.

Incarnational love which fosters solidarity within the community is "sustainable" by itself. It is not transitory or instrumental for any higher goals such as reciprocity or equality of treatment. Moltmann's Christology offers a theological argument for the non-transitory nature of incarnational love. He argues that Christ's incarnation is not contingent upon sin. The dual nature of Christ also affirms that his incarnation is eternal. Incarnational love is not transient nor is it conditional upon the circumstances that surround the community. When solidarity is the goal of personal relationships, any material difference between persons need not be considered evil, though incarnational love tends to equalize this difference. For the sake of solidarity, the strong can continue to give and sacrifice for the weak without seeking equal return. This "uneven" relationship is not necessarily tragic, for self-giving is not necessarily detrimental to the self. Besides, love and strength is received from God, not generated from within humanity. In fact, it is God who bestows gifts and strengths to particular persons and makes them strong so that they can share what they have received with others in the community. Therefore, incarnational love is a better alternative to the equal-regard love that Browning advocates. While equal-regard love aims at reciprocity and equality, incarnational love aims at solidarity while recognizing the differences between persons. Solidarity does not demand equality but the identification of the strong with the weak and the empowerment of the weak by the strong such that shared life becomes possible. In the process, differences between persons are reduced. Incarnational love enhances equality between persons. Unlike equal-regard love, it does not diminish coherence between family members but instead fosters solidarity between them, resulting in a community where both justice and cohesion are achieved at the same time.

This notion of incarnational love is particularly pertinent to the parent-child relationship. When children are young, parents are "stronger" and incarnational love encourages them to "lower" themselves to seek solidarity with their children. This "lowering" does not mean that parents should become children themselves. It means that parents should give up what they own – resources, time, career prospect, etc. – such that the needs of their children are catered for. It also means that they should understand the needs of their children according to their respective developmental stages and each child's particular characteristics. The self-sacrifice involved is not necessarily detrimental to the self but can instead bring fulfillment to fathers and mothers. The love of the strong for the weak is described as "motherly love" by Erich Fromm. This type of love is characterized by the inequality between persons: "where one needs all the help, and the other gives it." Fromm argues that "motherly love" is instinctive, a part of the mother's self-love when she feels that the infant is still part of herself.[75] But the quality of "motherly love" that prompts the strong to love the weak is not limited to mothers alone. In *Fatherhood: The Dao of Daddy*,[76] various thinkers discuss how fathers ought to love their children through protecting them from danger,[77] guiding them to maturity through "tough love,"[78] modeling, discipline,[79] and mercy.[80] While fathers may love their children differently than mothers, these expressions all describe actions from a person of greater maturity and authority to a person who needs help. "Motherly love," a love of the strong for the weak motivated by the needs of the weak, is common to both fathers and mothers, though how this love is expressed can be quite different between the genders. It is perhaps better to name this love specific to the father "fatherly love" as a counterpart to "motherly love." It is true that fathers, due to their lower level of physical connection with their infant child, do not develop fatherly love as instinctively as mothers. Yet fatherly love can be fostered through "rites of passage" into fatherhood, such as active involvements during pregnancy and after the infant is born,

---

75. Erich Fromm, *The Art of Loving* (New York: Harper & Brothers, 1956), 50

76. Lon Nease and Michael W. Austin, ed., *Fatherhood: The Dao of Daddy* (Malden, MA: Wiley-Blackwell, 2010).

77. Dan Florell and Steffen Wilson, "How Should I Parent? Fathering That's Fun and Effective," in *Fatherhood: The Dao of Daddy*, eds. Lon Nease and Michael Austin, (Malden, MA: Wiley-Blackwell, 2010), 77–78.

78. Andrew Terjesen, "Does My Father Care? Paternalism, Care Ethics, and Fatherhood," in *Fatherhood: The Dao of Daddy*, eds. Lon Nease and Michael Austin, (Malden, MA: Wiley-Blackwell, 2010), 65–76.

79. Andrew Komasinski, "Maybe Happiness is Loving Our Father: Confucius and the Rituals of Dad," in *Fatherhood: The Dao of Daddy*, eds. Lon Nease and Michael Austin, (Malden, MA: Wiley-Blackwell, 2010), 110–120.

80. Stephen Joseph Mattern, "The Heart of the Merciful Father," in *Fatherhood: The Dao of Daddy*, eds. Lon Nease and Michael Austin, (Malden, MA: Wiley-Blackwell, 2010), 130–141.

and the telling of stories about becoming fathers.[81] Being present at the child's birth also fosters the emotional bond of the father toward his child and helps him transition into fatherhood emotionally.[82] Fatherly love can be as strong as motherly love. In a sociological study of fatherhood, a father comments on his experience with his son: "I never realised [sic] how much I'd love him." Another describes himself "falling head over heels in love" with his children.[83] The promotion of fatherly love can help alleviate the "male problematic" that worries Browning. It is a variation of incarnational love and aims at solidarity and the sharing of lives between fathers and their children. Unlike equal-regard love, incarnational love recognizes the material differences between parents and children, as well as between man and woman. It can respond to the concrete situations of the family better.

Incarnational love aims to bring all into solidarity with Christ. Parents should empower their children toward maturity so that shared life becomes possible. Unlike equal-regard love, parents do not need to bring their children into reciprocity with themselves. Instead, parents should bring them to the likeness of Christ so they, too, can respond faithfully to God. The love that children receive from their parents need not be paid back to their parents but should be offered to God and neighbors. This is how, using Waters's words, the "familial narrative becomes enfolded into God's story."[84] As the difference in strength between parents and children narrows as the children grow up, the focus of incarnational love should also shift from leveling their strengths to fostering mutuality between them. In other words, when children become adults, solidarity is no longer achieved through "lowering" of parents and maturing of children but through the sharing of life, understanding, and affection between them. However, incarnational love does not demand the elimination of differences between family members. In case a child is permanently infirm and remains dependent throughout her life, incarnational love would still encourage her parents to

---

81. Kimberley Fink-Jensen, "The Born Identity: Becoming Daddy," in *Fatherhood: The Dao of Daddy*, eds. Lon Nease and Michael Austin, (Malden, MA: Wiley-Blackwell, 2010), 34–39.

82. Esther Dermott, *Intimate Fatherhood: A Sociological Analysis* (London: Routledge, 2008), 66–67.

83. Ibid., 68.

84. Waters, *Family in Christian*, 243.

continue caring for her though there might not be hope of her reciprocating. In case a parent had failed to bring up her child but needs care herself in her old age, incarnational love would also demand her child to offer care in spite of their history. Differences in strength are common, even inevitable, among family members. These differences can be temporary, permanent, diminishing, or widening. Our parents will eventually grow old and become dependent. Our spouse, siblings, or other relatives can become sick or destitute in many different ways. Incarnational love calls the "strong" in the family to care for the "weak," even without the likelihood of future reciprocity. It is the solidarity and the sharing of life among family members that compels us to love our family this way.

The manner in which incarnational love is expressed in the family depends on the material circumstances and can assume different forms. For instance, the Catholic tradition names responsibility for human persons as an expression of familial love. This responsibility is first between the husband and wife and then extends to their children.[85] Incarnational love in terms of responsibility is not only directed from parents to their children. Social scientists use the term "intergenerational solidarity" to characterize the help and support offered between generations. This solidarity is an important factor that affects the willingness of adult children to care for their elderly parents.[86] Solidarity within the family can be further extended beyond the parent-child relationships. Sociologists Howard and Kathleen Bahr advocate the notion of "grants" instead of "exchanges" within the extended family. While "exchanges" is predicated upon reciprocity, "grants" is altruistic and does not expect return. But within an integrative system of many members, all become givers as well as receivers. It does not mean that the "grants" that one gives always balance what she receives. Yet the "influence of grants multiplies and spreads like the proverbial ripple on the water." The Bahrs also point out that the sacrifices that are required of grants promote solidarity within the family. It is through voluntary giving

---

85. Pope John Paul, *Fruitful and Responsible Love* (New York: Seabury Press, 1979), 18–27.

86. Tonya M. Parrott and Vern L. Bengtson, "The Effects of Earlier Intergenerational Affection, Normative Expectations, and Family Conflict on Contemporary Exchanges of Help and Support," *Research on Aging* 21, no. 1 (Jan 1999): 76.

among family members that solidarity is promoted.[87] In the Christian tradition, C. S. Lewis uses the word "affection" to describe love among family members. He contends that affection allows "warm comfortableness" and "satisfaction in being together" to develop between people of very different characteristics. It is another expression of solidarity and incarnational love between family members. Experience tells us that it is common for a person to have family members drastically unlike her and share little interest with her compared to her friends. If not for familial affection, these people would not normally come together.[88] If not for the solidarity and the sharing of life, familial affection could not have been fostered among them.

5.4.3 From Erotic Love to Unfolding Love

Next we turn to Thatcher's sexual ethics which emphasize the sharing of life between man and woman especially in the sexual aspect. The wisdom that he offers is that sexual love is essential to the family. Cahill defines the family as "an organized network of socioeconomic and reproductive interdependence and support *grounded in biological kinship and marriage.*"[89] Natural ordering stipulates that sex is ordered to procreation.[90] Without sex, there is no procreation, biological kinship, and the family. St Paul also sees sex as an important part of marriage and exhorts Christian couples to pay "conjugal debt" to each other.[91] Psychological studies show that sexual satisfaction is positively correlated to relational satisfaction, love, and commitment. In other words, those who are committed and satisfied with their relationships tend to also be satisfied with the sex they have in the relationship. Therefore, sexual satisfaction is a "barometer for the quality of marriage."[92]

Thatcher's emphasis on sexual intimacy stems from his view that God's love is primarily eros and that this erotic love is foremost expressed through

---

87. Howard M. Bahr and Kathleen S. Bahr, *Toward More Family-Centered Family Sciences: Love, Sacrifice, and Transcendence* (Lanham, MD: Lexington, 2009), 103.

88. C. S. Lewis, *The Four Loves* (London: Geoffrey Bles, 1960), 42–43.

89. Cahill, *Family*, x–xi. My emphasis.

90. See section 2.6.1.

91. 1 Cor 7:3.

92. Susan Sprecher, "Sexual Satisfaction in Premarital Relationships: Associations with Satisfaction, Love, Commitment, and Stability," *The Journal of Sex Research* 39, no. 3 (Aug 2002): 190.

the body. The incarnation, he argues, shows that even God desires erotic union with human beings and so sexual intimacy is an indispensable dimension of human relationality. However, I have argued that the eschatological transformation of sexuality and marriage releases the imperative of sexual expression in this age; relationality no longer entails sexual expression. Another psychological study concludes that many couples who experience involuntary celibacy due to physiological or psychological reasons still choose to remain in their relationships. Despite their frustrations over the lack of sex, many are still happy with their relationships mainly because of the friendship and shared life that they have established.[93] This shows that while sex is an important aspect of marriage, it is not essential for happy marriages. It is true that high sexual satisfaction is a "barometer" of good marital relationship, yet the former is not a necessary condition of the latter. It is more accurate to say that sex is essential to the family only with respect to the origin creation where procreation is an imperative. In the new creation, spiritual kinship will replace biological kinship while marriage and sex will cease in the household of God.

However, the non-essentiality of sex in human relationality does not mean that eros ceases to inform us. Erotic love is not just sex. It is, as Thatcher points out, a desire for union between persons – though he quickly equates this union with sexual intercourse.[94] Paul Tillich agrees with his definition of "desire for union," saying that "Love is the drive towards the unity of the separated." He continues to argue that the union of the lovers presupposes an original unity and a subsequent estrangement of this unity. Love desires to overcome the separation and reunite the estranged.[95] We can further say that where there are persons who belong to an original unity, there is love between them. Any estrangement between these persons entails their desire to be reunited. To distinguish it from other kinds of love, I will call this desire for reunion "erotic love" where "erotic" does not necessarily carry any sexual connotation. It is obvious that erotic love

---

93. Denise A. Donnelly and Elisabeth O. Burgess, "The Decision to Remain in an Involuntarily Celibate Relationship," *Journal of Marriage and Family* 70, no. 2 (May 2008): 529–530.

94. Thatcher, *God, Sex, and Gender*, 65–66.

95. Paul Tillich, *Love, Power, and Justice: Ontological Analysis and Ethical Applications* (New York: Oxford University Press, 1954), 25.

informs human relationality; the desire for union between lovers, between parents and their children, and between friends clearly demonstrates it. The creation narratives also describe all human beings arising from one person – an original oneness. The creation of Eve from Adam, argues Kass, suggests that Adam's love for Eve "seeks merging, reunion, fusion." This love aims at the "restoration of some lost bodily wholeness" and is possessive, prompting Adam to announce: "She is mine, she is me."[96] Augustine extends this original oneness to embrace the whole human race, saying that "God's intention [in creating humanity from one individual] was that in this way the unity of human society and the bonds of human sympathy be more emphatically brought home to man [sic], if men were bound together not merely by likeness in nature but also by the feeling of kinship."[97] Therefore, this original oneness informs human relationality so human persons attach to one another through the "feeling of kinship" and live in communities instead of as solitary individuals.

Besides its importance in human relationality, erotic love is also an aspect of love within the Godhead. Jesus claims that "the Father and I are one."[98] The Son came from the Father into the world, and again he left the world and went back to the Father.[99] The relationship between the Son and the Father that stems from this original oneness is again described as love,[100] and according to our definition, is erotic love. Furthermore, erotic love also informs divine-human relationality. It is true that humanity and God do not belong to an original oneness; human beings are creatures and do not share God's divine nature. Yet as we bear the *imago Dei*, God's love for the world is directed to us. God created the world out of love, says Barth, but the creation is nothing but "the road to the covenant" between God and humanity.[101] God's love within the creation finds its object in humanity. In love, God seeks and saves us. Christ's redemption enables us to "become

---

96. Leon Kass, *The Beginning of Wisdom: Reading Genesis* (New York: Free Press, 2003), 102–103.
97. Augustine, *City of God*, Book XII.22, 502.
98. John 10:30.
99. John 16:28.
100. John 17:22–23.
101. Barth, *Church Dogmatics Vol. 3.1*, 231.

God" so that we can unite with God and share God's abundant life. C. S. Lewis contends that God's erotic love for humanity is shown in the image of Christ as the bridegroom of the church.[102] This wedding image suggests that erotic love between God and humankind is mutual; both God and human beings desire union with each other. St Paul says that he gives up all things so that he may "gain Christ and be found in him,"[103] that is, "to be united completely with" Christ.[104] Augustine's famous prayer "our heart is restless until it rests in you" expresses our erotic desire for God and resonates among Christians throughout the ages.[105] Erotic love, the love between estranged persons who belong to an original union, is found within the Trinity, among persons, and between God and humanity.

Erotic love has a definite object. The lover desires not pleasure nor benefits nor other persons, but only the beloved herself.[106] This makes erotic love intense yet exclusive. The exclusivity of erotic love is important on this side of the eschaton where the biological family of the original creation still has not ceased and fidelity remains a good of marriage. Exclusive love between man and woman promotes marriage stability. Our erotic love for our own family, in conjunction with our preference for those close to us,[107] allows us to fulfill our duty in caring for our family members. While erotic love may keep us faithful to our spouse and to God, the same love may equally blind us from what lies outside of the object of our love. When we focus solely on the object of our erotic love, other persons fade away. Erotic love is inward-directing, luring the lovers to close in upon themselves to the exclusion of outsiders. Perhaps this is why Thatcher's "betrothal solution," while focusing solely on erotic love between the couple, excludes children from their relationship. Anders Nygren challenges this "egocentric" character of erotic love and contends that the "theocentric" love of agape should be the only

---

102. Lewis, *Four Loves*, 92.
103. Phil 3:8–9.
104. Peter Thomas O'Brien, *The Epistle to the Philippians: A Commentary On the Greek Text* (Grand Rapids, MI: Eerdmans, 1991), 392.
105. Augustine, *Confessions,* trans. Henry Chadwick (Oxford: Oxford University Press, 1991), 3.
106. Lewis, *Four Loves*, 109–111.
107. See section 5.4.1 above.

attitude of life that is Christian.[108] His denunciation of eros stems from a particular understanding of this love. He posits self-centeredness and self-serving as the core meaning of eros: "Eros does not seek the neighbour [sic] for himself; it seeks him in so far as it can utilise [sic] him as a means for its own ascent."[109] Nygren's definition of eros thus assigns an egocentric motivation to erotic love. While Thatcher and Tillich define eros as a desire for union between lovers without naming the motivation behind this desire, Nygren posits self-serving as the only motivation. Nygren's concept of eros is in fact narcissism, a love of the self only. It is true that erotic love, a desire for union with the beloved, can be motivated by the narcissistic self. Yet it can also be motivated by a concern over the wellbeing of the beloved. It is commonly observed that estranged lovers do not only wish to reunite with their beloved; they also wish their beloved well. In fact, the wellbeing of those in love frequently depends on their ability to see each other, and their desire to see each other is also imbricated with their desire to give oneself for the benefit of the other. Hence, Ann Belford Ulanov is correct to argue that erotic love can in fact "pull us across the borders of ego-concern toward otherness."[110] This concept of erotic love breaks loose the narcissistic self and is other-directing. Therefore, erotic love should not be reduced to narcissism. Perhaps it is more accurate to say that erotic love between friends and couples is motivated by a combination of both self-serving and other-directing desires. Nygren is wrong to denounce eros completely. His error, contends Stephen Post, is caused by his abstraction of love from the communal setting, leading him to posit only two possible types of love: the other-directing agape and the self-directing eros.[111] He proceeds to pit one in total opposition to the other, claiming that they represent "two ultimate standards of value confronting one another" so Christians should rid themselves of all acquisitive desire, egocentrism, and

---

108. Anders Nygren, *Agape and Eros,* trans. Philip S. Watson (London: SPCK, 1957), 205–207.

109. Ibid., 214.

110. Ann Belford Ulanov, "Two Sexes," in *Men and Women: Sexual Ethics in Turbulent Times*, ed. Philip Turner (Cambridge, MA: Cowley, 1989), 22.

111. Stephen G. Post, *A Theory of Agape: On the Meaning of Christian Love* (Lewisburg, PA: Bucknell University Press, 1990), 79–89.

loving others based on their worth.[112] This form of other-regard love overlooks mutuality, which is another important aspect of Christian love. Love in a community is much more complicated than simply other-regard versus self-regard. Erotic love is not necessarily incompatible with Christian love; it may even characterize the love within the Godhead and between God and humanity, as discussed above. Contrary to Nygren, erotic love should not be totally renounced. Nevertheless, he is correct to warn us of the inward-directing tendency associated with erotic love and a corrective to its exclusionary nature is needed.

The corrective can be found in Trinitarian theology. As God is not the Father alone, God's love is not narcissistic self-love. The presence of the Son within the Godhead breaks loose the narcissistic love of the Father. Love between the Father and the Son, as discussed, can be described as erotic love. But we have also suggested that this erotic love is not confined to within the Father-Son relationship. Christ's incarnation, his taking on human nature, extends this love to humanity. Moltmann states, "Through the incarnation of the Son *the Father* acquires a twofold counterpart for his love: his Son and his image," that is, humanity.[113] Christ's incarnation "throws open" God's love, extending it to beyond the Father-Son dyad, and "acquires" for the Father another object of love. Moltmann continues, "*the Son* becomes the first-born among many brethren. Through this he throws open to his brothers and sisters his relationship of sonship to the Father. . . . In fellowship with the only begotten Son, people become co-opted sons and daughters of the Father."[114] Therefore, God loves humankind *through* the Son; we are loved by God because we have become brothers and sisters of his Son. Besides, God loves humankind *because* the Father loves the Son; God treats us the same way as the Father treats his Son, that is, in love. God's love for humanity, conceived through this notion of "co-opted sonship," is not simply an extension of love toward a "wholly other" but entails God's solidarity with the object of love. In other words, the "throwing open" of God's love is also a "throwing open" of the Godself. When God "opens up" and considers humanity as part of the Godself, he

---

112. Nygren, *Agape and Eros*, 210.
113. Moltmann, *Trinity and the Kingdom*, 121. Original emphasis.
114. Ibid. Original emphasis.

then loves us as he loves himself. This shows that God's love and God's solidarity with others are one and the same thing: when God loves someone, he wishes solidarity with that same one; when God wishes solidarity with someone, he loves that same one. This is another way of saying that the incarnation – God's solidarity with the world – demonstrates God's love for the world and God's love for the world entails the incarnation. God's love for humankind is thus God's love of himself, that is, a form of erotic love. This erotic love does not lead God to close in upon himself precisely because God wishes to "throw himself open" and find solidarity with others. As such, God's love always flows outward toward the others.

Robert Jenson also argues that God's outflow of love, or God's expanding solidarity with others, is intrinsic to God's triune nature. In his argument he does not appeal to Christology or the incarnation but to pneumatology. The common error in understanding the Spirit, he observes, is that the Spirit is perceived not as a personal agent but as the bond of love between the Father and the Son. This reduces the Trinity to a binary relationship, allowing no third party in the community. Following Hegel's thoughts, Jenson analyzes the possibility of the formation of free subject within this binary structure: for a person to be free for one another and thus love others freely, she must be both subject and object in the encounter. While she can be subject to herself, the other must be present so that she can become an object. However, if the other evades her, she cannot become an object and her freedom to love is eclipsed. The other can enslave her by withholding reciprocity in their encounter. Thus, free love is easily eclipsed in binary structures, and relationships are reduced to struggles for domination.[115] The solution, argues Jenson, is the presence of a third party within the encounter:

> If I am to be your object and you mine, so that we may be subjects for each other, there has to be one for whom we are both objects, and whose intention for us is our love for each other. I have no choice but to defend myself against being your object so long as you, with whom I am paired for freedom or

---

115. Robert W. Jenson, *Systematic Theology, Vol. 1, The Triune God* (Oxford: Oxford University Press, 1997), 155–156.

bondage, are the one who objectifies me. And you must defend yourself in the same way. But if another, whose intention for you and me is precisely our mutual love, objectifies us by that very intention, we are free to love each other.[116]

The Spirit, a personal agent within the Godhead, liberates the Father and the Son to love in freedom. Free love is only possible when persons in the community are liberated from the binary structure by an "intrusive third-party."[117] Love is free only when the inward-directing erotic love is intruded upon by a third party, turning love outwards to those outside. Jensen's Trinitarian doctrine shows that God's outflow of love and God's expanding solidarity with others is not contingent upon the creation or the incarnation but is intrinsic to God's triune nature. As triune, God is not only love, he is also free. Freedom, an essential element of personhood, throws open the erotic love between persons and directs their love outwards to others.

Jenson immediately sees an ethical implication of this Trinitarian doctrine in the context of the family. He says, "God has arranged that the mutuality of married love – the invariable paradigm of I-Thou relatedness – shall be achieved by acts whose term is the child – a paradigm of the intrusive third party – whose free agency or suffered absence is the final bond between the couple."[118] Thomas Breidenthal expresses this "intrusive third party" in an even more negative tone, saying that "children are interlopers. . . . Women may experience them as invaders of their bodies, and even the most loving husbands and wives must resign themselves to the fact that their daughters and sons come between them and erase their privacy."[119] Instead of seeing children as "intrusive third parties," "interlopers," or "invaders," Waters more positively considers them initiators of an "unfolding" love in the family. Based on O'Donovan's notion of created order, he argues that the one-flesh unity between man and woman is ordered to procreation, which extends and unfolds the exclusive marital love to parental love that includes fellowship with their child. Marital love, an

---

116. Ibid., 156.
117. Ibid.
118. Ibid.
119. Breidenthal, *Christian Households*, 140–141.

erotic and exclusive love, is the origin of familial love which unfolds and expands into parental love.[120] Perhaps we can step back and say that erotic love between the married couple first breaks loose the narcissistic self-love of each. To use the creation story as an illustration: The creation of Eve from Adam turns Adam from his self-directing narcissistic love toward the other-directing erotic love. What is "not good" in Adam – his loneliness and narcissism – is overcome by his outward-directing love towards Eve. This Eve, this "other," is part of himself and his love for her is in fact an extended erotic love of himself. Then the reunion of the estranged, the marital love between Adam and Eve, continues to unfold into parental love through procreation. Their child, though being an "other," is again originated from their one-flesh union. Their love for this child is a further extension of their erotic love between themselves. In this story, erotic love is repeatedly extended to incorporate larger spheres of relationships, yet the unfolding love is always linked with an erotic love of the self.

The unfolding of familial love, however, is not only determined by the flesh. The birth of a child, contends Waters, is not merely the beginning of a relation that parallels the marital relationship; it signifies the extension of a common and shared life of the family that began with the marriage. This common and shared life provides a place of "mutual and timely place of belonging" that enables each member to practice the virtues pertaining to the *telos* of the family according to the roles that God assigns to each.[121] Viewed from this wider purpose of the family, and in light of the eschatological transformation of the family, the family in this age is not merely a place for biological procreation but also a social sphere that welcomes adopted children, singles, and even strangers. It is the familial history, not merely kinship, which draws the boundary around the family. However, Waters believes that both biological and social dimensions of the family should be kept in tension; the former avoids the reduction of marriage and parenthood into mere contracts and human artifacts, and the latter prevents the family from collapsing in upon itself.[122] While looking forward to the eschaton, the family follows a "providential trajectory" towards

---

120. Waters, *Family in Christian*, 181.
121. Ibid., 181–182.
122. Ibid., 185–191.

its *telos* in Christ. Waters expresses, "Together, parents with children initiate a patterned movement being drawn towards a greater end, which over time draws them out as an association built upon, but greater than, what preceded it. The family is related to a providential trajectory in that this expansive quality is being drawn towards a transformation of the very affinities of which it is comprised."[123] A closer look at this notion of the family reveals that it heeds the four dualities of human existence: body and spirit, man and woman, individual and community, and present and future. For the duality between body and spirit, this notion affirms that bodily structure provides the connection between parents and children, yet bloodline alone does not dictate the familial association; the biological and historical bases of the family are held in tension. For the duality between man and woman, the family is an extension from an original oneness between the man and the women. Children emerge from this oneness yet each member is a distinctive person, receiving God's calling in her particular roles. But owing to the original oneness, the family is not merely an agglomeration of discrete persons gathering out of consent. Guided by the providential trajectory that looks forward to the eschaton, the duality of individual and community is characterized by an unfolding love that originates from the couple and extends outward. This unfolding love reminds us of the extension of God's love, first within the Trinity and then through the incarnation of the Son. In the presence of the Son, the narcissistic self-love of the Father is broken loose. In the presence of the Spirit, love between the Father and the Son becomes free. When the Son takes on human nature, the Father's erotic love for the Son extends to embrace humanity. It is according to this unfolding love of God that the erotic love between man and woman unfolds and extends, incorporating their biological children, adopted children, and other singles and strangers into the family. As discussed, Christ's incarnation shows us that God's love and God's solidarity with the object of love is inseparable. In the same way, the unfolding of familial love is concurrent with the solidarity that a family member finds with others. When solidarity extends from a person toward her spouse, child, and others, her love also unfolds toward them.

---

123. Ibid., 207.

However much this unfolding love extends outwards, it can never traverse the boundary of the family and become universal and disinterested. The family on this side of the eschaton is, and will ever remain, grounded in special and preferential relationships. As the link between the present age and the eschaton is characterized by a historical discontinuity instead of an undisrupted progression, the natural household will never become the eschatological household of God. Therefore, the unfolding familial love cannot replace the agape love that Christians are called to practice. Unlike the unfolding erotic love of the family, agape love is purely other-regard and disinterested; it does not seek the benefit of the self or the cultivation of friendship and mutuality. As Christians, bearing special duty towards our family does not excuse us from practicing the agape love of neighbor, especially when particular situations call us to such love. Perhaps Meilaender's reflections can shed light on how we should think about familial love and agape love. He says that agape love "can, without denigrating the natural love of [family] given us by the Creator, move us to try to live even now as if the process by which the partial, preferential loves are transformed into nonpreferential neighbor-love were completed."[124] Within the family we learn to love one another through friendship and incarnational love. We also embrace newcomers and outsiders through an unfolding love. In a way, the natural family is a "school of love" that trains us how to love one another and guides us toward a more universal love of neighbors. Yet this "school," while grounded in the original creation, is in itself inadequate. It must be complemented by the eschatological community of the church so that the universal and impartial love of Christ can be fully witnessed in the world. The natural household, no matter how inclusive it becomes, is never identical with the household of God. In the resurrection, the natural household will give up its place as the elemental form of human association and be replaced by the universal household of God. Now that we are still on this side of the eschaton, the eschatological community of the church embraces both marriage and singleness as complementary witnesses. Marriages in the church today not only bear witness to the original creation but also, as Germain Grisez says, "manifests that heaven will be

---

124. Meilaender, *Friendship*, 34–35.

an intimate, interpersonal, communion in which human bodily persons will find their fulfillment." Yet the ecclesial communion is also unlike the familial communion, for the complementary witness of singleness "manifests that heavenly communion will be inclusive . . . and will surpass the limitations of the most intimate communion men and women can experience in this life."[125] But for the church community to be inclusive, there must, as Breidenthal avers, "be sufficient distance between the members of the body, so that new people can get in . . . *until the Lord's return.*"[126] Before the *parousia*, we must continue to learn agape love through welcoming strangers into the church. The inclusiveness of the church community, in turn, can remind families to "throw open" the special relationships between their members, training them into practicing unfolding love in the family.

5.4.4 From Unilateral Love to Mutual Love

Finally, we turn to the ethics of complementarianism and examine what insight it offers concerning love between man and woman. Love, as it appears in this gender ethics, is demanded from the husband alone and not from the wife. It is because complementarians construct their gender ethics from a literalist interpretation of only a few scriptural passages. The passages that govern their family ethics are the New Testament household codes, where husbands are exhorted to love and not to submit while wives are admonished to submit and not to love. Complementarians strictly follow these biblical codes and advocate distinctive roles and functions between husbands and wives in the family. This leads them to the curious situation of restricting love to only one person amidst all family members. Thus, love is not a general principle from which specific ethical guidelines are developed. Instead, it is a practical rule that stems from some higher ethical principle. The love that the husband should show his wife is then reduced to certain tasks and functions that he should perform. This is why in Piper's definition of "biblical manhood," the word "love" disappears completely, replaced by the exhortation "to lead, provide for and protect women."[127]

---

125. Germain Gabriel Grisez, *The Way of the Lord Jesus, Vol. 2, Living a Christian Life* (Quincy, IL: Franciscan Press, 1993), 609–610.

126. Breidenthal, *Christian Households*, 14. Original emphasis.

127. Piper, "Vision of Biblical Complementarity," 36.

Knight also says that the Ephesian and Colossian household codes express the marital relationship "in the *key terms* 'be subject' for wives and 'head' for husbands."[128] Although husbands are explicitly exhorted to love in the household codes, Knight completely replaces this language of love with the notions of headship and subjection. Our discussions in chapter 4 show that an authority structure between male and female governs the moral vision of complementarianism. It is the principle of male headship that determines what love means: love should be expressed as male responsibilities in leadership, provision, and protection. For instance, Clark says that "love" in the household codes does not refer to the husband's erotic love to his wife but to "activities like feeding and sheltering." Furthermore, this kind of duty-love "corresponds to the wife's subordination to her husband."[129] Knight explicates what this "correspondence" between husband and wife means. He says that "love" in the household codes refers to the duty of the one in higher authority toward the one of lower authority and corresponds to the submission of the one of lower authority toward the one of higher authority.[130] In other words, only those in higher authority can love. This is why complementarians do not speak of the wife's love for her husband, for she is of lower authority and cannot possibly "love" him.[131] All she should do is to submit to him. However, this "correspondence" between love and submission is problematic, as it risks turning love into a tool of

---

128. Knight, "Husbands and Wives," 177. My emphasis.

129. Clark, *Man and Woman*, 81.

130. Knight, "Husbands and Wives," 171.

131. In *Recovering Biblical Manhood and Womanhood*, a major complementarian publication, there are 42 entries to the word "love" in the index, compared with 92 entries to "male headship" and "male leadership." Most of the 42 entries about "love" refer to the husband's love of his wife. There are five instances that the word refers to the wife's love for her husband. Two of them use the word "love" to describe the wife's submission to her husband as voluntary and so the emphasis is still on her submission (166, 168). In another instance, it is argued that the love of the husband for his wife and the love of the wife for her husband are different, thus repeating the notion that submission, not love, is the guiding principle for wives (240). The remaining two instances refer to the exhortation "encourage the young women to love their husbands" in Titus 2:4. Yet this exhortation in Titus is only mentioned in passing and does not go into the construction of the headship-submission model (223, 362). The biblical exhortation for wives to love their husbands evidently contradicts the notion of love as duty only applicable to the one of higher authority. Perhaps this is why complementarians omit this verse in constructing their gender ethics. As a result, love between husband and wife is one-sided from the husband, who holds higher authority, to the wife, who should submit to his authority.

coercion and manipulation. Dietrich Bonhoeffer observes, "Because Christ stands between me and others . . ., I must release the other person from every attempt of mine to regulate, coerce, and dominate him [sic] with my love." Otherwise the other person is not free and cannot "be loved for what he is."[132] Unilateral love that "corresponds" to submission is not Christian love, for it is manipulative and suffocates free love between persons. I have shown that complementarians posit authority, not love, as the essence of interpersonal relationship.[133] For instance, in Ware's Trinitarian doctrine, the relationship among the three persons is described solely in authority difference. Even the Spirit, who is usually associated with love, is described in terms of his function to assist the other Persons' work, for the Spirit is of lower authority than the other two.[134] The language of love is subsumed under the principle of authority in their doctrines and ethics. Furthermore, as complementarians believe that love can simply be reduced to specific functions and duties, we can even say that the notion of love is irrelevant in their ethics; the language of authority, leadership, submission, roles, and duties are themselves adequate to construct their gender theory. This is surprising as complementarians claim that their gender ethics is divinely ordained. The heart of the Christian message – God is love – simply disappears from this Christian ethics.

The problem with complementarianism, as discussed in chapter 4, is the universalizing of particular moral exhortations and the elevating of specific rules to timeless principles. Roles and duties become fixed, rendering their gender ethics inadequate in the changing cultural and economic environment. Complementarians aim to formulate a gender ethic that promotes familial relationships that are pleasing to God, but they err in starting from functions and duties instead of ethical principles. Complementarianism therefore falls into the trap of legalism where morality is based on codes written in Scripture. In his analysis of Jewish legalism in Jesus's time, Paul Ramsey points out that when morality is based on written codes, more and

---

132. Dietrich Bonhoeffer, *Life Together*, trans. John W. Doberstein (San Francisco, CA: Harper & Row, 1954), 35–36.

133. See section 4.2.3.

134. Ware, *Father, Son, and Holy Spirit*, 105–108.

more rules are required to clarify how the codes should be observed.[135] This has also happened in complementarian gender ethics. For instance, when Knight attempts to apply the biblical exhortation "I do not allow a woman to teach or exercise authority over a man" (1 Tim 2:12), he offers detailed rules such as at what age should boys stop being taught by women, and what para-church institutions should be considered "church."[136] Another characteristics of Jewish legalism, contends Ramsey, is an insistence on sticking to the written codes and their own interpretive tradition to the exclusion of other traditions.[137] This is also observed in the complementarian writings. Ramsey also observes that advocates of Jewish legalism did not aim to put extra burden on those who wish to obey by complicating the rules. On the contrary, they tried to make it easier to observe the codes by clarifying them with more and more rules.[138] Perhaps all 856 pages of Grudem's massive work, *Evangelical Feminism and Biblical Truth: An Analysis of More Than One Hundred Disputed Questions*, stem from his benevolent attempt to clarify the codes through meticulous explanations and arguments.[139] However, Ramsey contends that legalism is not Christian ethics. Jesus's life, he observes, demonstrates that the fulfillment of human need, or the love of neighbor, determines how moral codes should be interpreted and applied. Christian ethics aims at fulfilling the law not through a fervent observation of codes but a freedom from them.[140] He states, "Love led [Jesus] to be downright unconcerned about laws he had been trained to cherish."[141] Instead, the love command in Christian ethics is "*infinitely superior to*" and "*incommensurable* with" all other commands.[142] But freedom from written codes does not mean that Christian ethics entails no rules, for love requires actions from us. Ramsey says that love "defines for

---

135. Paul Ramsey, *Basic Christian Ethics* (Chicago, IL: University of Chicago Press, 1980), 51.
136. Knight, "Family and the Church," 354–356.
137. Ramsey, *Basic Christian Ethics*, 52.
138. Ibid., 50.
139. Grudem, *Evangelical Feminism*.
140. Paul Ramsey, *Basic Christian Ethics* (Chicago, IL: University of Chicago Press, 1980), 51–56.
141. Ibid., 56.
142. Ibid., 65. Original emphasis.

the Christian what is right, righteous, obligatory to be done among men."[143] Therefore, general rules of conduct can be deduced from love.[144] It is true that Christ frees us from codes into obedience to the love command. Yet being obligated by the love command, we must perform the duties that correspond to the roles we play. As a result, moral codes and duties are derived from love; they do not dictate what love should look like. The New Testament household codes are thus an application of Christ's love within a particular historical setting; they should not come around and define what love encompasses. As such, the exhortation for wives to submit to their husbands, children to obey their parents, and servants to obey their masters, are an example of how wives, children, and servants should express their love in the household within a particular cultural setting. It is mutual love among all household members, not unilateral love of the husband, that undergirds all familial relationships. While the complementarian gender ethic is not based on love, it fails to offer us wisdom about how we can witness Christ's love in the family. Nevertheless, this discussion reminds us that love is free and cannot be solidified into unchanging codes, lest we fall into legalism. But love also demands actions. In the family, this means the carrying out of duties is indispensable if we are to express love. Finally, as love is the "infinitely superior command," all must obey it and the relationship within the family is that of mutual love. All family members should witness Christ's love by loving one another, though how love should be expressed varies from person to person according to one's own roles and particular circumstances.

5.5 Conclusions

This chapter summarizes the results of our earlier conversations with the three different schools of Christian thoughts on gender. Then the four dualities of human existence – between mind and body, man and woman, individual and community, and present and future – are formulated. I argue that these dualities form a *framework* within which gender ethics should

---

143. Paul Ramsey, *Deeds and Rules in Christian Ethics* (New York: Charles Scribner's Sons, 1967), 108.
144. Ibid., 128.

be constructed. My thesis is that inside this framework, *Christ's love* is the moral vision that informs the relationship between man and woman as well as among family members. From the life, death, resurrection, and exaltation of Christ, three kinds of love that are relevant to familial relationships are identified: friendship, incarnational love, and unfolding love. It must be emphasized that these three kinds of love are not distinct from one another; they simply describe different facets of the same love of Christ. As such, there is overlap between them. Most notably, all three kinds of love share the same theme of solidarity. In fact, when we adopt Christ's love – a love that accomplishes reconciliation – as our moral vision, solidarity between persons naturally becomes the common theme among the different expressions of love. But as each particular familial relationship has its own specific features, we would also expect Christ's love, or the theme of solidarity, to manifest differently among the different relationships. The three kinds of love described in this chapter, while emphasizing different aspects of relationality, become pertinent to the different types of familial relationships. Friendship, with its emphasis on mutuality, communion, and covenant, is especially pertinent to the relationship between husband and wife. While incarnational love encourages identification between persons and empowerment of the weak, it is especially relevant to the parent-child relationship. Unfolding love guards family members against the egocentric tendency of familial love and is especially pertinent to the family's relationship with its neighbors. Therefore, friendship, incarnational love, and unfolding love roughly correspond to Barth's three spheres of human fellowship: man and woman, parents and children, and near and distant neighbors.[145] Solidarity within each of these relationships is achieved through the different emphases of the three kinds of love. For friendship, solidarity is achieved through union and sharing between equal partners; for incarnational love, through empowering and taking on the reality of a materially different other; and for unfolding love, through incorporating the unfamiliar other into one's own community.

The family is a "school of love." Through practicing Christ's love in the family, each member bears witness to a love which is of God, not of human

---

145. Barth, *Church Dogmatics Vol. 3.4*, 116.

origin. A person's act of love also reminds others of their own obligation to love. The resulting mutual love among family members bears witness to Christ's love in the world. Yet love in the family, though always extending and unfolding outwards, always seeks solidarity and communion. The natural family is thus inadequate and must be complemented by the eschatological community of the church in which Christians learn disinterested love towards strangers. On this side of the eschaton, we must look forward to the *parousia* where the natural and exclusive family will be replaced by the all-inclusive household of God, in which all members will practice the perfect love of Christ. We began our investigation of human relationality with man and woman. But our investigation leads us to an expanding community which incorporates all of humanity in the end. Therefore, sexual ethics, family ethics, and communal ethics are all related to one another. This reveals the very nature of personal relationship: the outflow of love from the triune God, the procreative expansion of the biological family in the original creation, and the breaking of the biological bond in the eschaton all bear witness to this expansive nature of relationality between persons. The relationship between man and woman simply cannot stop at themselves alone.

CHAPTER 6

Witnessing Christ's Love: The Ephesian Household Code

In the previous chapter, I argued that Christ's love is the moral vision that informs all familial relationships. My thesis is that friendship, incarnational love, and unfolding love are the three kinds of love conceived through the life, death, resurrection, and exaltation of Christ. Although all three kinds of love are needed in every type of familial relationship, each is particularly pertinent to one of the three spheres of human fellowship: friendship to the fellowship between man and woman, incarnational love to the fellowship between parents and children, and unfolding love to the fellowship between family members and their neighbors. Christians should practice these kinds of love in the family to bear witness to Christ's love for us. This final chapter offers a reading of the Ephesian household code (Eph 5:21–6:9) using this understanding of Christ's love. Two main tasks will be carried out. First, through a survey of some common interpretive approaches, I argue that any proper interpretation and application of the household code requires an understanding of Christ's love. Second, a reading of the Ephesian household code is carried out to illuminate and clarify the meanings of the different kinds of love and to shed light on how these scriptural exhortations can be applied in the contemporary family.

An obvious reason for selecting the household code is that it contains the most explicit discussions on household management and familial relationships. New Testament texts are chosen as their authors have experienced the Christ event, causing their view of the family to no longer be confined to that of the original creation. The Ephesian household code, instead of those found in Colossians 3:18–4:1 or 1 Peter 2:11–3:12, is selected due to its extensive and in-depth discussions on the relationship between man and woman, the main focus of our investigation. Besides, hermeneutical and theological reasons also contribute to the selection of the Ephesian household code. These reasons will become clear in the following discussions.

6.1 A Survey of Contemporary Interpretations

6.1.1 Literalist Interpretation

In this section, I outline four major approaches to interpreting the Ephesian household code in contemporary literature. The first one is a literalist approach adopted by the complementarians. As discussed in chapter 4, this approach assumes that the "plain texts" of Scripture are universal moral codes and should be adopted in all ages and across all cultures. The Ephesian household code, with its assignment of headship to the husband, is a major text for complementarians to establish the hierarchical authority structure within the family.[1] The analogy between the Christ-church relationship and the husband-wife relationship is interpreted to mean that male headship is divinely ordained and transcultural.[2] Based on the notion of male headship and female submission, complementarians construct a gender ethic where men should assume the roles of leaders, providers, and protectors whereas women should be followers, nurturers, and dependents.[3] A milder form of this literalist approach is found in Barth's interpretation of the text "husband is the head of the wife" (Eph 5:23). Although he painstakingly argues that man and woman are of equal dignity, the plain text of Scripture compels him to say that subordination of women is a "real subordination" and the ordering between man and woman is "an irreversible order."[4] He refrains from probing into the contents of this "order" and only states that "man and woman are an A and a B," and that

---

1. Doriani, "Historical Novelty," 217.
2. Wayne Grudem, "The Key Issues in the Manhood-Womanhood Controversy, and the Way Forward," in *Biblical Foundations for Manhood and Womanhood*, ed. Wayne Grudem (Wheaton, IL: Crossway, 2002), 37.
3. Piper, "Vision of Biblical Complementarity," 31–59.
4. Barth, *Church Dogmatics Vol. 3.4*, 173.

"A precedes B, and B follows A."[5] No further moral implications are given. This leaves his discussions unsatisfying as the theological ordering between man and woman fails to infer any moral ordering between them. Thielicke advocates another mild form of literalist interpretation of the household code. He does not assign any theological ordering between man and woman, and his interest is in the practical matter of decision making within the family. For "normal" cases, he argues, decisions are made through discussions and agreements between the couple. In case where the couple cannot arrive at an agreement, then "in line with the tradition of Christendom based upon the Holy Scripture, . . . the father [should hold] the final decision." Thielicke specifically refers to Ephesians 5:23 in making this recommendation.[6] For him, the household code simply offers a moral tradition without inferring any doctrine. His argument is opposite to Barth's, who reads a theological ordering between man and woman from the household code without suggesting any practical implications. What is common to both of them, as well as to the complementarians, is a literalist adoption of the household code without considering the political and historical circumstances of the text. In chapter 4, I argued that reading scriptural exhortations as timeless moral codes fails to recognize their cultural embeddedness. Transplanting these codes directly into other cultures and times is often harmful. Therefore, the household code should be seen as specific instructions given to concrete Christian communities in history. It is the underlying moral principles behind these instructions, not the specific codes themselves, that inform our moral thinking today.

6.1.2 Feminist Interpretation

The second approach of interpretation addresses the harmful effect of reading the household codes as transcultural rules. This approach, adopted by some feminist biblical interpreters, criticizes the use of household codes to establish and perpetuate patriarchal structures in the church's history. Form and historical criticisms are used to uncover the historical origin of

---

5. Ibid., 169.
6. Thielicke, *Ethics of Sex*, 158.

the household codes.⁷ For instance, Elisabeth Schüssler Fiorenza opines that the household codes were adoptions of the pagan patriarchal order into the post-Pauline churches, motivated by a desire to soften the egalitarian Christian message in the contemporary patriarchal culture.⁸ The codes were of Greco-Roman or Jewish-Hellenistic origin, first codified by Aristotle, later revitalized in neo-Pythagorean and Stoic philosophy, and finally accepted by Philo and Josephus, who were Hellenized Jews contemporary with the authors of the New Testament household codes.⁹ Schüssler Fiorenza believes that the New Testament household codes were adopted from this pagan tradition, claiming that "the only Christian element in the Colossian code is the addition 'in the Lord.'"¹⁰ For the Ephesian household code, its focus on the relationship between husband and wife further "reinforces the cultural-patriarchal pattern of subordination"¹¹ and even "reasserts the submission of the wife to the husband as a religious Christian duty."¹² Rosemary Radford Ruether, on the other hand, locates the origin of the Scripture's patriarchy to the Old Testament laws which, she thinks, denigrate women to an inferior position. The New Testament household codes reaffirm the patriarchal social order and adopt it into the Christian community. This patriarchal order, or the "religion of the sacred canopy," condones dominance and servility and is a corruption of the true Christian faith.¹³ However, she does not abandon the Bible despite this corruption. Instead, she argues that there are "two religions within the biblical text."¹⁴

---

7. There are many varieties of feminist hermeneutical approaches. Carolyn Osiek classifies the approach adopted by Elizabeth Schüssler Fiorenza and Rosemary Radford Ruether as "liberationist," among the rejectionist, loyalist, revisionist, and sublimationist approaches. See "The Feminist and the Bible: Hermeneutical Alternatives," in *Feminist Perspectives on Biblical Scholarship*, ed. Adela Yarbro Collins (Chico, CA: Scholars Press, 1985), 97–103.

8. Elisabeth Schüssler Fiorenza, *In Memory of Her: A Feminist Theological Reconstruction of Christian Origins* (New York: Crossroad, 1983), 246.

9. Ibid., 254–259.

10. Ibid., 253.

11. Ibid., 269.

12. Ibid., 270.

13. Rosemary Radford Ruether, "Feminism and Patriarchal Religion: Principles of Ideological Critique of the Bible," *Journal for the Study of the Old Testament* 22 (1982): 56–58.

14. Ibid., 55.

The corrupt "religion of the sacred canopy" can be countered by the "prophetic faith," which sides with the poor and the oppressed in their struggle against the rich and powerful. This "prophetic faith" tradition is found in Isaiah, Jeremiah, Amos, Matthew, Luke, and Galatians.[15] In other words, a "true canon" should be created within Scripture while the "false canon" must be rejected. In fact, she produced a liturgy of "exorcism of patriarchal texts" where the Ephesian household code is read and then condemned as oppressive.[16] Schüssler Fiorenza, meanwhile, argues against splitting up the canon. She states that Scripture should be interpreted through a "feminist biblical hermeneutics" that challenges androcentrism. The household code should be retained as a "'dangerous memory' that reclaims our foremothers' and foresisters' sufferings and struggles through the subversive power of the critically remembered past."[17] Under her "feminist biblical hermeneutics," the household codes serve as a continuous reminder that the patriarchal structure has been oppressing women. Although the canon is not split, the effect is similar. A part of the canon is relegated to an inferior position to be criticized by a superior part of the canon or by a superior hermeneutical method.

The main weakness of this feminist hermeneutical approach is the creation of a "canon within canon." Carolyn Osiek argues that the formation of this feminist canon is based on an "almost partisan position" of filtering Scripture through the experience of women.[18] Besides, judging the value of the different canonical texts must involve an ideology external to Scripture. Jeffery Siker is correct to observe that Ruether's "prophetic faith" principle is an ideology that she constructed. As the narrative nature of Scripture means that there is no certain way to determine which prophets truly speak for God, her "prophetic critique" is a "rather flat ideology" imported from outside for pitting one prophet against another.[19] Similarly, Richard Hays

---

15. Ibid., 59–64.

16. Rosemary Radford Ruether, *Women-Church: Theology and Practice of Feminist Liturgical Communities* (San Francisco, CA: Harper & Row, 1985), 137.

17. Elisabeth Schüssler Fiorenza, *Bread Not Stone: The Challenge of Feminist Biblical Interpretation,* 10th ed. (Boston, MA: Beacon, 1995), 86.

18. Osiek, "Feminist and the Bible," 104.

19. Jeffrey S. Siker, *Scripture and Ethics: Twentieth-Century Portraits* (New York: Oxford University Press, 1997), 200–201.

criticizes Schüssler Fiorenza for subordinating the authority of Scripture under the authority of contemporary feminist experience[20] and reinterpreting Scripture using the "symbolic world of modern social science and political ideology."[21] Despite these criticisms, this feminist hermeneutical approach may still be valuable in uncovering and challenging the patriarchal elements latent in Scripture. The biblical text is, after all, produced with human participation and the possibility of human culture distorting divine revelation is real. This distortion may be brought in by cultural institutions that preserve the privilege of the powerful at the expense of the powerless.[22] Feminist hermeneutics, in some cases, can serve as a "countercultural witness" which challenges the dominant understanding and gives voice to the marginalized, as the whole of Scripture stands against oppression of the powerless so giving more weight to the disfranchised voices may be justified.[23] It is true that patriarchal distortion is found in Scripture, especially in narratives where the patriarchy of the Ancient Near East is assumed. But for our purposes, criticizing the household code with this feminist hermeneutic deprives these moral exhortations of their redemptive potential. It is true that applying them as literal moral codes today is to perpetuate ancient patriarchy. But rejecting them completely is to subject them to unnecessary critique using modern ideologies. Both hermeneutical approaches are anachronistic, ignoring the cultural background from which these household codes arise. Allen Verhey points out that Scripture is "strange" to us due to the cultural distance between the biblical world and our contemporary world.[24] Brian Brock further argues that this "strangeness" is not only temporal and cultural, but also moral. When assessing the different interpretations of the household code, Brock argues that the texts are "difficult" not only because of the cultural gap between the biblical authors and us, but because the exhortations "clash with deeply held

---

20. Hays, *Moral Vision*, 280.
21. Ibid., 278.
22. Charles H. Cosgrove, *Appealing to Scripture in Moral Debate: Five Hermeneutical Rules* (Grand Rapids, MI: Eerdmans, 2002), 91.
23. Ibid., 113–114.
24. Verhey, *Remembering Jesus*, 50.

contemporary moral presuppositions."²⁵ He continues, "exegetical maturity in Christian ethics consists in engaging one's efforts to examine claims that a text is morally hard . . . [and] to let it burrow into and confront our moral presuppositions."²⁶ The cultural and moral "strangeness" of Scripture means that we must recognize the cultural gap that separates us from the first-century Christians so we do not apply the household codes as timeless instructions. We must also allow the texts to speak to us and challenge us, instead of us rejecting them based on our own presuppositions.

6.1.3 Cultural Interpretation

This leads to the third approach which reifies the redemptive elements of the household code by contrasting it with its contemporary culture. Lynn Cohick suggests that the Ephesian household code was written against the honor-shame culture of the ancient Roman world where social categorization was crucial. In that culture, everyone had her own place according to her social status, and relationship was asymmetrical and only people of the higher rank could bestow benefits upon those in lower ranks. The household code, according to Cohick, challenges this social stratification by claiming equality of all in Christ. It encourages oneness, reciprocity, and love between husband and wife, thereby subverting the honor-shame culture of the time.²⁷

Instead of focusing on the social background, John Howard Yoder compares the Ephesian household code with its contemporary Stoic literature and identifies several important differences between them. The Stoic household codes, he observes, emphasize individual achievement of the male head and address him alone, implying that he is the sole moral agent in the household. But the Ephesian household code focuses on relationships and mutuality among all members and exhortations are also directed to wives and slaves. This implies that wives and slaves are of equal moral standing with the male head so it becomes necessary to exhort them into voluntary subordination. Yoder avers that this voluntary subordination is

---

25. Brian Brock, *Singing the Ethos of God: On the Place of Christian Ethics in Scripture* (Grand Rapids, MI: Eerdmans, 2007), 49.

26. Ibid.

27. Lynn H. Cohick, *Ephesians: A New Covenant Commentary* (Cambridge, UK: Lutterworth Press, 2013), 129–142.

"revolutionary subordination," subverting the patriarchal assumptions of the New Testament times. Besides, the exhortation for husbands to love their wives is unknown in the Stoic literature. Scripture does not consecrate the existing patriarchal order but relativizes and undercuts it. In fact, the household code outlines a "whole new order" within which voluntary subordination presents us with the freedom to live within the structures of the world yet not confined by them.[28] The household code, interpreted this way, is thoroughly redemptive when held up against its contemporary cultural background.

Yoder's interpretation of the household code challenges the modern assumption which asserts that subordination equals inequality and that freedom means liberation from all structures. Unlike the feminist biblical interpreters, he does not filter Scripture through an external ideology but allows it to challenge us. It is true that his interpretation offers valuable insights into the Christian notion of freedom and servitude. It does not, however, provide gender ethics. In particular, he does not address the cultural difference between the first-century Greco-Roman world and the late-modern western world and how the household code can be applied in today's families. All he does is to suggest that in the economic and political structure of the New Testament times, subordination practiced by Christian wives is "revolutionary subordination" that accords with the ethics of Jesus. In other words, he simply uses the household code as a springboard to launch into challenging the modern biblical interpretation methods, while failing to offer any contemporary application of its moral exhortations. Similarly, Cohick's cultural interpretation does not offer concrete suggestions on how to apply the specific instructions today. All she offers to married couples today are general affirmations about the redemptive and unitive power of the gospel.[29]

6.1.4 Historical Interpretation

The fourth approach affirms the redemptive elements of the household code in its own context while also attempting to apply it today. Unlike the

---

28. John Howard Yoder, *The Politics of Jesus: Vicit Agnus Noster*, 2nd ed. (Grand Rapids, MI: Eerdmans, 1994), 168–187.

29. Cohick, *Ephesians*, 141.

complementarians, adherents of this approach consider that the instructions are culturally embedded so they do not apply them directly as transcultural rules. They also do not share Yoder's opinion that the household code is fully redemptive and the subordination exhortations are radically subversive. Instead, they think that the code still retains certain patriarchal elements. The New Testament instructions, they observe, present some major improvements compared with their contemporary non-Christian literature. The subordination exhortations still demonstrate some lingering patriarchy which must be purged nowadays. To retain the redemptive dimensions of the household code yet reject its patriarchal elements, adherents of this approach construct a historical "trajectory" of biblical gender ethics. For instance, William Webb argues that the biblical canon is moving toward an elevation of women's status and greater gender equality. The Old Testament laws offer more protection to women against abuse compared with their contemporary culture. The New Testament materials present even greater elevation of the women's status. Although the household code, especially its exhortations for the wives to submit, appears patriarchal in the modern culture, it is the exhortations for husbands to love their wives that are radical and strange in their original setting. A "redemptive movement" of gender equality is observed in Scripture, though full equality had not been achieved when the New Testament was written.[30] Since the "movement" has already started, we should carry it forward to today's setting.[31] Samuel Terrien performs a similar but more elaborate reconstruction of this "movement" using biblical theology. Instead of seeing a continuous progress from patriarchy to equality, he argues that the biblical literature "presents a tidal movement of action and reaction, of progress and regress" concerning the relationship between man and woman.[32] The creation narratives depict woman as the "crown of creation" that helps man with his loneliness.[33] Stories of the patriarchs portray the ancestresses of

---

30. William J. Webb, *Slaves, Women and Homosexuals: Exploring the Hermeneutics of Cultural Analysis* (Downers Grove, IL: InterVarsity, 2001), 76–81.

31. Ibid., 167.

32. Samuel L. Terrien, *Till the Heart Sings: A Biblical Theology of Manhood and Womanhood* (Grand Rapids, MI: Eerdmans, 2004), 210.

33. Ibid., 17.

the Hebrew nation as "heroines of valor, of courage, and of wit," making decisions in their freedom.[34] Even the prophets promoted gender equality.[35] This elevated status of woman presents a notable contrast to other cultures of the Ancient Near East. But with the birth of Judaism during the Babylonian exile, a concern over purity and the emphasis on the rite of circumcision sharpened the distinction between the sexes, excluded women from cultic service, and devalued them.[36] Jesus challenged this patriarchy in Judaism in his dealings with women. The Samaritan woman who met Jesus at Jacob's well was an "apostle" and Mary Magdalene was the "midwife of Christianity."[37] Women participated equally with men in the infant church where gender equality was practiced.[38] St Paul, in Terrien's assessment, was a "half-liberated legalist" who espoused gender equality in Galatians 3:26–28 but justified hierarchy in 1 Corinthians 11:3. Terrien says that when writing the First Corinthian passage, St Paul "evidently suffered from theological immaturity."[39] Gender equality experienced in the young church deteriorated further when the faith tradition was handed over to the second generation. The Ephesian household code, written by St Paul's followers, privileged church order over the status of women and hence blunted the radical gender equality promoted by their predecessors.[40] Despite these "progress and regress," there is a "steady direction, an entelechy, a teleology" that moves toward an "equilibrium between masculine and feminine experiences of being human."[41] According to Terrien's historical reconstruction, the Ephesian household code belongs to a "regress" in this "steady progress" toward gender equality. In the final analysis, though the household code is redemptive compared with its contemporary patriarchal culture, it does not represent the end point of gender ethics. Browning and his team adopt the same view, that the Ephesian household

---

34. Ibid., 30–31.
35. Ibid., 70.
36. Ibid., 71–86.
37. Ibid., 122–137.
38. Ibid., 153–158.
39. Ibid., 164.
40. Ibid., 183–188.
41. Ibid., 210.

code "never fully escaped the patriarchal language of patriarchy" and so the "trajectory" toward full equality should be continued today.[42]

This fourth approach is better than the earlier approaches as it considers the two differences that are crucial to applying the household code today: the difference between the scriptural exhortations and its contemporary culture, and the difference between the New Testament world and our world. Besides, the household code is not discarded as evil but is appreciated as redemptive, contributing to a trajectory that promotes gender equality today. However, this approach has other weaknesses. Advocates must explain why the author of the household code did not promote the fully redemptive version of gender ethics in their time. For those who say that the household code represents a "regress" in the "trajectory," they also need to explain why such a regression was necessary. For instance, Craig Keener contends that as the social implications of the gospel was too radical for the Greco-Roman world, the household code was necessary to alleviate the concerns of the Roman elites if the Christian faith was to propagate among them.[43] The household code was thus written as a strategy for successful evangelism. Similarly, Bonnie Thurston argues that by encouraging Christian women to conform to the expectations of the Roman society, they could be exempt from facing criticisms in the wider society.[44] James Dunn argues in the similar way, saying that when the hope of an imminent *parousia* was fading among the second or third generation Christians, they were "settling down to a more conformist ethic," and the household code demonstrates this shift.[45] All these interpreters assume that the author of Ephesians was concerned over what outsiders think about Christian behavior and how Christians should "settle down" in the world. However, Jerry Sumney is correct to observe that Ephesians focuses mainly on "innerecclesial [sic] relations." He contends that "Ephesians does not attend to the effects that church members' lives have on outsiders. This letter ties

---

42. Browning et al., *From Culture Wars*, 146–147.

43. Craig S. Keener, *Paul, Women and Wives: Marriage and Women's Ministry in the Letters of Paul* (Peabody, MA: Hendrickson, 1992), 146–148.

44. Bonnie Bowman Thurston, *Women in the New Testament: Questions and Commentary* (New York: Crossroad, 1998), 140–141.

45. James D. G. Dunn, "The Household Rules in the New Testament," in *The Family in Theological Perspective,* ed. Stephen C. Barton (Edinburgh: T&T Clark, 1996), 54–55.

proper ethics to proper teaching; living the Christian life helps one maintain correct doctrine."[46] Besides, the letter promotes Christian solidarity by emphasizing the distinctiveness of the church from the world. Hence Christians should stop living as "gentiles" or "children of darkness" and start living as "children of light."[47] Therefore, it would be rather inconsistent for the author of Ephesians to exhort Christian distinctiveness in one part of the epistle yet promote a conformist ethic in the household code.[48] Daniel Darko conducts a detailed analysis of the Ephesian *parenesis* (Eph 4:17–6:9) that includes both the contrast between believers and unbelievers as well as the household code. He concludes that "there is a consistent rhetoric of differentiation running through 4.17–6.9 alongside a consistent use of shared ethical values."[49] Any moral value shared by the household code and its contemporary literature does not imply that the church was conforming to the world. Rather, the household code provides "christological motivations" to these shared values and uses them to promote mutuality within the church.[50] Timothy Gombis also argues that the author of Ephesians is not interested in apologetics or in establishing a "common ground" between the Christian community and the pagan world. Instead, the author emphasizes that Christians and non-Christians are incompatible. The household code is a "manifesto for the New Humanity, painting in broad strokes a vision for how believers ought to conduct themselves in new creation communities, thus epitomizing the triumph of God in

---

46. Jerry L. Sumney, "Ephesians," in *The New Testament and Ethics: A Book-by-Book Survey*, ed. Joel B. Green (Grand Rapids, MI: Baker Academic, 2013), 64–65.

47. Ibid., 65. Harold Hoehner concurs, arguing that the Ephesian household code does not have any apologetic function but serves to promote unity within the church. Harold W. Hoehner, *Ephesians: An Exegetical Commentary* (Grand Rapids, MI: Baker Academic, 2002), 727.

48. Some interpreters recognize this inconsistency but insist to interpret the household code as advocating a conformist ethic. For instance, Minna Shkul writes, "While on the one hand, Ephesians demands countercultural distancing from the surrounding non-Israelite world and its impurity, it does, on the other hand, encourage conservative acceptance of social hierarchy and patriarchal models typical of the surrounding social world." Minna Shkul, *Reading Ephesians: Exploring Social Entrepreneurship in the Text* (London: T&T Clark, 2009), 205.

49. Daniel K. Darko, *No Longer Living as the Gentiles: Differentiation and Shared Ethical Values in Ephesians 4.17–6.9* (London: T&T Clark, 2008), 99.

50. Ibid.

Christ."⁵¹ In other words, the household code is not a regression from a former egalitarian ethics under social pressure; it is an embodiment of the gospel within the sphere of the household.⁵² This view does not deny the cultural embeddedness of the household code; the texts are still particular exhortations to concrete communities in history and reflect the cultural characteristics of the time so they should not be adopted as universal moral instructions. But contrary to the adherents of the fourth approach, the household code should still be considered fully redemptive in the economic and political circumstances of the early church households. The task of Christian ethics is to examine how it is redemptive in its original setting and adopt its redemptive elements to our contemporary setting.

Another weakness of this approach is that its adherents measure "redemptiveness" only in terms of gender equality. This criterion leads them to criticize the household code as only partially redemptive. But the Christian vision of the household is not patriarchal or egalitarian, but evangelical or gospel-centered.⁵³ In O'Donovan's words, evangelical ethics springs from the life, death, resurrection, and exaltation of Christ.⁵⁴ Therefore, the redemptiveness of the household code should not be viewed through the ideal of gender equality but should be understood through the work of Christ. Besides, judging the household code based on equality alone renders it uninformative in our construction of gender ethics today. All we look for in the texts are phrases that support or undermine equality while neglecting the rich and intricate exhortations concerning human relationships. Furthermore, when full equality is deemed as lacking in the household code, it is reduced to a point along the historical trajectory toward the ideal of gender equality. Now that the modern world has surpassed the household code in gender equality, the texts are deemed archaic and cease to inform us today. More importantly, gender ethics constructed from such an approach is reduced to a flat notion of equality, unable to enlighten us

---

51. Timothy G. Gombis, "A Radically New Humanity: The Function of the *Haustafel* in Ephesians," *Journal of the Evangelical Theological Society* 48, no. 2 (June 2005): 319.

52. Ben Witherington III, *The Letters to Philemon, the Colossians, and the Ephesians: A Socio-Rhetorical Commentary on the Captivity Epistles* (Grand Rapids, MI: Eerdmans, 2007), 321.

53. Breidenthal, *Christian Households*, 57.

54. O'Donovan, *Resurrection and Moral Order*, 11–13.

on the intricate relationships between man and woman and among family members today.

6.1.5 Theological Interpretation

It appears that we have to agree with Yoder that the household code is fully redemptive. But as discussed above, Yoder's interpretation only offers a critique of the modern biblical interpretation methods and fails to provide a viable gender ethics for today. Our task is to bring his approach forward in time so that the household code can also help us understand gender relationships today. Yoder's failure to bridge the household code and our contemporary world is due to the very method he uses: comparing the household code with its contemporary Stoic literature. Although he has shown how the household code was redemptive in the first century, the comparison is stranded in a world two millennia away from us. As the household code is culturally embedded while the culture is constantly shifting, Yoder's method is only valid for comparing the household code with its contemporary literature. It would fail if we try to compare the household code against our modern-day literature. It is precisely this anachronistic comparison that leads the feminist biblical interpreters to reject the household code as hopelessly patriarchal. Unfortunately, a modern-day version of the household code is not available for comparison with our contemporary literature to show how the gospel is redemptive in today's world. Therefore, Yoder's method of comparing the household code with its contemporary literature cannot offer a viable gender ethic for today.

James Hering offers a way out of this impasse. In his book, *The Colossian and Ephesian* Haustafeln *in Theological Context: An Analysis of Their Origins, Relationship, and Message*, he performs a thorough investigation of the literature contemporary with the New Testament household codes, including the writings of Plato, Aristotle, pseudo-Aristotle who wrote the *Oeconomica*, Philo, Musonius Rufus, and Plutarch. He observes that these ancient writers demonstrate a wide range of thoughts concerning household management. In their writings are elements and notions both different and similar to the household codes. For instance, Musonius advocates ontological equality between man and woman, reciprocity and mutual love in marriages, and sharing of responsibilities between husband and wife. These notions are similar to those found in the Ephesian household code, indicating that the New Testament instructions are not as radical as others interpreters assumed them to be.[55] Besides, Plutarch's instructions to women are also strikingly similar to those found in the Ephesian household code but the reasons behind the two sets of exhortations are different.[56] Hering points out that the wide variety of thought patterns among these ancient thinkers defies a seamless progression or a consensus on gender relationship in the period. For this reason, he concludes that it is "difficult . . . to attribute elements of the New Testament household code to a particular author, context or period."[57] Other interpreters concur, saying that the New Testament household code is neither a simple adoption of pagan tradition nor a distinctively Christian creation. It grows out of a common concern of the wider society over the household, and this concern is also shared within the Christian community.[58] Therefore, unlike what Yoder assumes, the household code was not composed simply to subvert the pagan household tradition by advocating the notion of "revolutionary subordination." It was written out of the Christian community's concern over household management, namely, how family members should relate to one another in light of the Christian gospel.

If the household code is not apologetical in nature, then the key to its interpretation is not to compare it with its contemporary pagan literature but to understand it within its own literary and theological setting. Hering conducts such an investigation for the Colossian and Ephesian household codes. He observes that the book of Colossians emphasizes Christ's lordship and authority as depicted in the vertical, divine-human axis and the horizontal, intra-human axis.[59] This authority and lordship is not based on power alone but is relational, demonstrating Christ's benevolence to humanity. Christ's redemption first transforms the divine-human relationship

---

55. James P. Hering, *The Colossian and Ephesian* Haustafeln *in Theological Context: An Analysis of Their Origins, Relationship, and Message* (New York: Peter Lang, 2007), 247–252.

56. Ibid., 256–257.

57. Ibid., 260.

58. See Dunn, "Household Rules," 53; Stephen E. Fowl, *Ephesians: A Commentary* (Louisville, KY: Westminster John Knox, 2012), 179–180; Ernest Best, *A Critical and Exegetical Commentary on Ephesians* (Edinburgh: T&T Clark, 1998), 521; Witherington, *Letters*, 319–320.

59. Hering, *Colossian and Ephesian*, 63.

and then the intra-human relationship, where Christ is located at the intersection of the two axes. Salvation is understood as Christians forming new allegiance with Christ and submitting to the benevolent lordship of Christ. A common salvation for all implies egalitarianism. Salvation as reception and identification with Christ informs the behavior of Christians.[60] The ethics of the Colossian epistle, including its household code, should be understood with the notion of Christ as Lord and as the eschatological judge. For this reason, the slave-master exhortation in the Colossian household code is expanded where the "lordship" language takes on concrete, ethical form. The master-slave relationship in the household code does not merely point to a social relationship but also embodies a theological meaning where all believers are slaves of Christ the Lord.[61] This suggests to the superordinate members (husbands, fathers, masters) that the household is under a new management under Christ, the new head of the household. The subordinate members are also addressed directly and given order of preference, indicating an attainment of equal status with the superordinate members and an ultimate identity in Christ.[62] The contents of the Colossian household code are integrated into the theme and theology of the whole epistle and the household code must in turn be interpreted within this theological context.

Hering proceeds to the Ephesian household code, assuming the priority of the Colossian epistle and that Ephesians is dependent on this older epistle. Although there are common elements between the two epistles, he observes that Ephesians presents its own theology and its household code transforms the ethic found in the Colossian household code.[63] While the author of Colossians emphasizes the vertical "heavenly-earthly" axis, the author of Ephesians shifts the focus to the horizontal "heathen-Christian" bifurcation. The difference between heaven and earth is transformed to reflect the conflict between the church and the world, with the result that the church's role is elevated in the life of believers. Reconciliation in Colossians, understood in the vertical divine-human axis, is expanded in Ephesians

---

60. Ibid., 65–71.
61. Ibid., 75–78.
62. Ibid., 80–83.
63. Ibid., 130.

to describe the intra-human reconciliation between Jew and Gentile. The direct and individual paradigm of master-slave relationship is replaced by a more general relationship characterized by the church community. The church takes on the fullness of Christ, who loves the church. The lordship of Christ over Christians in Colossians is transformed into the love of Christ for the church in Ephesians. The church becomes the regulatory authority for human relationships, and Christian life is perceived as participation in the church community. The body metaphor becomes significant in describing the relationship between Christ and the church; the word *sōma* refers solely to the church and not to the physical body and head of this *sōma* is Christ, who loves his body. Compared with Colossians, the theme of love plays a much more prominent role in Ephesians. While Colossians introduces love as the guiding ethical principle, Ephesians interprets this love through the example of Christ. Love becomes the defining marker in the saving work of Christ, in the relationship among Christians, and in the building up of the church. It is not coincidental that Christ becomes exemplar of love in the Ephesian household code. The designation of Christ as "the beloved" also implies that Christ is not only the mediator of salvation but also the mediator of God's love. Love becomes the common element between the vertical and the horizontal axes, and the mediation of Christ is foremost through the mediation of love. As such, the ethical principle that governs inter-human relationships is characterized by God's love through Christ, whose love stands in contrast to the world. The key to moral behavior is therefore the knowledge and imitation of Christ, and in particular, the knowledge and imitation of his love. For this reason the author of the Ephesian household code expanded the husband-wife exhortations to reflect this emphasis on love.[64] The love of husband to his wife is an expression of Christ's love in concrete interpersonal relationships. It is a continuation of God's love through Christ to the church, and the love described in the household code is not limited to that of the husband, for all family members are also members of the church. As the author is interested in both the husband-wife and Christ-church relationships, descriptions of Christ as head, the church as body, and the cleansing and nourishing of

---

64. Ibid., 158–183.

the church are also inserted into the husband-wife exhortations.[65] Same as for the master-slave exhortation in the Colossian household code, the husband-wife exhortation in the Ephesian household code is not only concerned with a social relationship but also furnishes theological meanings to the relationship between Christ and the church: "The [household code] functions, then, as parenetic instruction to husband and wife, which draws upon the profound mysteries of the Christ-church relationship; in similar manner, it can also be characterised [sic] as theological instruction, in which the author presses the human analogy with dramatic effect."[66] For the parenetic function of the household code, it is the theology of the whole epistle, not the adoption or subversion of pagan traditions, that informs the interpretation of the moral exhortations. The person of Christ and his love for the church is the key to understanding the Ephesian household code. At the conclusion of his investigation, Hering says:

> The uniquely Christian element of the [household code] . . . lies . . . in the nature of [the person of Christ] (as appertained in the events of salvation: his incarnation, suffering, resurrection and pending return in glory and judgement [sic]) and the believer's intimate union with him. The New Testament [household codes] and their regulation cannot be understood as uniquely Christian without the mediation of Christ, and all that this may imply. Each household relationship, then, is construed in reference to Christ and his work in the church. Elements such as sacrificial love and divine retribution differ from their Hellenistic counterparts only insofar as they are Christ's love and Christ's justice. The Christian [household code] does not introduce unheard of principles to the regulation of the household, as we have seen. It only introduces Christ.[67]

Therefore, an understanding of Christ's love as revealed in his life, death, resurrection, and exaltation is indispensable in the interpretation

---

65. Ibid., 188–192.
66. Ibid., 201.
67. Ibid., 261.

of the Ephesian household code. Instructions of the household code are concrete moral exhortations given to particular Christian communities in history. These instructions are predicated upon Christ's love, which is unchanging through the ages. From the household code, we witness how Christ's love was practiced two millennia ago, and today we should bear witness to this same love in our own situation. This is how we bridge the New Testament world and our world. Barth believes that Scripture bears witness to God's past revelation and at the same time promises future revelations.[68] The biblical writers point us to God's past revelation using human words embedded in history. Interpreters of Scripture must study the texts and understand them in their historical setting. These human words bear witness to God's living Word which continuously communicates to all generations, including us in our situation today.[69] Summarizing Barth's view of Scripture, Francis Watson says that there is an "inner circle" of biblical writers, or the "first addressees" who witnessed God's past revelation and recorded it in Scripture. God's Word continues to communicate to the world through this "inner circle" to the "outer circle," from the "first addressees" to the "secondary addresses," who are the interpreters of Scripture in the subsequent generations.[70] Seen in this light, Scripture is God's "living speech" which continues to address us today. We are "contemporaneous" with the biblical writers, hearing God's direct command in Scripture:

> The witness of the Bible does not, therefore, refer to a temporary expression of the divine command which we have to divest of its temporary character if we are to deduce from it an eternal content valid for us. It refers to the divine command which has eternal and valid content for us precisely in its temporary expression, and demands that we should hear and respect it in our very different time and situation.[71]

---

68. Karl Barth, *Church Dogmatics Vol. 1.1, The Doctrine of the Word of God*, eds. G. W. Bromiley and T. F. Torrance, trans. G. W. Bromiley (Peabody, MA: Hendrickson, 2010), 111.

69. Barth, *Church Dogmatics Vol. 1.2*, 463–472.

70. Francis Watson, "The Bible," in *The Cambridge Companion to Karl Barth*, ed. John Webster (Cambridge, UK: Cambridge University Press, 2000), 60–61.

71. Karl Barth, *Church Dogmatics Vol. 2.2, The Doctrine of God*, eds. G. W. Bromiley and T. F. Torrance, trans. G. W. Bromiley, J. C. Campbell et al. (Peabody, MA: Hendrickson,

The historical situation of the biblical writers is in the past; we cannot assume that we are still living in their exact cultural environment. Still, Christ is alive yesterday, today, and tomorrow. It is in beholding Christ's love that the author of Ephesians wrote the household code, and it is in recognizing the same love that we interpret and apply the household code in our own culture today. Stephen Fowl offers a similar suggestion. In his recent commentary on the Ephesian household code, he writes, "when faced with very different social contexts, Christians should extend the same Christ-focused practical wisdom to prescribe quite different ways of living faithfully in those new contexts."[72]

This discussion shows that the proper way to interpret and apply the Ephesian household code is through an understanding of Christ's love as revealed in his life, death, resurrection, and exaltation. I contend that the notion of Christ's love developed in chapter 5 can serve as the hermeneutical key to unlock the Ephesian household code. This code, unlike that found in 1 Peter, assumes that all members in the household are believers.[73] It is within this Christian household that mutual love among members can serve as a witness to Christ's love. Besides, Hering's analysis also shows that Christ's love undergirds the theology of the Ephesians epistle and its household code. This differs from the emphasis on Christ's lordship in the Colossians epistle. The household code in the Ephesians epistle, instead of those in Colossians or 1 Peter, is the most suitable one to study for our purposes. In the remainder of this chapter, I attempt to read the Ephesian household code through the notion of Christ's love developed in this book.

6.2. Interpreted through Christ's Love

The Ephesian household code contains instructions concerning three pairs of household relationships: wives and husbands, children and parents, and slaves and masters. Exhortations to the specific groups begin in 5:22, where wives are addressed first. Grammatically 5:22 is linked to 5:21, which, in turn, is a phrase that points further back to the previous verses. Concepts

---

2010), 706–707.

72. Fowl, *Ephesians*, 181.

73. Ernest Best, *Essays on Ephesians* (Edinburgh: T&T Clark, 1997), 191–192.

of the family also underlie the paragraph that precedes the household code (4:17–5:20).[74] Therefore, the Ephesian household code is not a standalone paragraph but is grammatically and thematically connected to the rest of the epistle. For our purposes, it is adequate to follow most modern commentators and delimit the household code to 5:21–6:9.

6.2.1 Mutual Subordination

> Subordinating to one another out of reverence for Christ.
> (Eph 5:21)

The absence of a finite verb in the verse that follows (5:22) requires that the verb "to subordinate" (*hupotassō*) be supplied from this verse. Hence, 5:21 and 5:22 are tied together grammatically. "Subordinating to one another" is also the fourth participial clause that supplements the main clause, "be filled with the Spirit," in 5:18. This verse is again grammatically connected with the moral exhortations that precede it. Thus, 5:21 is a "bridge"[75] or "fulcrum"[76] linking the previous and the following sections. In the previous verses (5:18–21), Christians are encouraged to be filled with the Spirit (5:18) through giving thanks to the Father (5:20) and fearing Christ (5:21). The exhortations invoke all three persons of the Trinity and are directed to all Christians. Serving as a "bridge," 5:21 is also the beginning of the household code. Therefore, 5:21 is the governing principle for all household relationships; the exhortation to "subordinate to one another" is the overarching principle for all household relationships: between wives and husbands, children and parents, and masters and slaves.[77]

"Subordinating to one another" echoes the theme of "forbearing one another in love" (4:2),[78] "be kind to one another," "forgiving one an-

---

74. Margaret Y. MacDonald, *The Power of Children: The Construction of Christian Families in the Greco-Roman World* (Waco, TX: Baylor University Press, 2014), 86–87.

75. Ralph P. Martin, *Ephesians, Colossians, and Philemon* (Atlanta, GA: John Knox), 67.

76. Thomas B. Slater, *Ephesians* (Macon, GA: Smyth & Helwys, 2012), 151.

77. Fowl, *Ephesians*, 186; Hoehner, *Ephesians*, 719–720.

78. John Muddiman, *A Commentary on the Epistle to the Ephesians* (London: Continuum, 2001), 257.

other" (4:32), and "to walk in love" (5:2) in the earlier parts of the epistle.[79] Subordination and love are intricately related. Francis Watson argues that as the command to love is given to all Christians, all members in the Christian household should practice love, even though, in the household code, husbands are the only ones who are exhorted to love.[80] The actual practice of Christian love entails subordination of the one who loves, for the incarnational love of Christ demands self-limitation and even self-sacrifice. Gilbert Bilezikian also observes that "among spouses it is possible to submit without love, but it is impossible to love without submitting."[81] Similarly, Andrew Lincoln says that "submission and love can be seen as two sides of the same coin."[82] In other words, the husband, father, and master should also practice subordination even though the household code does not specifically require them to do so. The word "one another" (*allēlois*) implies that love and subordination should be mutual.[83] Mutuality means that all persons involved should practice love and subordination, though the exact way to do so may vary from person to person. In the exhortations that follow (5:22–6:9), the author offers ways for each person in the family to practice love and subordination within the cultural environment of the early church.

It should be noted that mutual love and subordination corresponds to the notion of friendship formulated in chapter 5. As discussed, friendship affirms the importance of special relationships. Since special relationships entail special demand, when a person is called into a family and thus into special relationships, she is required to subordinate herself under the demands of these special relationships. However, mutual love is not the same as reciprocal love; its *telos* is not reciprocity but the sharing of life and the deepening of relationships among family members. One's practice of mutual love and subordination is not contingent upon the behavior or

---

79. Andrew T. Lincoln, *Word Biblical Commentary, Vol. 42, Ephesians* (Nashville, TN: Thomas Nelson, 1990), 363.

80. Watson, *Agape, Eros, Gender*, 244.

81. Gilbert G. Bilezikian, *Beyond Sex Roles: A Guide for the Study of Female Roles in the Bible* (Grand Rapids, MI: Baker, 1985), 168.

82. Lincoln, *Ephesians*, 393.

83. Ibid., 154–156; Clinton E. Arnold, *Ephesians* (Grand Rapids, MI: Zondervan, 2010), 402.

situation of the other, though a return of love is welcomed and can greatly enhance their relationship. Although much has changed since the author penned the Ephesian household code, the demand for mutual love and mutual subordination among family members has not. The exhortation "to subordinate to one another" has become even more pertinent to our late-modern culture where people enter into families expecting self-fulfillment, love others only if others love them back, and conceive of love in terms of emotions and freedom instead of actions and subordination. Therefore, God's love for us through Christ's friendship with us should continue to remind us of our obligation to love and to subordinate ourselves in our family.

The participle "subordinating" (*hupotassomenoi*) should be interpreted as the middle voice instead of passive voice, giving agency to the person receiving the exhortation so that subordination is voluntary.[84] As subordination is out of love, and love must be free and voluntary, so subordination must also be voluntary. The verb means "ordering of something underneath something else"[85] or "subordination of someone in an ordered array to another who is above the first, that is, in authority over that person."[86] Most interpreters translate the verb as "submit" rather than "subordinate," arguing that the latter can imply inferiority.[87] This translation is understandable if subordination and super-ordination takes place between persons, for inferiority implies unequal dignity. Yoder suggests that subordination can also be understood with respect to an order: "Sub*ord*ination is the acceptance of an *order*."[88] When subordination takes place with regard to an *order* and not a *person*, then subordinating oneself underneath an order does not jeopardize equal dignity between persons as long as everyone subordinates under the same order. I contend that the order that holds

---

84. Although the form of the participle is either middle or passive, many commentators argue that it should be interpreted as middle. See Hoehner, *Ephesians*, 731–732; Derek Tidball and Dianne Tidball, *The Message of Women: Creation, Grace and Gender* (Downers Grove, IL: InterVarsity, 2012), 241; Peter T. O'Brien, *The Letter to the Ephesians* (Grand Rapids, MI: Eerdmans, 1999), 411.

85. Frank Thielman, *Ephesians* (Grand Rapids, MI.: Baker Academic, 2010), 372.

86. O'Brien, *Letter to the Ephesians*, 411.

87. Hoehner, Ephesians, 717.

88. Yoder, *Politics of Jesus*, 172. Original emphasis.

authority above all persons is the household order. It is true that in the household code, subordination is literally spoken of with regard to other persons and not toward the household order. Yet the exhortations are addressed only to persons within the household and not to those outside: if a woman is single, there is no husband for her to subordinate under; if a child is orphaned, her obedience is no longer directed to her own parents; once a slave is manumitted, she does not need to obey her pervious master anymore. Hence, subordination only becomes necessary when a person is called into her particular roles within the household order and terminates when she ceases to remain a member. Seen in this light, a person actually submits herself under the household order more than another person. The "one another" in the exhortation, therefore, refers not so much to the other household members but to the household community as a whole. When subordination in the household code is understood this way, *mutual* subordination can be logically coherent. Some interpreters postulate that the difficulty with 5:21 is how "subordination" can be "to one another," as it seems impossible for a person of authority to "subordinate" under her subjects.[89] If subordination takes place between persons, the statement is a "paradox."[90] But when one's subordination is with respect to the household order, then all members can place themselves under it and "subordination to one another" can be logically coherent. One application of this notion of subordination is in the understanding of marriage as a contract versus a covenant. When marriage is thought of as a contract, then the two persons involved stand above the contract as its creators. They hold all the decision power concerning the fate of their marriage and no external authority can step in to avoid its dissolution. Subordination also has no place in the contract, either between persons or with respect to the contract itself. But when marriage is treated as a covenant, both persons should subordinate under the *order* of marriage through the covenant. The household order, not the will of the two persons, then holds the higher authority over the marriage relationship. Accordingly, the words "subordinate to one another" means that when a man and a woman enter into marriage, they immediately

---

89. Thielman, *Ephesians*, 372–373; Walter L. Liefeld, *Ephesians* (Downers Grove, IL: InterVarsity, 1997), 140–141.

90. Muddiman, *Commentary*, 256.

subordinate themselves under the household order. Understanding subordination with respect to the household order implies that the family is an *institution* of God's created order, and the household code serves to affirm and regulate this institution. For this reason, the family is not merely a *social construct* which can be deconstructed and reconstructed at will.

Yoder continues, saying that "[s]ub*ord*ination is the acceptance of an *order*, as it exists, but with the new meaning given to it by the fact that one's acceptance of it is willing and meaningfully motivated."[91] The "new meaning," he says, comes from the new order of gender equality that subverts the old patriarchal order. When Christ brings about this new order, female agency is affirmed and subordination becomes "revolutionary." The affirmation of equality and female agency makes subordination "willing and meaningfully motivated." However, I contend that this new order is not only a subversion of the patriarchal structure and an affirmation of female agency. More importantly, it is predicated upon the eschatological transformation of marriage brought about by Christ, who inaugurates a new era where spiritual kinship has replaced biological kinship as the most essential bond between human persons. In this new order, people are relieved of the imperative to procreate so that singleness – a witness to the eschaton – becomes a parallel and equal witness to marriage – a witness to the original creation. Singleness, marriage, and parenthood become different vocations assigned by God. When God calls one into marriage or parenthood, and when one responds to this calling in obedience, then one also chooses to subordinate oneself voluntarily under the order of the household. Freedom in God's calling and freedom in one's response become the basis of one's subordination under the household order. This freedom, as discussed in chapter 2, is not freedom from limitation but freedom through welcoming and engaging with limitations.[92] As such, subordination under limitations – the limitations determined by God – is the precondition to freedom. Subordination becomes "revolutionary," not merely due to an affirmation of female agency, but because the assignment and acceptance of all household roles is out of freedom. It is through accepting the limitations that

---

91. Yoder, *Politics of Jesus*, 172. Original emphasis.
92. See section 2.6.2.

correspond to the familial roles that freedom is realized. Therefore, "revolutionary subordination" is not limited to wives but is also embraced by husbands, children, parents, slaves, and masters. It is through subordinating under the household order that husbands love their wives, children honor their parents, parents nourish and educate their children, slaves obey their masters, and masters treat their slaves with good will. It is also through subordination under the household order that everyone exercises her true freedom in the family.

Besides bringing about the eschatological transformation of marriage, Christ also replaces the *paterfamilias* as the head of the household. The author of Ephesians claims that when God raised Christ from the dead, "he has put all things under his feet and has made him the head over all things" (1:22). The new order that Christ inaugurates subverts the patriarchal structure not by affirming female agency but by dismissing the *paterfamilias* as the head of the household. For this reason, subordination of each household member is "out of reverence for Christ" (5:21). When Christ becomes the head of the household, all members become equal by subordinating under the same authority. It is by displacing the *paterfamilias* that mutuality among members can be realized. Cohick points out that in asymmetric relationships, such as those between the *paterfamilias* and the rest of the household in the Greco-Roman honor-shame culture, the bestowal and receipt of benefits can only be unilateral.[93] When Christ becomes the head of the household, the *paterfamilias* is relieved of his superior position which precludes mutuality between himself and the other members of the household. This displacement, however, does not abolish the household roles that stem from the original creation; it only relativizes them and prepares for their cessation in the eschaton. As long as this age has not passed away, household roles are still relevant. For this reason, the author of Ephesians continues to offer exhortations to the six household roles relevant in the early church cultural settings. Today we still live on the same side of the eschaton. Familial roles are still important, though how family members relate to one another has become very different. Therefore, we still need to construct our own family ethics relevant to our

---

93. Cohick, *Ephesians*, 132.

Witnessing Christ's Love: The Ephesian Household Code

own circumstances. The ethics must continue to regard Christ as the head of the household and encourage mutual love and subordination among family members.

6.2.2 Subordination of Wives

> Wives to your own husbands as to the Lord because the husband is the head of the wife in the same way that Christ is head of the church – he himself is Savior of the body. But as the church subordinates to Christ, so also wives to husbands in everything. (Eph 5:22–24)[94]

The words "wives" (*gunaikes*) and "husbands" (*andrasin*) can refer to women and men in general. Context dictates that they should be translated as "wives" and "husbands." Inserting the word "own" (*idiois*) indicates that subordination is only toward the wife's own husband as opposed to men in general.[95] Hence, this verse does not advocate male headship and female submission in general. The clause "as to the Lord" does not mean that husbands are lords of their wives, for "husbands" are plural but "the Lord" (*kuriō*) is singular and can only refer to Christ. The author is saying that wives should subordinate themselves under "their own husbands" as an aspect of their subordination under the headship of Christ.[96] As wives are exhorted to subordinate "because the husband is the head of the wife," many interpreters attempt to understand the meaning of subordination through the word "head" (*kephalē*). As discussed in chapter 4, complementarians aver that the word should only mean "authority" while egalitarians argue that it should mean "source." Others suggest that it can also mean "prominence."[97] All these meanings are probable, especially in the largely patriarchal cultural of the early church; we do not need to advocate one single meaning to the exclusion of all others.[98] However, the meaning

---

94. Translation adopted from Thielman, except *hupotassō* is translated into "subordinate" instead of "submit." Thielman, *Ephesians*, 371.

95. Hoehner, *Ephesians*, 730–732.

96. F. F. Bruce, *The Epistles to the Colossians, to Philemon, and to the Ephesians* (Grand Rapids, MI: Eerdmans, 1984), 384.

97. Hoehner, *Ephesians*, 739; Liefeld, *Ephesians*, 144.

98. Further discussion about the meaning of *kephalē* is given below.

of *kephalē* is best understood within its literary context. The author of Ephesians says that "husband is the head of the wife *in the same way that* Christ is head of the church." The meaning of *kephalē* should be understood through the relationship between Christ and the church.[99] In fact, in the whole hortatory paragraph concerning the wife-husband relationship (5:22–33), the relationship between Christ and church is used exclusively to describe the relationship between husband and wife. Frank Thielmann argues that in Ephesians, headship of Christ over the church refers not to authority or source, but to the work he did to reconcile the church to God. This meaning is further affirmed by the clause that follows: "he himself is Savior of the body" (5:23). The two clauses in 5:23 therefore correlate between Christ's role as head and his role as savior.[100] However, the emphatic "himself" (*autos*) limits the role of savior to Christ alone, precluding the interpretation that the husband is the savior of his wife.[101] Within the context, husband as *kephalē* of his wife does not primarily mean that he is of higher authority, is her source of livelihood, or is her savior. Instead, the metaphor implies reconciliation. Besides, *kephalē* is used in conjunction with *sōma* (body) in 5:23. The same pair of metaphors also appears in 1:22–23 and 4:15–16. Together, these two words form a combined metaphor which suggests unity and harmony between two parties.[102] John Muddiman is correct, then, to say that subordination of the wife is for "making peace"[103] and for Harold Hoehner to conclude that "[the husband's] headship and the wife's submission are for the sake of harmony."[104]

Unity and harmony within the household is the motivation behind the exhortation that admonishes wives to "subordinate to their own husbands." As discussed above, their subordination is foremost with respect to the household order rather than toward their own husbands; it is for the sake of the household order, not for the sake of their husbands *per se*, that wives are to subordinate themselves. This subordination is "in everything"

---

99. Arnold, *Ephesians*, 399.
100. Thielman, *Ephesians*, 378–379.
101. O'Brien, *Letter to the Ephesians*, 414–415.
102. Hoehner, *Ephesians*, 740; Cohick, *Ephesians*, 140.
103. Muddiman, *Commentary on the Epistle*, 51.
104. Hoehner, *Ephesians*, 740.

(5:24), implying that subordination should be unconditional, not dependent on the behavior of their husbands or other members.[105] Furthermore, through the principle of mutual love and subordination, other members should also subordinate to one another for the sake of household unity. The phrase "as the church subordinates to Christ" (5:24) reminds every household member who belongs to "the church" – not only wives – to subordinate under Christ's lordship and the household order. Seen in this light, the Ephesian household code enriches our understanding of Christ's love: practicing this love not only bears witness to Christ's love for us, it also fosters unity and harmony within the household. Christ's reconciling work with respect to the church is mentioned in the exhortation, suggesting that marriage and household unity is not simply a human endeavor but depends on the reconciliation that Christ accomplishes. In other words, Christ's headship over the household is necessary for members to practice mutual love and subordination so that the household can achieve unity and harmony. It is through emulating Christ's love that household members love one another, and it is also through his reconciliation that they reconcile with one another. The practice of mutual love and reconciliation within the Christian household in turn bears witness to Christ's love and reconciliation. Peace within the Christian household testifies to the peace accomplished in Christ.

In the household code, though mutual subordination is exhorted in 5:21, only wives are explicitly enjoined to subordinate to their husbands and husbands are not told to subordinate to their wives. Instead, husbands are admonished to love, an admonition not given to wives. This gender difference in the household code creates difficulty if we wish to apply the exhortations in contemporary gender ethics. Two questions must be addressed. First, if Christ affirms equal dignity between man and woman and subverts the patriarchal household structure, why does the author of the household code still spell out such distinctive exhortations based on gender? This first question can be addressed by invoking the mind-body duality that informs human existence. As discussed in chapter 2, the body – and thus sexual difference – is important in constructing gender ethics,

---

105. O'Brien, *Letter to the Ephesians*, 417–418.

otherwise alterity and relationality is lost and human persons cannot flourish as concrete man or woman. Besides, sexual difference will remain in the resurrection although marriage and procreation will cease. Therefore, being a man or a woman is essential to a person's existence. Equal dignity between man and woman by no means obliterates sexual difference. Recognizing the significance of sexual difference, the author of the household code gives different sets of exhortations to wives and husbands to affirm and reify this difference. In other words, the presence of gender-specific exhortations in the household code suggests that gender ethics should not be reduced to a flat notion of gender equality. Gender ethics of all ages, similar to the household code of the early church, should also offer insights specific to man and woman.[106] However, the conception of gender and the roles of man and woman vary with culture. This leads to our second question: If the conception of gender is not universal, how can the culturally-bound household code enlighten us today? To answer this question, we must understand the principles that motivate the author of the household code to offer each specific exhortation in its own context.

In the household code, wives are unilaterally exhorted to subordinate "because the husband is the head (*kephalē*) of the wife" (5:22). We can understand why this exhortation is unilateral by examining the meaning of the word *kephalē* in the original socio-political context. As discussed, interpreters mainly debate between two alternative meanings of the word: authority versus source. I contend that each meaning suggests a reason why the author only exhorted wives to subordinate. Complementarians argue that *kephalē* should only mean authority.[107] They believe that husbands have authority over their wives and female subordination stems from the "God-given roles" of male as leader and female as follower in the family.[108] In chapter 4, I argued that complementarians err in assigning an inherent

---

106. Francis Watson also writes, "In the 'household code' (5.22–6.9), it is acknowledged that differences persist within the 'one body.' . . . The new, common identity relativizes differences, but it does not erase them. Within the one body, there are still men and women, parents and children, slave-owners and slave. They are one but they are also different. . . . [If] the difference between woman and man, wife and husband . . . had been eradicated, there could be no specific address to wives and husbands." Watson, *Agape, Eros, Gender*, 226–227.

107. Bryan Chapell, *Ephesians* (Phillipsburg, NJ: P & R, 2009), 275.

108. Arnold, *Ephesians*, 380.

hierarchy between the sexes, thereby universalizing a particular mode of gender conception. However, there were practical reasons for husbands to be leaders and make important household decisions in the early churches. A recent study of the first-century eastern Mediterranean household indicates that most men married at around thirty years of age when they had become economically sufficient to start a household. But there was no need for women to acquire any prescribed skills or attain any economic status before marriage. Besides, fathers usually married their daughters young to avoid pregnancy outside of wedlock. As a result, it was common for mature men to marry women who were ten to fifteen years younger.[109] Due to this difference in maturity, men were usually advised to take responsibility for their wives, educating them in the skills to manage the household.[110] It was for the sake of the household, not the gratification of her husband, that a young wife was required to follow the instructions and leadership of her more mature husband. In fact, the distinction between young wives and children could be inconspicuous at times. Writing in this cultural setting, it is reasonable for the author of the household code to command wives to subordinate to their husbands as children ought to obey their parents.[111] In other words, *kephalē* can mean authority and leadership in this context. This authority comes from maturity and experience, not from a God-ordained hierarchy.

The second meaning of the *kephalē* is "source." Interpreters frequently assign theological meanings to this word. For instance, Bilezikian argues that as the second creation narrative describes that man is the "source of life" to woman, the proper response of the woman – the recipient of this gift – is the "reciprocal gift of self." Subordination is thus a reciprocating response of the wife upon receiving her husband's initiating gift of life.[112] However, the book of Genesis names the woman "the mother of all who live" (3:20) and "acquirer of man" (4:1). St Paul also says "just as woman came from man, so man comes through woman" (1 Cor 11:12). These texts

---

109. William R. G. Loader, *Making Sense of Sex: Attitudes towards Sexuality in Early Jewish and Christian Literature* (Grand Rapids, MI: Eerdmans, 2013), 33.

110. Ibid., 35–36.

111. MacDonald, *Power of Children*, 35.

112. Bilezikian, *Beyond Sex Roles*, 166–167.

make it difficult to determine who initiates the "gifting of life." In fact, biology dictates that the woman bears a heavier burden when giving birth to new life. As a result, Bilezikian's explanation is not entirely satisfactory, for we can equally argue that it is the man who should reciprocate and subordinate to the women for her gift of life. Rather than grounding the "source of life" in theology, I contend that the husband as his wife's "source" can simply be understood through the economic setting of the time. A household in the first-century Mediterranean world was foremost a place for "a group of people bound together by close kinship, who live together and make a living together." Residence and subsistence, instead of companionship, was the main purpose of the household.[113] Seen in this light, the age difference between the married couple not only means that the husband was usually more mature; it also means that livelihood of the household mostly depended on him. For a woman living in the New Testament times, her husband was her "source," more in the sense of "livelihood" rather than "life" itself. The dire conditions of widows described in the New Testament also testify to this socioeconomic situation. I. Howard Marshall continues to argue that as "the husband is the person on whom the wife depends. . ., therefore submission is appropriate."[114] In other words, subordination is an appropriate response to the one who provides for the self. This does not mean that economic power gives one a higher status so as to demand subordination from others; the household code never tells husbands to demand subordination from their wives – only wives are encouraged to voluntarily subordinate to their husbands. It only means that voluntary subordination – limiting the self for the sake of the household – is an appropriate response when one recognizes that one's livelihood depends on the other. In the early church, it was usually the wives who depended on their husbands, so only wives were exhorted to subordinate.

These two reasons – husband as the more mature partner and the major provider – explain why wives were unilaterally exhorted to subordinate

---

113. Halvor Moxnes, "What Is Family? Problems in Constructing Early Christian Families," in *Constructing Early Christian Families: Family as Social Reality and Metaphor*, ed. Halvor Moxnes (London: Routledge, 1997), 23.

114. I. Howard Marshall, "Mutual Love and Submission in Marriage: Colossians 3:18–19 and Ephesians 5:21–33," in *Discovering Biblical Equality without Hierarchy*, 198.

to their husbands in the New Testament context. But as discussed above, subordination of the wives is not only toward their husbands but more importantly toward the household order. We have to ask the question: Is there anything in the household order that demands subordination from the wives more than from the husbands? We have to remember that on this side of the eschaton, the natural family is always predicated upon the original creation. Although the eschatological transformation of the family removes the imperative to marry and procreate, those called into marriage must continue to live in the ways of the married, and those called into parenthood must continue to live in the ways of the parent. When a couple is called to procreate, God decides through the created order that the woman is to carry the child and bear a heavier biological burden than man. This difference in burden is especially acute in the New Testament world where reliable contraception was nonexistent, medicine was primitive, and nutrition was deficient. Many women died in childbirth, and early and constant childbearing harmed their health.[115] Despite the advancements of modern medicine, the biological burden associated with childbirth is still heavy. As recent as in 2008, 258,000 maternal deaths were recorded globally, most of which happened in developing countries. In sub-Saharan Africa, it was estimated that for every 100,000 live births, there were as many as 640 women dying from childbirth.[116] A report issued in 2004 states that in developing countries, childbirth was the leading cause of death for young women aged 15 to 19.[117] Even in developed countries, there were still 1,700 maternal deaths in 2008.[118] In the first step of procreation – giving birth, women already bear a much heavier burden then men. This differential burden continues into the initial period after childbirth as only the mother can nurse the infant. Even if her husband is eager to help, the created order dictates

---

115. Carolyn Osiek, "The New Testament Teaching on Family Matters," *HTS Teologiese Studies* 62, no. 3 (2006): 825.

116. WHO, UNICEF, UNFPA, and World Bank, *Trends in Maternal Mortality: 1990 to 2008* (Geneva: World Health Organization, 2010), 18.

117. Susan Mayor, "Pregnancy and Childbirth Are Leading Causes of Death in Teenage Girls in Developing Countries," *British Medical Journal* 328, no. 7449 (15 May 2004): 1152.

118. WHO, UNICEF, UNFPA, and World Bank, *Trends in Maternal Mortality: 1990 to 2008*, 18.

that he can only support the mother and the child at the side and cannot directly share her burden of gestation, delivery, or lactation. In chapter 2, I argued that the body and sexual difference is important in sexual ethics. The significance of sexual difference is the most prominent in the biological process of giving birth. Once a woman receives the calling to procreate, she must subordinate herself under the created order, bear the child, and take on the associated burden and risks which cannot be shared by her husband. This offers another reason why, in the household code, subordination is demanded from the wives more than from the husbands.[119] This does not imply that husbands do not need to voluntarily subordinate themselves to the order of procreation and help raise their children. The unilateral exhortation given to women only serves to remind them that the created order demands subordination from them more than their husbands with respect to the structural difference between man and woman.

Nevertheless, as Christ has removed the imperative to procreate, subordination with regard to childbearing is not coerced but is out of freedom. Barth says that freedom is not from limitation but through accepting and engaging with the limitations that God assigns us. It through subordinating herself under the created order and taking on the limitations associated with childbirth that a woman exercises her freedom within the family. This way, in Cahill's words, motherhood can be "an avenue of fulfillment and flourishing for women."[120] Besides, the wife's subordination is not toward her husband but toward the household with Christ as head. It is for the sake of Christ that she bears the child, not for the desire of herself, her husband, or others in the family. We are reminded of Mary, who, upon the Annunciation, gladly accepted God's calling and bore the burden to become Jesus's mother. Joseph also received his calling of fatherhood and submitted under God's will. Scripture clearly tells us that they did not become parents out of their own desire – either spiritually or physically, but out of obedience to the true head of their family. Mary subordinated herself "in everything" (Eph 5:24) while she carried Jesus and gave birth to him. Yet her subordination was above all toward God, not primarily toward

---

119. The household code includes instructions to children and fathers, thus procreation in the household is assumed.

120. Cahill, *Sex, Gender, and Christian Ethics*, 89.

her husband. Joseph also loved Mary, and his love was foremost expressed in obeying God to marry her despite doubts, thus subordinating himself under the household order. Now we continue with this love that the household code admonishes husbands to express.

6.2.3 Love of Husbands

> Husbands, love your wives, just as Christ also loved the church and gave Himself up for her, so that He might sanctify her, having cleansed her by the washing of water with the word, that He might present to Himself the church in all her glory, having no spot or wrinkle or any such thing; but that she would be holy and blameless. So husbands ought also to love their own wives as their own bodies. He who loves his own wife loves himself; for no one ever hated his own flesh, but nourishes and cherishes it, just as Christ also does the church, because we are members of His body. For this reason a man shall leave his father and mother and shall be joined to his wife, and the two shall become one flesh. This mystery is great; but I am speaking with reference to Christ and the church. Nevertheless, each individual among you also is to love his own wife even as himself, and the wife must see to it that she respects her husband. (Eph 5:25–33 NAB)

The author continues to use the analogy between Christ-and-church and husbands-and-wives in this paragraph. The analogy serves two purposes. The first involves an "upward" movement from human to Christ. The human marriage imagery – the joining of the man and his wife to become one flesh – offers insights into the relationship between Christ and the church.[121] Through the human image of bridal washing,[122] beautifying, nourishing, and cherishing of the wife, Christ's love for the church is depicted.[123] Although the fallen and temporary human marriages can

---

121. Muddiman, *Commentary on the Epistle*, 271; Hoehner, *Ephesians*, 778.
122. Although many commentators argue that "washing of water" (5:26) refers to baptism, some argue that it can also refer to the bridal bath. See Lincoln, *Ephesians*, 375; O'Brien, *Letter to the Ephesians*, 422–423; Hoehner, *Ephesians*, 753–754.
123. Thielman, *Ephesians*, 370.

never truly represent the perfect and eternal union between Christ and the church, the author is not deterred from describing Christ's love for the church using human images. In fact, an image of a perfect bridegroom is conjured up and projected onto Christ and an image of the perfect bride onto the church. Hence, Christology and ecclesiology are developed in the same passage.[124] This leads some interpreters to comment that 5:22–33 is primarily about the union of Christ and church instead of human marriages.[125] But the household code is, after all, a set of exhortations concerning household relationships. Although the author develops Christology in the same passage, his main purpose is still parenetic, giving practical advises to household members. The Christ-and-church and husbands-and-wives analogy serves a second purpose: a "downward" movement from Christ to human. The Christ-church relationship is a "prototype"[126] or a "typology"[127] of human marriage. However, care must be exercised to interpret this "typology," for the analogy between Christ-and-church and husbands-and-wives is not exact in every aspect.[128] There are things that Christ does to the church that husbands can never do their wives. Earlier I mentioned that the husband is not the Lord (5:22) or savior of his wife (5:23). Similarly, he cannot sanctify her (5:26) or make her holy and blameless (5:27).[129] It is therefore crucial to decide which aspect of the Christ-church relationship can be adopted to the marital relationship. Fowl suggests a way to do so, saying that "husbands cannot present their wives to themselves as holy and blameless, without blemish or wrinkle. Nevertheless, the self-giving, other-regarding love that Christ displays for the church is the same love that husbands are to display for their wives."[130] It is the quality of Christ's love, not his exact actions, that informs the "prototype" of human marital relationships. Emulating Christ's love and not his actions is in fact imperative

---

124. Lincoln, *Ephesians*, 389.

125. Edgar J. Goodspeed, *The Meaning of Ephesians* (Chicago, IL: University of Chicago Press, 1933), 61–62; Claude Chavasse, *The Bride of Christ: An Enquiry into the Nuptial Element in Early Christianity* (London: Faber & Faber, 1939), 77.

126. Lincoln, *Ephesians*, 352.

127. O'Brien, *Letter to the Ephesians*, 432–435.

128. Fowl, *Ephesians*, 190.

129. Liefeld, *Ephesians*, 147.

130. Fowl, *Ephesians*, 190.

when we recognize our creatureliness. As creatures, we can never perform the same acts as God. Yet we should emulate God in attitude and motivation while performing acts of love. This is the key to interpreting the Christ-and-church and husbands-and-wives analogy in the household code.

Now we apply this principle to the exhortations given to the husbands (5:25–32).[131] The main exhortation ("husbands, love your wives") is given in 5:25a, followed by the reason, means, and purpose of the exhortation. The same exhortation is restated but amplified in 5:28a ("love their own wives as their own bodies"). Following this restatement are the two grounds that support the amplified exhortation (5:28b–32.) The structure of this section is as follows:[132]

Exhortation	5:25a	Husbands, love your wives
Reason	5:25b	as Christ also loved the church
Means	5:25c	gave himself up for her
Purpose	5:26–27	sanctify her, present to himself the church in all her glory
Amplification	5:28a	husbands ought also to love their own wives as their own bodies
Grounds 1	5:28b–30	He who loves his own wife loves himself . . . his own flesh
Grounds 2	5:31–32	becoming one flesh . . . great mystery

As the Christ-church relationship serves as the typology of the husband-wife relationship, husbands are exhorted to love their wives because Christ loved the church. Christ's love is demonstrated in his self-giving, which brought about the sanctification and holiness of the church. The sacrificial love of Christ on the cross and his willingness to die for others is clearly implied.[133] Husbands are admonished to love their wives with the same

---

131. The hortatory paragraph that concerns the wife-husband relationship (5:22–33) includes two major exhortations – one to the wives (5:22–24) and another to the husbands (5:25–32). These two exhortations are restated at the end (5:33). The focus is now on the second exhortation which is directed to the husbands. See Edna Johnson, *A Semantic and Structural Analysis of Ephesians* (Dallas: SIL, 2008), 209–210.

132. Adopted from Johnson, *Semantic and Structural Analysis*, 209–210.

133. Glenn H. Graham, *An Exegetical Summary of Ephesians*, 2nd ed. (Dallas: SIL, 2008), 484.

willingness to sacrifice themselves. However, the effects of Christ's love on the church – her sanctification and cleansing described in 5:26–27, are confined to the Christ-church relationship and should not be extended to the husband-wife relationship.[134] These two verses only serve to depict Christ's love for the church through human images. In other words, these human images are projected "upward" to describe the Christ-church relationship. This "upward" projection entails spiritualizing the human images: "washing of water" is interpreted to mean redemption,[135] baptism by water,[136] or baptism by the Spirit,[137] while "having no spot of wrinkle" means morally blameless.[138] Because human husbands cannot effect such spiritual cleansing on their wives, their love should not emulate these actions of Christ. In other words, 5:26–27 do not contain moral exhortations to the husbands; they only describe the author's Christology and ecclesiology.

Despite these difficulties, some interpreters still advocate "applying" 5:26–27 as moral codes by encouraging husbands to emulate Christ's actions described in these two verses. Two weaknesses arise from this "application." First, through emulating Christ, the husband invariably elevates himself to a higher spiritual status than his wife, jeopardizing the spiritual equality between them. For instance, based on 5:26, Bryan Chapell argues that "it is the husband's responsibility to aid his wife in sanctification by making sure that the Word of God is present in the home."[139] Sanctification of the wife becomes the responsibility of the husband, and a spiritual hierarchy is set up between them. Second, as 5:26–27 are expressions of Christology using human marital images, and as human images are culturally embedded, "applying" them entails forcing the New Testament cultural setting into our own situation. For instance, when the author uses the "perfect bridegroom" image of his time to describe Christ, applying the passage as moral codes either forces the New Testament image into our understanding of a "good husband" or reads our own cultural assumptions

---

134. Witherington, *Letters*, 324–325.
135. Hoefner, *Ephesians*, 752–754.
136. Liefeld, *Ephesians*, 146–147.
137. Arnold, *Ephesians*, 387–388.
138. Lincoln, *Ephesians*, 377.
139. Chapell, *Ephesians*, 280.

into the text. In an attempt to find moral relevancy of the phrase "in all her glory" (5:27), Chapbell says that "husbands are to express their appreciation for the beauty (internally and externally) of their spouses.... We diminish our wives and our marriages when we do not tell our wives of their beauty (external and internal) as part of our rejoicing in what God has provided."[140] The contemporary western notion of a "good husband," who verbally appreciates the beauty of his wife, and a "good wife," who appears beautiful in the eyes of her beholder, is read back into Scripture. But what Scripture actually says is that out of love, Christ sanctified the church and made her spotless – a task which cannot be accomplished by the human husband to his wife.

Therefore, while husbands are exhorted to love their wives with the sacrificial love of Christ, 5:25–27 does not explicate the exact way to do so. Instead, Christ's love as discussed in chapter 5 can help us understand this love. Sacrificial love means subordinating one's own benefit under the benefit of others. Practicing sacrificial love entails subordination, so husbands are in fact admonished to subordinate themselves to their wives through loving them. The principle of mutual love and mutual subordination within marital relationships is again affirmed. Christ's sacrificial love is expressed through giving up his own life, so there is a time for husbands to give up their lives for their wives. However, Clinton Arnold is correct to say that it is "[not] necessary for every husband to die for his wife, but it most assuredly means that every husband must deny himself of time, resources, and self-gratification to express his love for his wife."[141] The *telos* of sacrificial love is the other's benefit. The benefit to the church within the Christ-church relationship is her sanctification, glory, spotlessness, holiness, and blamelessness through the work of Christ. The benefit to the wife within the marital relationship, though not explicated in 5:26–27, is further amplified in the following verses (5:28–32).[142]

In 5:28, the original exhortation "husbands, love your wives" is amplified by adding the words "as their own bodies." Instead of simply saying

---

140. Ibid., 281.
141. Arnold, *Ephesians*, 383.
142. The word "so" (*houtōs*) at the beginning of 5:28 ties the verse to 5:25b "just as Christ loved the church." Arnold, *Ephesians*, 390; Hoehner, *Ephesians*, 763.

the husbands ought to love their wives "as themselves" (see 5:33), "their own *bodies*" is mentioned,[143] thereby emphasizing the bodily and the material. In fact, the words *sōma* (body) and *sarx* (flesh), whose meanings are synonymous here[144] – appear a total of four times in 5:28–32.[145] The apparently mundane phrase "no one ever hated his own flesh" and language of "cherish" and "nourish" (5:29) add to the materialistic nature of the exhortation. It should be noted that exhorting husbands to love their wives "as their own bodies" does not imply a merging or a confusion of the two persons, for the analogy with the Christ-church relationship precludes it: Christians, as members of Christ's body, do not merge with Christ into a single person (5:29–30) and so wives as bodies of their husbands does not imply an abolition of individuality.[146] Besides, describing the wife as the body of her husband does not suggest hierarchy between them, for nowhere in the household code are husbands exhorted to act as "heads" of their wives – headship is only mentioned in the exhortations to the wives. The emphasis on the body only serves to highlight the mundane and bodily aspect of the marital relationship;[147] the husband's love for this wife should be expressed through "nourishing" and "cherishing" of the "flesh." In God's material creation, marital love involves providing food, nursing, clothing,[148] expressing natural affection, and sexual love.[149] Marriage is not merely the mingling of minds but also the imbricating of two persons under the same roof, sharing with each other material things, food, finance, and bodies. Entangling with each other in the material realm entails subordination under the created order and the acceptance of limitations. Marital love – a willing and beneficent regard for the other – is an expression of freedom in limitation and the witnessing of Christ's love through the mundane. Under the principle of mutual love, both husband and wife are to love each

---

143. Muddiman, *Commentary on the Epistle*, 267.

144. O'Brien, *Letter to the Ephesians*, 427; Slater, *Ephesians*, 159.

145. A major textual variation adds "part of his flesh and bone" after "his body" in 5:30. Emphasis on the flesh and the material is even more prominent should this variation be adopted. Muddiman, *Commentary on the Epistle*, 268.

146. Liefeld, *Ephesians*, 148.

147. Martin, *Ephesians, Colossians, and Philemon*, 72.

148. O'Brien, *Letter to the Ephesians*, 427–428.

149. Lincoln, *Ephesians*, 374.

other by engaging in the material reality of the marriage life. As discussed in chapter 5, they should recognize the "heavy investment" and the absence of alternatives once they enter into marriage.

In 5:31, the author includes a quotation from Genesis to further explicate the Christ-church relationship: "For this reason a man shall leave his father and mother and shall be joined to his wife, and the two shall become one flesh" (quoting Gen 2:24). Although some interpreters think that the quotation refers exclusively to the husband-wife relationship and not the Christ-church relationship,[150] Thielman is correct to conclude that it "probably refers to both themes, but primarily to the unity of Christ and the church."[151] Similarly, Peter O'Brien argues that the "great mystery" (*mustērion*) in the following verse (5:32) refers to "the relationship between *Christ and the church*" where this relationship serves "*as a typology of marriage.*"[152] In other words, the author of the household code uses the Genesis quotation primarily to illustrate the Christ-church union,[153] which in turn provides an ethical model for Christian marriages.[154] The one-flesh quotation emphasizes the *union* between two entities. Then how does the Genesis quotation enrich our understanding of the "great mystery" of the celestial union, which in turn serves as the "typology" of the earthly union? Muddiman offers a useful insight. He points out that it is difficult to interpret the Genesis quotation as a literal correspondence or as an analogy.[155] Instead, it should be interpreted through an allegory which views the church as the bride of Christ:

> [S]ince the first Adam did not leave father and mother to be joined to his wife, the Genesis text must be referring to the last Adam who indeed abandoned family ties in order to devote himself to the Kingdom of God. And just as the body of the first Adam was the source of Eve at creation, so also the last Adam was the source of the Church at the moment of his

---

150. Muddiman, *Commentary on the Epistle*, 269.
151. Thielman, *Ephesians*, 388–389.
152. O'Brien, *Letter to the Ephesians*, 432. Original emphasis.
153. Thielman, *Ephesians*, 389.
154. O'Brien, *Letter to the Ephesians*, 433.
155. Muddiman, *Commentary on the Epistle*, 269.

self-sacrifice for her on the cross, and he will be united with her on the eschatological wedding day.[156]

According to this interpretation, the Genesis quotation suggests that Christ, the last Adam, "abandoned family ties" and "sacrificed himself on the cross" in order to unite himself with the church. Union is accomplished through Christ "leaving his family" – an allusion to his incarnation, and his "self-sacrifice" – an expression of his kenosis. In other words, Muddiman's allegorical interpretation suggests that Christ's incarnational love is the kind of love to which the author of Ephesians refers. As discussed in chapter 5, Christ's incarnational love advocates the sharing of life, recognizes the importance of material and bodily differences, seeks solidarity between persons, and empowers persons to find solidarity with Christ and with God. In other words, solidarity and unity is the *telos* of Christ's incarnation. In the same vein, O'Brien contends that marital unions that demonstrate unity bear witness to the meaning of "two becoming one." Unity between husband and wife is part of the unity between Christ and church, and even fulfills God's purposes in the unity for the cosmos. This unity is the "great mystery of the gospel."[157] Eugene Peterson says that unity is concerned with what lies "between." This "between" is beyond our control, and is thus a "mystery," demanding our subordination and humility.[158] It is exactly through his incarnation – subordinating under the created order and humbling himself – that Christ accomplishes the "great mystery," that is, the unity between himself and the church. The love mentioned in the household code is therefore the incarnational love of Christ.

The love of the husband as incarnational love can explain why, in the household code written in the early church settings, only husbands were exhorted to love while wives were not exhorted to do the same. As discussed above, wives alone were admonished to subordinate because they were usually much younger and less mature, and their husbands were usually the major provider of the household. In chapter 5, I argued that incarnational love is especially pertinent for relationships that involve material

---

156. Ibid., 270.
157. O'Brien, *Ephesians*, 434.
158. Eugene H. Peterson, *Practice Resurrection: A Conversation on Growing up in Christ* (Grand Rapids, MI: Eerdmans, 2010), 248.

differences. Practicing incarnational love means that the "strong" in the relationship should empower the "weak" through seeking solidarity with them. When the household code was written, wives were perceived to be the "weaker" ones in maturity and economic strength so husbands should love them and empower them. Earlier we also suggest that subordination is particularly pertinent to wives with regard to childbearing. They are admonished to subordinate, not so much toward their husbands, but under the order of procreation should they be called into motherhood. In the same token, incarnational love pertains more to husbands in the order of procreation. During pregnancy, childbirth, and immediately afterward, the wife and the infant are physically weaker compared with the husband. Fatherhood entails the practice of incarnational love that encourages husbands to "empower" these "weaker ones" through supporting them emotionally, helping them physically, understanding and providing for their needs. Although the wife may be "weaker" in this regard, she is not completely passive. She can empower her husband by helping him understand their needs so that he can perform the proper duties of a husband and a father. For this reason, mutual empowerment and mutual love should be practiced between the couple, though how to practice this love depends on the material difference between them. Recognizing the difference between the husband and the mother-child dyad does not imply any "hierarchy" between them. Instead, recognition of the difference is crucial so that everyone can embrace his or her particular roles and duties in the family. Together, they subordinate to the household order under Christ's lordship, living out the "mystery" of familial unity and bearing witness to Christ's love. Therefore, it is only through practicing this role-specific incarnational love, not the gender-neutral equal-regard love, can we maintain family cohesion and overcome the "male problematic."

In our contemporary culture, the differences in age, maturity, and resource contribution to the family have become much more equal between husbands and wives. If a modern-day household code is to be written, perhaps the exhortations would be more mutual and less unilateral. Yet sexual difference still remains significant, especially with regard to procreation. How subordination and love are practiced should still be qualitatively different between the husband and the wife. The differences in strength between the sexes still remain, though husbands are no longer perceived as being the "stronger" one in all aspects of life; each can be "strong" in different things. But it is still advisable that the "weaker" one should subordinate to the "stronger" one, who should in turn love and empowerment the "weaker" one to grow and mature. For instance, sociological studies reveal that females are biologically more suited to care for infants while males tend to be more congenial when interacting with older children.[159] Although these are general trends and not universal rules, couples who find themselves fitting this trend should have the "stronger" partner take the lead in performing the task that he or she is good at, while loving the "weaker" partner by empowering him or her to grow and mature. In a cross-cultural study, Rae Blumberg discovers that women devote a larger portion of their income to their families and keep less for their personal expenditure.[160] Based on this finding, Jack and Judith Balswick conclude that women are generally more willing to empower other family members than men.[161] In other words, women tend to practice self-sacrifice and to empower others more than men. This difference between the sexes is another reason why husbands need extra admonition to practice incarnational love so that they, like their wives, would also sacrifice themselves to empower others in the family. Hence, the unilateral exhortation to husband that they should "love their wives" is, to a certain extent, still valid today. Under the principle of mutual love, incarnational love should be practiced by both husband and wife so that both can grow and mature into the likeness of Christ. It is not for the sake of self-fulfillment or self-actualization, but for the sake of Christ – the head of the family – that each partner grows and matures. The Balswicks aptly describe this practice of mutual love and mutual empowerment within the contemporary family:

---

159. Alice S. Rossi, "Gender and Parenthood," *American Sociological Review* 49, no. 1 (Feb 1984): 13.

160. Rae Lesser Blumberg, "Income under Female versus Male Control: Hypothesis from a Theory of Gender Stratification and Data from the Third World," in *Gender, Family, and Economy: The Triple Overlap*, ed. Rae Lesser Blumberg (Newbury Park, CA: Sage, 1991), 97–127.

161. Jack O. Balswick and Judith K. Balswick, *The Family: A Christian Perspective on the Contemporary Home*, 4th ed. (Grand Rapids, MI: Baker Academic, 2014), 284.

Every couple begins marriage with similar and dissimilar (complementary) resources and skills. . . . In an empowering relationship, each partner's primary concern is how best to build up and encourage the other to reach his or her potential. . . . Marital empowerment can be direct, such as when spouses share a skill, expertise, information, or abilities. One partner teaches the other how to cook, how to read a map, how to interact socially, how to balance a checkbook, or how to share feelings openly. The aim is to help each overcome personal deficiencies that may be keeping the other person dependent. . . . Empowerment means not that each partner's strength must be duplicated in the other but that there is a willingness to build up the other and a commitment not to control or keep the other dependent.[162]

Understanding love between the couple as Christ's incarnational love, and emphasizing the bodily and the mundane in the family thus suggests this model of mutual empowerment between husbands and wives.

The "one-flesh union," besides stressing unity of the two, also suggests that the husband-wife relationship is exclusive.[163] "A man shall leave his father and mother" (5:31) reminds us that the husband-wife dyad is the most basic unit of the family and the origin of human association.[164] However, husband and wife should not close in upon themselves. The exhortation "husbands ought also to love their own wives as their own bodies" (5:28) alludes to the second great commandment: You shall love your neighbor as yourself (Lev 19:18; Matt 22:39). Loving one's wife can be thought of as an application of this commandment: as one's spouse is the closest neighbor to a person, one ought to love one's spouse the dearest.[165] By alluding to the second great commandment, the author of the household code reminds us that our spouse, though being the closest one, is not our only neighbor; our love should also embrace others. We are reminded of our discussions in chapter 5 that God's love is an unfolding of an erotic love that extends

---

162. Ibid., 283–284.
163. Witherington, *Letters*, 326.
164. Liefeld, *Ephesians*, 149; Slater, *Ephesians*, 159.
165. O'Brien, *Letter to the Ephesians*, 426.

from the Father to the Son and through the Son to the world. As such, the statement "he who loves his own wife loves himself" (5:28) does not imply egocentrism. Rather, loving one's spouse breaks loose one's narcissistic love of the self and sets off an outward movement of love, first toward one's spouse, then toward their children, and finally toward strangers who are included into the family. With this, we turn to the next set of exhortations that concerns children and parents.

6.2.4 Children and Parents

> Children, obey your parents in the Lord, for this is right. Honor your father and mother (which is the first commandment with a promise), so that it may be well with you, and that you may live long on the earth. Fathers, do not provoke your children to anger, but bring them up in the discipline and instruction of the Lord. (Eph 6:1–4 NAB)

Children are first commanded to obey (*hupakouete*) their parents. This is how children express mutual subordination in the parent-child relationship (5:21).[166] The imperative "to obey" demands absolute obedience from children and is stronger than the voluntary subordination demanded from wives.[167] The husband-wife relationship is qualitatively different from the parent-child relationship. In the context of the household code, children are old enough to be addressed directly but still in the process of being brought up by their parents (6:4).[168] They are not married yet, for absolute obedience toward one's parents is no longer required when she leaves them and cleaves to her spouse.[169] The exhortation to obey one's parents is temporally bound, depending on one's maturity. The clause "in the Lord" does not mean that obedience is demanded because their parents are Christians, but because children themselves are "in the Lord"[170] and obeying their par-

---

166. Lincoln, *Ephesians*, 403.
167. O'Brien, *Letter to the Ephesians*, 441; Thielman, *Ephesians*, 396; Witterington, *Letters*, 335–336.
168. Arnold, *Ephesians*, 415.
169. Hoefner, *Ephesians*, 789.
170. Thielman, *Ephesians*, 397;

ents is an expression of their obedience to the Lord.[171] John Coons argues that obedience is an imperative for an immature child to pursue and obtain human goods that are founded upon the "order of truth and correct conduct." A child, being inexperienced and inadequate in knowledge, has no other option but to seek help from others concerning the moral questions that she encounters. Only through obeying a "mature other" can she perform the correct conduct and conform to the order of truth.[172] In her immaturity, she is unable to see the correct way, but her obedience is "the endorsement of the hope to find it."[173] Obedience involves faith and humility: having faith in the "mature other" who can instruct her into truth, and recognizing her own immaturity and limitation in humility. Hence, the recognition of our limitation and creatureliness entails obedience. Since all human beings are God's creatures born into God's created order, everyone must learn to obey God and subordinate themselves under God's created order. For this reason "the first office in the community that a human being holds is the office of child."[174] Even Christ himself did not come as an adult but was born an infant. As a child, he obeyed his parents (Luke 2:51), and as a human person, he "learned obedience" and was "made perfect" through suffering (Heb 5:8–9).

Now every child must obey a "mature other" who instructs her into truth. The household code reveals that this "mature other," according to God's created order, are her parents.[175] For this reason, obeying one's parents is "right" (6:1), not only because it is a "correct" thing to do, but also because it allows one to be "righteous" (*dikaion*) in the eyes of God.[176] As discussed, the subordination of wives is not primarily to their husbands

---

171. Lincoln, *Ephesians*, 402.
172. John E. Coons, "Luck, Obedience, and the Vocation of Childhood," in *The Vocation of the Child*, ed. Patrick M. Brennan (Grand Rapids, MI: Eerdmans, 2008), 76–89.
173. Ibid., 91.
174. Vigen Guroian, "The Office of Child in the Christian Faith: A Theology of Childhood," in *The Vocation of the Child*, ed. Patrick M. Brennan (Grand Rapids, MI: Eerdmans, 2008), 106.
175. Elmer John Thiessen avers that "The primary authority of parents to educate is natural and part of the creation order." Elmer John Thiessen, "The Vocation of the Child as a Learner," in *The Vocation of the Child*, ed. Patrick M. Brennan (Grand Rapids, MI: Eerdmans, 2008), 398.
176. Muddiman, *Commentary on the Epistle*, 273.

but to the household order. In the same vein, the obedience of children is not only toward their parents, but more importantly toward God. In fact, a child's obedience to her parents is the first step in her learning to obey God.[177] This anticipates the exhortations to fathers in 6:4 that they are to "bring them up in the discipline and instruction *of the Lord*." Although all parents wish to pass their own moral convictions to their children,[178] Christian parents are admonished to instruct their children not according to their own convictions but according to the knowledge and obedience of the Lord.[179] We are reminded of the notion of incarnational love, which, I argued, is the most pertinent to the parent-children relationship. Incarnational love encourages the "strong" one in the relationship to "lower herself" and find solidarity with the "weak" one. This "lowering oneself" is not the *telos* of incarnational love; solidarity of all with Christ is. When parents love their children with incarnational love, the aim is neither for the parents to become like children nor for the children to become like parents, but for all to become like Christ. Parents are exhorted to bring them up, discipline them, and instruct them into the ways of the Lord. Children, on the other hand, are also commanded to obey their parents "in the Lord."

Through the household order, God determines that the parent-child relationship is a special one.[180] It is special in a sense that parents do not need to bring up other children, only "your" (*humōn*) children (6:4).[181] In the same way, children should obey "your" (*humōn*) parents, not all adults (6:1). But special relationships entail special duties. The exhortation "*bring them up* in the *discipline* and *instruction* of the Lord" implies that the parent-child relationship is not only limited to biological linkage but also entails other parental duties. The word "bring up" (*ektrephete*) implies "to nourish"[182] and "to nurture,"[183] "discipline" (*paideia*) aims at the "forma-

---

177. Hoefner, *Ephesians*, 788–789.
178. Coons, "Luck, Obedience," 96.
179. O'Brien, *Letter to the Ephesians*, 446.
180. William Werpehowski, "In Search of Real Children: Innocence, Absence, and Becoming a Self in Christ," in *The Vocation of the Child*, ed. Patrick M. Brennan (Grand Rapids, MI: Eerdmans, 2008), 66.
181. Hoefner, *Ephesians*, 796.
182. Lincoln, *Ephesians*, 407.
183. Hoefner, *Ephesians*, 797.

tion of the adult,"[184] and "instruction" (*nouthesia*) refers to "verbal admonition or correction."[185] In other words, parenting is a task that involves multiple responsibilities necessary to help a child mature. Once a couple is called into parenthood, a special relationship with their child is formed, and they must shoulder the corresponding special duties. These duties impose limitations on them. Yet it is through navigating these very limitations they can freely love, for parental love is above all expressed through voluntary self-giving in an environment of limited resources and contending demands. As discussed in chapter 5, the family is a "school of love" where members are trained in different kinds of love. If the relationship with one's spouse trains one mutual and subordinating love, the presence of one's child trains one incarnational love which demands sacrifice and "lowering" of the self. The arrival of the child also opens up the relationship between husband and wife, for parental love is an expression of unfolding love which throws open the otherwise closed relationship. It is often through bringing up one's own children that one appreciates the difficulties that other parents face and learns to accept and love other children. Hence, the love that parents unfold to their own children does not stop at them but extends to embracing others. "Unfolding" also implies that the nature of love is changing over time. When a child is born, the relationship between husband and wife is immediately changed to accommodate this "intruding" person. Parental love is first trained through the new relationship parents have with their child. As the child matures, the parent-child relationship also changes. Both parents and children must adjust their love toward each other to accommodate for these changes. This leads us to the second exhortation to children.

Children are also commanded to "honor" their father and mother (6:2). Here the author quotes the fifth commandment of the Decalogue,[186] where the word "honor" in Hebrew means "to make heavy." Children should show "weighty respect and dignity" to their parents.[187] Honoring one's par-

---

184. MacDonald, *Power of Children*, 80.
185. O'Brien, *Letter to the Ephesians*, 446.
186. Bruce, *Epistles*, 397.
187. Marcia J. Bunge, "'Best Practices' for Nurturing the Best Love of and by Children: A Protestant Theological Perspective on the Vocations of Children and Parents,"

ents is not the same as obeying them. To obey means "to do what one is told" or "to carry out someone's order."[188] It assumes that instruction has been given by someone else. Obedience is thus reactive, a response to someone else's initiating action. But to honor is much more active; the one who honors usually takes the initiative to express respect and dignity. Obedience also presumes that the one who obeys is less mature or is of lower authority. But honoring others is not predicated upon such difference. Some commentators believe that honoring has a wider scope of application than obeying: while all children should honor their parents, only young children need to obey them. When the child is young and dependent, honoring her parents means obeying their instructions. But for adult children who have left home, honoring entails showing respect and taking care of their parents in their old age, and not necessarily obeying all their instructions.[189] Coons contends that the child's obedience "should correlate inversely with the child's age and experience . . . and eventually shrink to an honorific deference."[190] By issuing two commands to children, the author of the household code suggests that the parent-child relationship changes with the growing maturity of the children and the expression of love between them should also change accordingly. The notion of incarnational love, the kind of love which is pertinent between the "strong" and "weak" ones, can inform children how to love their parents under all circumstances. Incarnational love calls for solidarity between persons and with Christ. When children are young, they should love their parents by obeying them so that they themselves can grow into the likeness of Christ. When parents are old and become weak, children should respect and care for them so that they can continue to witness Christ in their old age. Parents, on the other hand, should give fewer direct instructions to their children as they mature. Instead, incarnational love demands parents of adult children to continue seeking solidarity through understanding and supporting them. Elderly parents should also accept the care given them from their children, for it is

---

in *The Best Love of the Child: Being Loved and Being Taught to Love as the First Human Right*, ed. Timothy P. Jackson (Grand Rapids, MI: Eerdmans, 2011), 242.

188. Hoehner, *Ephesians*, 786.
189. Arnold, *Ephesians*, 416; Hoehner, *Ephesians*, 789.
190. Coons, "Luck, Obedience," 89.

appropriate to accept the honor due them from their children. Accepting care also stems from recognizing one's creatureliness and acknowledging the special relationship that God assigned one so that one can learn how to love and receive love in the family. Mutual love and mutual subordination also characterizes the parent-child relationship; each should subordinate to the household order and express love to one another according to each one's particular situation. For this reason the household code exhorts parents not to "provoke your children to anger" (6:4). Although children may be less mature and need guidance and instructions, they are nonetheless human persons of equal dignity, worthy of respect. Parents should not treat them as mere property,[191] and should avoid "excessively severe discipline, unreasonably harsh demands, abuse of authority, arbitrariness, unfairness, constant nagging and condemnation, subjecting a child to humiliation, and all forms of gross insensitivity to a child's needs and sensibilities."[192] With the coming of Christ, children are already equal members with their parents in the Christian community. Jesus even says that those entering the kingdom of heaven must become like children.[193] It is true that in the original creation – due to the bodily and temporal nature of our existence – parents should bring up their young children, who, in turn, should obey their parents. But to heed the present-future duality of our existence, both parents and children must look forward to the resurrection where the special relationship between them will cease and they will enjoy a fully mutual relationship, becoming more like equal friends than unequal superiors and subordinates. Therefore, in this age, parents and children should prepare for the eschaton by cultivating friendship among them as the children mature.

It is noted that only fathers are directly exhorted in the household code; mothers are not addressed directly. In the Greco-Roman culture, the male head usually held sole authority over the whole household. This may be the reason why only fathers were commanded to bring up and instruct their children.[194] The exhortation to children – "obey your *parents*" (6:1) – implies that mothers also give instructions to them. To command fathers

---

191. Witherington, *Letters*, 338.
192. Lincoln, *Ephesians*, 406.
193. Matt 18:3.
194. Slater, *Ephesians*, 161; Hoehner, *Ephesians*, 794–795.

alone (6:4) does not imply limiting the parenting duties to fathers; it only emphasizes the importance of paternal involvement in parenting. Indeed, according to Browning, the "male problematic" is an issue that disrupts the human family so an emphasis on the father's duties toward his family is fitting in the household code.

6.2.5 Slaves and Masters

> Slaves, obey your fleshly masters with fear and trembling in the sincerity of your heart, as to Christ, not in mere appearance as people-pleasers but as slaves of Christ, doing the will of God from the inner person, working as slaves with goodwill, as for the Lord and not for human beings, because you know that each person who does something good will be repaid for this from the Lord, whether slave or free. And masters, do the same things for them, with the result that you give up the threat of violence, because you know that their Master and yours is in heaven, and there is no favoritism with him. (Eph 6:5–9)[195]

The author next addresses the slave-master relationship. Slaves were common in the Greco-Roman households. As slaves could be acquired with little cost, many non-elites – such as artisans, soldiers, peasants, and even other slaves – owned slaves.[196] Selling oneself into slavery due to poverty and debt was also common.[197] It is true that slaves were considered properties and could be abused and tortured.[198] But in practice they frequently enjoyed good relationships with the rest of the household.[199] The slaves exhorted in the household code were household slaves working in urban settings, not those working in the mines or the fields. While having urban households to depend on, they were not the most impoverished in

---

195. Translation adopted from Thielman. Thielman, *Ephesians*, 405.

196. Justin J. Meggitt, *Paul, Poverty and Survival* (Edinburgh: T&T Clark, 1998), 129–131.

197. Ibid., 58.

198. Keener, *Paul, Women and Wives*, 200.

199. Darko, *No Longer Living*, 95.

the Empire.[200] Being addressed directly in the household code implies that they were normally considered part of the household.[201] Many slaves received education and training in specialized skills for the benefit of their masters; some even became doctors, teachers, writers, and accountants.[202] Manumission could be expected after ten to twenty years of diligent service.[203] Thereafter, they could retain a client-patron relationship with their former masters to ensure livelihood.[204] The inclusion of slaves into the Greco-Roman households was mainly out of economic benefit, for the households and often the slaves themselves. Although the system of slavery could be abusive, manumission and upward mobility was still possible for many slaves.

Understanding the socioeconomic background of the household code, however, does not help us formulate how the slave-master exhortations can be applied today. As slavery is now illegal in every nation of the world,[205] contemporary ethics must strive to eradicate any lingering practice of slavery instead of regulating it. Thus the household code exhortations which aim to regulate the slave-master relationship appear to have no direct relevance to the modern world. However, some contemporary interpreters still advocate applying the passage today. Two types of application are common. First, the texts are used as a resource in the contemporary strife against unjust power structures and racism. Some interpreters think that the equalizing tendency and subversive elements within the exhortations imply that slavery should ultimately be abolished, though the author of the household code did not campaign for such social changes. For instance, Slater says that "Our twenty-first-century sensitivities correctly would have Ephesians advocate the abolition of slavery."[206] Cohick also argues that the author "undercuts the power of the institution of slavery and its attending reliance

---

200. Keener, *Paul, Women and Wives*, 197–198.
201. Ibid., 200.
202. Arnold, *Ephesians*, 421.
203. Lincoln, *Ephesians*, 417.
204. Arnold, *Ephesians*, 421.
205. Kevin Bales, *Disposable People: New Slavery in the Global Economy*, rev. ed. (Berkeley, CA: University of California Press, 2012), xxviii.
206. Slater, *Ephesians*, 163.

on social rank and status."[207] This offers resources to support the abolition of slavery and the struggle against racism in the modern world.[208] This hermeneutical method analyzes the power relationship between persons in the private and applies the result into the social and political sphere. While political implications can certainly be drawn from private relationship, this hermeneutical method ignores the personal nature of the household code exhortations and simply uses them as a springboard to launch into advocating certain political agenda. In other words, the exhortations cease to inform the private household relationships. The second way to apply the passage recognizes the personal nature of the exhortations. As the institution of slavery has been abolished, advocates of this hermeneutical method turn to the contemporary employee-employer relationship as a counterpart to the slave-master relationship in the New Testament world. For instance, Hoehner says that the passage teaches both employees and employers how to treat others in ways pleasing to the Lord.[209] Similarly, Chapell contends that "An employee has the obligation to demonstrate Christ's integrity and service, and an employer has the obligations to demonstrate Christ's justice and mercy."[210] Although they both recognize that the slave-master and employee-employer relationships are very different, they still consider them similar enough so that the household code can inform the contemporary workplace relationships. It is true that this hermeneutical method recovers the personal dimension of the household code. Yet the sphere of application is moved from the household to the workplace. While the economic aspect of the relationship is retained, the familial aspect is dismissed. In today's world, an employee does not belong to her employer's family nor does she have any necessary dealings with her employer's family members. Unlike the New Testament slave-master relationship which is enmeshed within other household relationships, the employee-employer relationship today is isolated from her other relationships. It is even considered appropriate or "professional" for a person to separate her workplace and her private relationships. Applying the slave-master exhortations to the

---

207. Cohick, *Ephesians*, 149.
208. Ibid., 149–151.
209. Hoehner, *Ephesians*, 816.
210. Chapell, *Ephesians*, 324.

employee-employer relationship therefore bends the original context of the household code and severs the slave-master exhortations from the rest of the *parenesis*.

This analysis shows that the slave-master admonition is most appropriately applied to a particular type of special relationship. This special relationship is formed within the household but is predicated upon economic benefits instead of biology or kinship. In the New Testament setting, the slave-master relationship belonged to this type of special relationship but in modernity, it is the household-employer and household-servant relationship that belongs to this category. This special relationship is initiated by an economic contract, which may be terminated when the terms of the contract have been fulfilled or through mutual consent of the persons involved. The relationship is still formed within the context of the family, which is "a place of timely and mutual belonging."[211] It is the "mutual belonging" of the employer family and the servant in the same household, not merely the sharing of residence between persons, that gives their relationship a familial character.[212] The legal historian Evelyn Atkinson, upon surveying the changing concept of household servants over the course of industrialization, concludes that the home of the employer is never simply a workplace for a household servant. This "workplace," even for modern domestic servants, always retains the characteristics of the family.[213] This implies that the contemporary employer-servant relationship, similar to other familial relationships, should be guided by the principle of mutual love and subordination. Today the employment of live-in domestic servant is not uncommon. In fact, neo-liberal globalization in the recent decades boosted the export of domestic servants from developing nations such as the Philippines, Indonesia, Sri Lanka, Thailand, and India to wealthier

---

211. Waters, *Family*, 175.

212. Therefore, friends who simply share an apartment but who do not eat or spend time together are less like a "family" compared with the household employer and servant who are both involved in maintaining the household.

213. Evelyn Atkinson, "Out of the Household: Master-Servant Relations and Employer Liability Law," *Yale Journal of Law & the Humanities* 25, no. 2 (Summer 2013): 270.

regions such as the Middle East, Hong Kong, Singapore, and Malaysia.[214] In Hong Kong there are about 285,000 – or 4 percent of the total population – of foreign domestic servants.[215] Most of these migrant workers live in the same apartments with their employers for extended periods of time. A worker may even serve in the same family for over ten years and virtually becomes part of her employer's family.[216] It is within these households that the slave-master exhortations of the household code become relevant, shedding light on the special relationship between the employer family and the servant.

The relationship between the employer family and the domestic servant is in itself a subject worthy of further theological investigation. Comprehensive assessment of this relationship or detailed hermeneutics of the master-slave exhortations of the household code is beyond the scope of this book. For our purposes, I will limit our discussions to the notion of unfolding love which informs the inclusion of domestic servants into families today. Just like a couple who unfolds their marital love to parental love and welcomes their children into the family, the family unfolds their familial love to their domestic servant and includes her into their household. It is through this notion of extending relationship that Friedrich Schleiermacher reflects on the relationship between masters and domestic servants. He observes that welcoming domestic servants into one's own household is difficult: "to receive people into the house as household companions, people originally strange to the house, is in itself a heavy burden."[217] This burden can only be lightened by love.[218] It is even more difficult for the domestic servants themselves as they are separated from their own families and grafted into households that are strange to them. To address this, the employers should, out of love, "provide for them a

---

214. Rosie Cox, *The Servant Problem: Domestic Employment in a Global Economy* (London: I. B. Tauris, 2006), 23.

215. Hans J. Ladegaard, "Demonising the Cultural Other: Legitimising Dehumanisation of Foreign Domestic Helpers in the Hong Kong Press," *Discourse, Context and Media* 2 (2013): 132.

216. For instance, my family in Hong Kong employed a migrant domestic servant who served my grandmother from 1999 until her death in 2010.

217. Friedrich Schleiermacher, *The Christian Household: A Sermonic Treatise*, trans. Dietrich Seidel and Terrence N. Tice (Lewiston, NY: Edwin Mellen, 1991), 95.

218. Ibid., 96.

substitute [home] for their being separated from their own loved ones."²¹⁹ This "substitute home" is only temporary, for the servants must eventually leave, become independent, or even start her own family. During the time of "mutual belonging" in the employer's household, the employer family should help her move toward this goal. When the time is ripe for her to leave, they should not hinder her but to rejoice in her moving forward. This is how the employer family can serve their domestic servant out of Christian love. When such mutual love and service is practiced, a "new and finer relationship . . . is developed . . . [and the servant] was regarded full-heartedly as one who belonged to the house and who could heartily participate in everything that took place there."²²⁰ Within such a household, the servant would serve in freedom and regard her role in the household as a matter of Christian calling, which is not inherently inferior to that of her employer.²²¹ After the servant leaves her employer's household, they can continue their relationship not as superior and inferior, but as equals, or even friends. Schleiermacher's discussions on domestic servants, though given nearly two centuries ago, are still relevant today. Again, the different kinds of familial love as discussed in chapter 5 are needed in the employer-servant relationships. It is incarnational love that motivates the employer to recognize the servant's need and offer a "substitute home" for her and help her move forward in life. It is mutual love, mutual service, solidarity, and eventually friendship that they seek between them. But to begin their relationship within the household, an unfolding love that welcomes the servant into the family must first be practiced.

6.3 Conclusions

The unfolding love of the Christian family does not stop at domestic servants. In his sermonic treatise on the Christian household, Schleiermacher continues discussing Christian hospitality and charity under the purview of the household. He observes that hospitality exudes from a "household that does not close itself away from the rest of the world but that temporarily

---

219. Ibid., 100.
220. Ibid., 101.
221. Ibid., 102.

takes others unto itself and in this way maintains connections with the outside."²²² Practicing hospitality destabilizes the boundary of the family, opening it up into an expanding fellowship. By inviting a lonely neighbor into one's own family gathering, by offering temporary shelter to a stranger in need, or by adopting an orphan into the family, the Christian household unfolds familial love outward and enfolds others into the family. While hospitality is concerned with "taking others in," charity complements hospitality that it commands one to "give oneself out" so the destitution of one's neighbor can be alleviated.²²³ It is interesting to note that Schleiermacher suggests that charity should be a collective act organized by the church community instead of an individual act performed by discrete Christians. In other words, individual Christians should give to the church community, which in turn should distribute the gifts to the poor. This arrangement, argues Schleiermacher, is necessary to avoid vanity of the ones who give and inferior feeling of those who receive.²²⁴ Practical issues aside, this view has in fact been anticipated by our earlier theological reflections on the family. As discussed in chapter 5, the family is constituted of special relationships where mutuality and the sharing of life is the *telos* of these relationships. Charity or agape love, however, is not interested in building sustained or mutual relationships. It is the disinterested attribute of agape love that is not characteristic of special relationships. As all familial relationships are special relationships, the family alone is inadequate for Christians to practice the universal love of agape. Therefore, the eschatological community of the church is necessary to complement the family so Christians can practice agape love on this side of the eschaton. Yet ultimately all familial and special relationships will cease in the resurrection; the natural household will give way to God's household. The kinds of the love practiced in the earthly family – friendship, incarnational love, and unfolding love – will then be perfected into agape love in God's all-inclusive and universal household.

From the beginning of creation, God made them male and female. God further placed them within the four dualities of human existence

---

222. Ibid., 124.
223. Ibid., 140–145.
224. Ibid., 153–154.

– mind-body, man-woman, individual-community, and present-future. In God's creation, the original male-female relationship brings forth complex human relationships. Different persons are assigned different roles, complicating and enriching the relationships within the family. In this book I formulated three notions of love – friendship, incarnational love, and unfolding love – to guide us in understanding and navigating these complex familial relationships. The author of the Ephesian household code pinpoints three of these household relationships and offers corresponding moral exhortations to the early church community. The household code admonitions are by no means exhaustive; they are only representative samples that set the tone for proper Christian familial relationships.[225] The familial roles are also overlapping and the identities of persons are transitional. For instance, servants can be parents themselves and parents who have young children to instruct may also have elderly parents to respect and honor.[226] Among these complex, overlapping, and changing relationships, it is Christ's love revealed in his life, death, resurrection, and exaltation that offers us the moral vision to love one another in the family. Within our own earthly families we are trained to love one another, and through practicing Christ's love in the family, we bear witness to Christ. In the end, it is the perfect love that we look forward to: the love between Christ the bridegroom and the church his bride – the universal household of God.

---

225. Witherington, *Letters*, 324.
226. MacDonald, *Power of Children*, 150.

Bibliography

Allen, Diogenes. *Love: Christian Romance, Marriage, Friendship*. Eugene, OR: Wipf & Stock, 2006.

Amato, Paul R., and Lydia H. Hayes. "'Alone Together' Marriages and 'Living Apart Together' Relationships." In *Contemporary Issues in Family Studies: Global Perspectives On Partnerships, Parenting and Support in a Changing World*, edited by Angela Abela and Janet Walker, 31–45. Chichester, West Sussex: Wiley & Sons, 2014.

Anderson, Joel. "Is Equality Tearing Families Apart?" In *Mutuality Matters: Family, Faith, and Just Love*, edited by Herbert Anderson, 93–106. Lanham, MD: Rowman & Littlefield, 2004.

Aquinas, Thomas. *Summa Contra Gentiles*. Translated by Dominican Fathers. London: Burns Oates & Washbourne, 1928.

Aristotle. *Nicomachean Ethics*. Translated by Joe Sachs. Newbury, MA: Focus/R. Pullins, 2002.

Arnold, Clinton E. *Ephesians*. Grand Rapids, MI: Zondervan, 2010.

Athanasius. *The Incarnation of the Word of God*. Translated by a Religious of CSMW, New York: MacMillan, 1946.

Atkinson, Evelyn. "Out of the Household: Master-Servant Relations and Employer Liability Law." *Yale Journal of Law & the Humanities* 25, no. 2 (Summer 2013): 205–270.

Augustine. *City of God*. Translated by Henry Scowcroft Bettenson. London: Penguin, 1984.

⸺. *Confessions*. Translated by Henry Chadwick. Oxford: Oxford University Press, 1991.

⸺. "The Good of Marriage." In *The Fathers of the Church: Saint Augustine Treatises on Marriage and Other Subjects*. New York: Fathers of the Church, 1955.

Bahr, Howard M., and Kathleen S. Bahr. *Toward More Family-Centered Family Sciences: Love, Sacrifice, and Transcendence*. Lanham, MD: Lexington, 2009.

Bales, Kevin. *Disposable People: New Slavery in the Global Economy*. Revised ed. Berkeley, CA: University of California Press, 2012.

Balswick, Judith K., and Jack O. Balswick. "Marriage as a Partnership of Equals." In *Discovering Biblical Equality: Complementarity without Hierarchy*, 2nd ed., edited by Ronald W. Pierce and Rebecca Merrill Groothuis, 448–463. Downers Grove, IL: InterVarsity, 2005.

Balswick, Jack O., and Judith K. Balswick. *The Family: A Christian Perspective on the Contemporary Home*, 4th ed. Grand Rapids, MI: Baker Academic, 2014.

von Balthasar, Hans Urs. *Theo-Drama: Theological Dramatic Theory*. Vol. 2 of *The Dramatis Personae: Man in God*. Translated by Graham Harrison. San Francisco, CA: Ignatius, 1990.

Barth, Karl. *Church Dogmatics*. Vol. 1.1 of *The Doctrine of the Word of God*. Edited by G. W. Bromiley and T. F. Torrance. Translated by G. W. Bromiley. Peabody, MA: Hendrickson, 2010.

———. *Church Dogmatics*. Vol. 1.2 of *The Doctrine of the Word of God*. Edited by G. W. Bromiley and T. F. Torrance. Translated by G. T. Thomson and Harold Knight. Peabody, MA: Hendrickson, 2010.

———. *Church Dogmatics*. Vol. 2.2 of *The Doctrine of God*. Edited by G. W. Bromiley and T. F. Torrance. Translated by G. W. Bromiley, J. C Campbell, et al. Peabody, MA: Hendrickson, 2010.

———. *Church Dogmatics*. Vol. 3.1 of *The Doctrine of Creation*. Edited by G. W. Bromiley and T. F. Torrance. Translated by J. W. Edwards, O. Bussey, and H. Knight. Peabody, MA: Hendrickson, 2010.

———. *Church Dogmatics*. Vol. 3.2 of *The Doctrine of Creation*. Edited by G. W. Bromiley and T. F. Torrance. Translated by H. Knight, G. W. Bromiley, J. K. S. Reid, and R. H. Fuller. Peabody, MA: Hendrickson, 2010.

———. *Church Dogmatics*. Vol. 3.4 of *The Doctrine of Creation*. Edited by G. W. Bromiley and T. F. Torrance. Translated by A. T. Mackay, T. H. L. Parker, H. Knight, H. A. Kennedy, and J. Marks. Peabody, MA: Hendrickson, 2010.

———. *Church Dogmatics*. Vol. 4.2 of *The Doctrine of Reconciliation*. Edited by G. W. Bromiley and T. F. Torrance. Translated by G. W. Bromiley. Peabody, MA: Hendrickson, 2010.

———. *Ethics*. Translated by Geoffrey W. Bromiley. New York: Seabury Press, 1981.

Batey, Richard A. *New Testament Nuptial Imagery*. Leiden: E. J. Brill, 1971.

Bennett, Jana Marguerite. *Water Is Thicker Than Blood: An Augustinian Theology of Marriage and Singleness*. Oxford: Oxford University Press, 2008.

Best, Ernest. *A Critical and Exegetical Commentary on Ephesians*. Edinburgh: T&T Clark, 1998.

———. *Essays on Ephesians*. Edinburgh: T&T Clark, 1997.

Bilezikian, Gilbert G. *Beyond Sex Roles: A Guide for the Study of Female Roles in the Bible*. Grand Rapids, MI: Baker, 1985.

Blankenhorn, David. *Fatherless America: Confronting Our Most Urgent Social Problem*. New York: Basic Books, 1995.

Blumberg, Rae Lesser. "Income under Female versus Male Control: Hypothesis from a Theory of Gender Stratification and Data from the Third World." In *Gender, Family, and Economy: The Triple Overlap*, edited by Rae Lesser Blumberg, 97–127. Newbury Park, CA: Sage, 1991.

Bonhoeffer, Dietrich. *Life Together*. Translated by John W. Doberstein. San Francisco, CA: Harper & Row, 1954.

Borland, James A. "Women in the Life and Teachings of Jesus." In *Recovering Biblical Manhood and Womanhood: A Response to Evangelical Feminism*, edited by John Piper and Wayne Grudem, 113–123. Wheaton, IL: Crossway, 2006.

Breazeale, Kathlyn A. *Mutual Empowerment: A Theology of Marriage, Intimacy, and Redemption*. Minneapolis, MN: Augsburg Fortress, 2008.

Breidenthal, Thomas E. *Christian Households: The Sanctification of Nearness*. Cambridge, MA: Cowley, 1997.

Brock, Brian. *Singing the Ethos of God: On the Place of Christian Ethics in Scripture*. Grand Rapids, MI: Eerdmans, 2007.

Brooks, Ann. *Gendered Work in Asian Cities: The New Economy and Changing Labour Markets*. Hampshire, UK: Ashgate, 2006.

Brown, Peter. *The Body and Society: Men, Women, and Sexual Renunciation in Early Christianity*. 20th anniversary edition. New York: Columbia University, 2008.

Browning, Don S., Bonnie J. Miller-McLemore, Pamela D. Couture, K. Brynolf Lyon, and Robert M. Franklin. *From Culture Wars to Common Ground: Religion and the American Family Debate*. Louisville, KY: Westminster John Knox, 1997.

Browning, Don S. *Equality and the Family: A Fundamental, Practical Theology of Children, Mothers, and Fathers in Modern Societies*. Grand Rapids, MI: Eerdmans, 2006.

———. *Marriage and Modernization: How Globalization Threatens Marriage and What to Do About It*. Grand Rapids, MI: Eerdmans, 2003.

———. "Response." In *The Equal-Regard Family and Its Friendly Critics: Don Browning and the Practical Theological Ethics of the Family*, edited by John Witte Jr., M. Christian Green, and Amy Wheeler, 246–262. Grand Rapids, MI: Eerdmans, 2007.

Bruce, F. F. *The Epistles to the Colossians, to Philemon, and to the Ephesians*. Grand Rapids, MI: Eerdmans, 1984.

Bunge, Marcia J. "'Best Practices' for Nurturing the Best Love of and by Children: A Protestant Theological Perspective on the Vocations of Children and Parents." In *The Best Love of the Child: Being Loved and Being Taught to Love as the First Human Right,* edited by Timothy P. Jackson, 226–250. Grand Rapids, MI: Eerdmans, 2011.

Cahill, Lisa Sowle. *Family: A Christian Social Perspective.* Minneapolis, MN: Fortress, 2000.

———. *Sex, Gender, and Christian Ethics.* Cambridge: Cambridge University Press, 1996.

Carson, D. A. "'Silent in the Churches': On the Role of Women in 1 Corinthians 14:33b–36." In *Recovering Biblical Manhood and Womanhood: A Response to Evangelical Feminism,* edited by John Piper and Wayne Grudem, 140–153. Wheaton, IL: Crossway, 2006.

Chan, Yiu Sing Lúcás. *The Ten Commandments and the Beatitudes: Biblical Studies and Ethics for Real Life.* Lanham, MD: Rowman & Littlefield, 2012.

Chandra, Anjani, Casey E. Copen, and William D. Mosher. "Sexual Behavior, Sexual Attraction, and Sexual Identity in the United States: Data from the 2006–2010." In *International Handbook on the Demography of Sexuality,* vol. 5, edited by Amanda K. Baumle, 45–66. New York: Springer Science + Business Media, 2013.

Chapell, Bryan. *Ephesians.* Phillipsburg, NJ: P & R, 2009.

Chavasse, Claude. *The Bride of Christ: An Enquiry into the Nuptial Element in Early Christianity.* London: Faber & Faber, 1939.

Clark, Stephen B. *Man and Woman in Christ: An Examination of the Roles of Men and Women in Light of Scripture and the Social Sciences.* Ann Arbor, MI: Servant Books, 1980.

Cohick, Lynn H. *Ephesians: A New Covenant Commentary.* Cambridge, UK: Lutterworth Press, 2013.

Cole, Graham A. *The God Who Became Human: A Biblical Theology of Incarnation.* Downers Grove, IL: InterVarsity, 2013.

Coleman, John. "Parenting Teenagers." In *Contemporary Issues in Family Studies: Global Perspectives on Partnerships, Parenting and Support in a Changing World,* edited by Angela Abela and Janet Walker, 203–214. Chichester, West Sussex: Wiley & Sons, 2014.

Collins, Raymond F. *Divorce in the New Testament.* Collegeville, MN: Liturgical, 1992.

———. *The Many Faces of the Church: A Study in New Testament Ecclesiology.* New York: Crossroad, 2003.

Coltrane, Scott, and Michele Adams. "Men's Family Work: Child-Centered Fathering and the Sharing of Domestic Labor." In *Working Families: The Transformation of the American Home,* edited by Rosanna Hertz and Nancy L. Marshall, 72–99. Berkeley, CA: University of California Press, 2001.

Coons, John E. "Luck, Obedience, and the Vocation of Childhood." In *The Vocation of the Child,* edited by Patrick M. Brennan, 75–103. Grand Rapids, MI: Eerdmans, 2008.

Cosgrove, Charles H. *Appealing to Scripture in Moral Debate: Five Hermeneutical Rules.* Grand Rapids, MI: Eerdmans, 2002.

Cott, Nancy F. *Public Vows: A History of Marriage and the Nation.* Cambridge, MA: Harvard University Press, 2002.

The Council on Biblical Manhood and Womanhood. "The Danvers Statement." In *Recovering Biblical Manhood and Womanhood: A Response to Evangelical Feminism,* edited by John Piper and Wayne Grudem, 469–471. Wheaton, IL: Crossway, 2006.

Cox, Rosie. *The Servant Problem: Domestic Employment in a Global Economy.* London: I. B. Tauris, 2006.

Darko, Daniel K. *No Longer Living as the Gentiles: Differentiation and Shared Ethical Values in Ephesians 4.17–6.9.* London: T&T Clark, 2008.

Davis, Deborah S., and Sara L. Friedman. "Deinstitutionalizing Marriage and Sexuality." In *Wives, Husbands, and Lovers: Marriage and Sexuality in Hong Kong, Taiwan, and Urban China,* edited by Deborah Davis and Sara Friedman, 1–38. Stanford: Stanford University Press, 2014.

De Vries, Roland J. *Becoming Two in Love: Kierkegaard, Irigaray, and the Ethics of Sexual Difference.* Eugene, OR: Pickwick, 2013.

Dermott, Esther. *Intimate Fatherhood: A Sociological Analysis.* London: Routledge, 2008.

Donnelly, Denise A., and Elisabeth O. Burgess. "The Decision to Remain in an Involuntarily Celibate Relationship." *Journal of Marriage and Family* 70, no. 2 (May 2008): 519–535.

Doriani, Daniel. "The Historical Novelty of Egalitarian Interpretations of Ephesians 5:21–22." In *Biblical Foundations for Manhood and Womanhood,* edited by Wayne Grudem, 203–231. Wheaton, IL: Crossway, 2002.

Duncan, J. Ligon, and Randy Stinson. "Preface (2006)." In *Recovering Biblical Manhood and Womanhood: A Response to Evangelical Feminism,* edited by John Piper and Wayne Grudem, ix–xiii. Wheaton, IL: Crossway, 2006.

Dunn, James D. G. "The Household Rules in the New Testament." In *The Family in Theological Perspective,* edited by Stephen C. Barton, 43–63. Edinburgh: T&T Clark, 1996.

Ebeling, Jennie R. *Women's Lives in Biblical Times.* New York: T&T Clark, 2010.

Ellul, Jacques. *The Technological Society.* New York: Vintage, 1964.

Farley, Margaret A. "The Church and the Family: An Ethical Task." *Horizons* 10, no. 1 (Mar 1983): 50–71.

———. *Just Love: A Framework for Christian Sexual Ethics.* New York: Continuum, 2006.

———. *Personal Commitments: Beginning, Keeping, Changing*. Revised ed. Maryknoll, NY: Orbis, 2013.

———. "The Role of Experience in Moral Discernment." In *Christian Ethics: Problems and Prospects*, edited by Lisa S. Cahill and James F. Childress, 134–151. Cleveland, OH: Pilgrim, 1996.

Fausto-Sterling, Anne. *Sexing the Body: Gender Politics and the Construction of Sexuality*. New York: Basic Books, 2000.

Fee, Gordon D. *The First Epistle to the Corinthians*. Grand Rapids, MI: Eerdmans, 1987.

———. "Praying and Prophesying in the Assemblies: 1 Corinthians 11:2–16." In *Discovering Biblical Equality: Complementarity without Hierarchy*, 2nd ed., edited by Ronald W. Pierce and Rebecca Merrill Groothuis, 142–160. Downers Grove, IL: InterVarsity, 2005.

Fimmel, Richard O. *Pioneer Odyssey*. Revised ed. Washington, DC: Scientific and Technical Information Office, National Aeronautics and Space Administration, 1977.

Fowl, Stephen E. *Ephesians: A Commentary*. Louisville, KY: Westminster John Knox, 2012.

Frame, John M. "Men and Women in the Image of God." In *Recovering Biblical Manhood and Womanhood: A Response to Evangelical Feminism*, edited by John Piper and Wayne Grudem, 225–232. Wheaton, IL: Crossway, 2006.

Fromm, Erich. *The Art of Loving*. New York: Harper & Brothers, 1956.

Gallagher, Maggie. "Reflections on Headship." In *Does Christianity Teach Male Headship? The Equal-Regard Marriage and Its Critics*, edited by David Blankenhorn, Don S. Browning, and Mary Stewart Van Leeuwen, 111–125. Grand Rapids, MI: Eerdmans, 2004.

Giles, Kevin. *The Eternal Generation of the Son: Maintaining Orthodoxy in Trinitarian Theology*. Downers Grove, IL: InterVarsity, 2012.

———. *The Trinity and Subordinationism: The Doctrine of God and the Contemporary Gender Debate*. Downers Grove, IL: InterVarsity, 2002.

Gillis, John R. "Marriages of the Mind." *Journal of Marriage and Family* 66, no. 4 (Nov 2004): 988–991.

Gittins, Anthony J. "In Search of Goodenough Families: Cultural and Religious Perspectives." In *Mutuality Matters: Family, Faith, and Just Love*, edited by Herbert Anderson, 167–180. Lanham, MD: Rowman & Littlefield, 2004.

Gombis, Timothy G. "A Radically New Humanity: The Function of the Haustafel in Ephesians." *Journal of the Evangelical Theological Society* 48, no. 2 (June 2005): 317–330.

Goodspeed, Edgar J. *The Meaning of Ephesians*. Chicago, IL: University of Chicago Press, 1933.

Graham, Elaine L. *Making the Difference: Gender, Personhood, and Theology*. Minneapolis, MN: Fortress, 1996.

Graham, Glenn H. *An Exegetical Summary of Ephesians*, 2nd ed. Dallas: SIL International, 2008.

Grant, George. *Technology and Empire*. Concord, Ontario: House of Anansi, 1969.

_____. *Technology and Justice*. Concord, Ontario: House of Anansi, 1986.

Grenz, Stanley J., and Denise Muir Kjesbo. *Women in the Church: A Biblical Theology of Women in Ministry*. Downers Grove, IL: InterVarsity, 1995.

Grisez, Germain Gabriel. *The Way of the Lord Jesus*. Vol. 2 of *Living a Christian Life*. Quincy, IL: Franciscan Press, 1993.

Groothuis, Rebecca Merrill. "'Equality in Being, Unequal in Role,' Exploring the Logic of Woman's Subordination." In *Discovering Biblical Equality: Complementarity without Hierarchy*, 2nd ed., edited by Ronald W. Pierce and Rebecca Merrill Groothuis, 301–333. Downers Grove, IL: InterVarsity, 2005.

Grudem, Wayne A. "Does kephalē ('Head') Mean 'Source' or 'Authority Over' in Greek Literature: A Survey of 2,336 Examples." *Trinity Journal* 6, no. 1 (Spring 1985): 38–59.

_____. *Evangelical Feminism: A New Path to Liberalism?* Wheaton, IL: Crossway, 2006.

_____. *Evangelical Feminism and Biblical Truth: An Analysis of More Than One Hundred Disputed Questions*. Wheaton, IL: Crossway, 2012.

_____. "The Key Issues in the Manhood-Womanhood Controversy, and the Way Forward." In *Biblical Foundations for Manhood and Womanhood*, edited by Wayne Grudem, 19–68. Wheaton, IL: Crossway, 2002.

_____. "The Meaning of *Kephalē* ('Head'): A Response to Recent Studies." In *Recovering Biblical Manhood and Womanhood: A Response to Evangelical Feminism*, edited by John Piper and Wayne Grudem, 425–468. Wheaton, IL: Crossway, 2006.

_____. "The Myth of Mutual Submission as an Interpretation of Ephesians 5:21." In *Biblical Foundations for Manhood and Womanhood*, edited by Wayne Grudem, 221–231. Wheaton, IL: Crossway, 2002.

_____. *Systematic Theology: An Introduction to Biblical Doctrine*. Leicester, England: IVP, 1994.

_____. "Wives Like Sarah, and the Husbands Who Honor Them: 1 Peter 3:1–7." In *Recovering Biblical Manhood and Womanhood: A Response to Evangelical Feminism*, edited by John Piper and Wayne Grudem, 194–208. Wheaton, IL: Crossway, 2006.

Gundry-Wolf, Judith M. "Christ and Gender: A Study of Difference and Equality in Gal 3,28." In *Jesus Christus Als Die Mitte der Schrift: Studien*

Zur Hermeneutik Des Evangeliums, edited by Christof Landmesser, Hans-Joachim Eckstein, and Hermann Lichtenberger, 439–477. Berlin: W. de Gruyter, 1997.

Guroian, Vigen. "The Office of Child in the Christian Faith: A Theology of Childhood." In *The Vocation of the Child*, edited by Patrick M. Brennan, 104–124. Grand Rapids, MI: Eerdmans, 2008.

Hallett, Garth L. *Christian Neighbor-Love: An Assessment of Six Rival Versions*. Washington, DC: Georgetown University Press, 1989.

Hamilton, Victor P. *The Book of Genesis*. Grand Rapids, MI: Eerdmans, 1990.

Hartopo, Yohanes Adrie. "The Marriage of the Lamb: The Background and Function of the Marriage Imagery in the Book of Revelation." PhD diss., Westminster Theological Seminary, 2005.

Hassey, Janette. "Evangelical Women in Ministry a Century Ago: The 19th the Early 20th Centuries." In *Discovering Biblical Equality: Complementarity without Hierarchy*, 2nd ed., edited by Ronald W. Pierce and Rebecca Merrill Groothuis, 39–57. Downers Grove, IL: InterVarsity, 2005.

Hauerwas, Stanley. *The Hauerwas Reader*. Edited by John Berkman and Michael G. Cartwright. Durham, NC: Duke University Press, 2001.

Hays, Richard B. *The Moral Vision of the New Testament: Community, Cross, New Creation*. New York: HarperOne, 1996.

Hering, James P. *The Colossian and Ephesian* Haustafeln *in Theological Context: An Analysis of Their Origins, Relationship, and Message*. New York: Peter Lang, 2007.

Hess, Richard S. "Equality with and without Innocence: Genesis 1–3." In *Discovering Biblical Equality: Complementarity without Hierarchy*, 2nd ed., edited by Ronald W. Pierce and Rebecca Merrill Groothuis, 79–95. Downers Grove, IL: InterVarsity, 2005.

Hick, John. *The Metaphor of God Incarnate: Christology in a Pluralistic Age*, 2nd ed. Louisville, KY: Westminster John Knox, 2006.

Ho, Petula Sik Ying. "An Embarrassment of Riches: Good Men Behaving Badly in Hong Kong." In *Wives, Husbands, and Lovers: Marriage and Sexuality in Hong Kong, Taiwan, and Urban China*, edited by Deborah Davis and Sara Friedman, 165–188. Stanford, CA: Stanford University Press, 2014.

Hoehner, Harold W. *Ephesians: An Exegetical Commentary*. Grand Rapids, MI: Baker Academic, 2002.

Hong Kong Legislative Council Subcommittee to Study the Subject of Combating Poverty. "Household Income Distribution in Hong Kong," LC Paper no. CB(2)2385/06-07(03), 3. Cited 8 August 2014. Online: http://www.legco.gov.hk/yr04-05/english/hc/sub_com/hs51/papers/hs510710cb2-2385-3-e.pdf.

Impett, Emily A., and Letitia Anne Peplau. "'His' and 'Her' Relationships? A Review of the Empirical Evidence." In *The Cambridge Handbook of Personal Relationships*, edited by Anita L. Vangelisti and Daniel Perlman, 273–291. New York: Cambridge University Press, 2006.

Instone-Brewer, David. *Divorce and Remarriage in the 1st and 21st Century*. Grove Biblical Series, vol. 19. Cambridge: Grove Books, 2001.

Jackson, Timothy P. "Judge William and Professor Browning: A Kierkegaardian Critique of Equal-Regard Marriage and the Democratic Family." In *The Equal-Regard Family and Its Friendly Critics: Don Browning and the Practical Theological Ethics of the Family*, edited by John Witte Jr., M. Christian Green, and Amy Wheeler, 123–150. Grand Rapids, MI: Eerdmans, 2007.

Jenson, Robert W. *Systematic Theology*. Vol. 1 of *The Triune God*. Oxford: Oxford University Press, 1997.

Jewett, Paul King. *Man as Male and Female: A Study in Sexual Relationships from a Theological Point of View*. Grand Rapids, MI: Eerdmans, 1975.

John Paul. *Fruitful and Responsible Love*. New York: Seabury Press, 1979.

Johnson, Edna. *A Semantic and Structural Analysis of Ephesians*. Dallas, TX: SIL International, 2008.

Kass, Leon. *The Beginning of Wisdom: Reading Genesis*. New York: Free Press, 2003.

Keener, Craig S. *Paul, Women and Wives: Marriage and Women's Ministry in the Letters of Paul*. Peabody, MA: Hendrickson, 1992.

Keller, Catherine. "Scoop Up the Water and the Moon Is in Your Hands: On Feminist Theology and Dynamic Self-Emptying." In *The Emptying God: A Buddhist-Jewish-Christian Conversation*, edited by John B. Cobb Jr. and Christopher Ives, 102–115. Maryknoll, NY: Orbis, 1990.

Klinenberg, Eric. *Going Solo: The Extraordinary Rise and Surprising Appeal of Living Alone*. New York: Penguin, 2012.

Knight, George W. III. "The Family and the Church: How Should Biblical Manhood and Womanhood Work Out in Practice?" In *Recovering Biblical Manhood and Womanhood: A Response to Evangelical Feminism*, edited by John Piper and Wayne Grudem, 345–357. Wheaton, IL: Crossway, 2006.

_____. "Husbands and Wives as Analogues of Christ and the Church: Ephesians 5:21–33 and Colossians 3:18–19." In *Recovering Biblical Manhood and Womanhood: A Response to Evangelical Feminism*, edited by John Piper and Wayne Grudem, 165–178. Wheaton, IL: Crossway, 2006.

_____. *The Role Relationship of Men and Women: New Testament Teaching*. Revised ed. Phillipsburg, NJ: P & R, 1985.

Ladegaard, Hans J. "Demonising the Cultural Other: Legitimising Dehumanisation of Foreign Domestic Helpers in the Hong Kong Press." *Discourse, Context and Media* 2 (2013): 131–140.

Lasch, Christopher. *Haven in a Heartless World: The Family Besieged.* New York: W. W. Norton & Co., 1995.

Lee, Eliza W. Y. *Gender and Change in Hong Kong: Globalization, Postcolonialism, and Chinese Patriarchy.* Honolulu, HI: University of Hawaii Press, 2003.

Leibholz, Gerhard. "The Nature and Various Forms of Democracy." *Social Research* 5, no. 1 (Feb 1938): 84–100.

Lesthaeghe, Ron. "The Second Demographic Transition in Western Countries: An Interpretation." In *Gender and Family Change in Industrialized Countries*, edited by Karen Oppenheim Mason and An-Magritt Jensen, 17–62. Oxford: Clarendon, 1995.

_____. "The Unfolding Story of the Second Demographic Transition." *Population and Development Review* 36, no. 2 (Jun 2010): 211–251.

Lewis, C. S. *The Four Loves.* London: Geoffrey Bles, 1960.

Liefeld, Walter L. *Ephesians.* Downers Grove, IL: InterVarsity, 1997.

Lincoln, Andrew T. *Ephesians.* Vol. 42 of *Word Biblical Commentary.* Nashville, TN: Thomas Nelson, 1990.

Loader, William R. G. *Making Sense of Sex: Attitudes Towards Sexuality in Early Jewish and Christian Literature.* Grand Rapids, MI: Eerdmans, 2013.

MacDonald, Margaret Y. *The Power of Children: The Construction of Christian Families in the Greco-Roman World.* Waco, TX: Baylor University Press, 2014.

Mahony, Rhona. *Kidding Ourselves: Breadwinning, Babies, and Bargaining Power.* New York: Basic Books, 1995.

Marshall, I. Howard. "Mutual Love and Submission in Marriage: Colossians 3:18–19 and Ephesians 5:21–33." In *Discovering Biblical Equality: Complementarity without Hierarchy*, 2nd ed., edited by Ronald W. Pierce and Rebecca Merrill Groothuis, 186–204. Downers Grove, IL: InterVarsity, 2005.

Marshall, Katherine. "The Family Work Week." *Perspectives on Labour and Income* 21, no. 2 (Summer 2009): 21–29. Cited 8 August 2014. http://search.proquest.com/docview/213987360?accountid=12861.

Martin, Ralph P. *Ephesians, Colossians, and Philemon.* Atlanta, GA: John Knox, 1991.

Mayor, Susan. "Pregnancy and Childbirth Are Leading Causes of Death in Teenage Girls in Developing Countries." *British Medical Journal* 328, no. 7449 (15 May 2004): 1152.

McLanahan, Sara, and Gary Sandefur. *Growing Up with a Single Parent: What Hurts, What Helps.* Reprint edition. Cambridge, MA: Harvard University Press, 1996.

Meggitt, Justin J. *Paul, Poverty and Survival.* Edinburgh: T&T Clark, 1998.

Meilaender, Gilbert. *Faith and Faithfulness: Basic Themes in Christian Ethics.* Notre Dame, IN: University of Notre Dame Press, 1991.
———. *Friendship: A Study in Theological Ethics.* Notre Dame, IN: University of Notre Dame Press, 1981.
———. *The Limits of Love: Some Theological Explorations.* University Park, PA: Penn State University Press, 1992.
———. *Things That Count: Essays Moral and Theological.* Wilmington, DE: ISI Books, 2000.
———. *The Way That Leads There: Augustinian Reflections on the Christian Life.* Grand Rapids, MI: Eerdmans, 2006.
Mercedes, Anna. *Power for Feminism and Christ's Self-Giving.* New York: T&T Clark, 2011.
Michaels, J. Ramsey. *The Gospel of John.* Grand Rapids, MI: Eerdmans, 2010.
Miller, John W. "The Problem of Men, Reconsidered." In *Does Christianity Teach Male Headship? The Equal-Regard Marriage and Its Critics*, edited by David Blankenhorn, Don S. Browning, and Mary Stewart Van Leeuwen, 65–73. Grand Rapids, MI: Eerdmans, 2004.
Miller, Mark A., and Richard H. Rahe. "Life Changes Scaling for the 1990s." *Journal of Psychosomatic Research* 43, no. 3 (1997): 279–292.
Miller, Patrick D. *The Ten Commandments.* Louisville, KY: Westminster John Knox, 2009.
Miller-McLemore, Bonnie. "Generativity, Self-Sacrifice, and the Ethics of Family Life." In *The Equal-Regard Family and Its Friendly Critics: Don Browning and the Practical Theological Ethics of the Family*, edited by John Witte Jr., M. Christian Green, and Amy Wheeler, 17–41. Grand Rapids, MI: Eerdmans, 2007.
———. "Sloppy Mutuality: Just Love for Children and Adults." In *Mutuality Matters: Family, Faith, and Just Love*, edited by Herbert Anderson, 121–135. Lanham, MD: Rowman & Littlefield, 2004.
Moltmann, Jürgen. *The Trinity and the Kingdom: The Doctrine of God.* San Francisco, CA: Harper & Row, 1981.
Moo, Douglas. "What Does It Mean Not to Teach or Have Authority Over Men? 1 Timothy 2:11–15." In *Recovering Biblical Manhood and Womanhood: A Response to Evangelical Feminism*, edited by John Piper and Wayne Grudem, 179–193. Wheaton, IL: Crossway, 2006.
Moxnes, Halvor. "What Is Family? Problems in Constructing Early Christian Families." In *Constructing Early Christian Families: Family as Social Reality and Metaphor*, edited by Halvor Moxnes, 13–41. London: Routledge, 1997.
Muddiman, John. *A Commentary on the Epistle to the Ephesians.* London: Continuum, 2001.

Musick, Kelly, Paula England, Sarah Edgington and Nicole Kangas. "Education Differences in Intended and Unintended Fertility." *Social Forces* 88, no. 2 (December 2009): 543–572.

Musick, Kelly, and Larry Bumpass. "Reexamining the Case for Marriage: Union Formation and Changes in Well-being." *Journal of Marriage and Family* 74 (Feb 2012): 1–18.

Nease, Lon, and Michael W. Austin, eds. *Fatherhood: The Dao of Daddy*. Malden, MA: Wiley-Blackwell, 2010.

Noack, Turid, Eva Bernhardt and Kenneth Aarskaug Wiik. "Cohabitation or Marriage? Contemporary Living Arrangements in the West." In *Contemporary Issues in Family Studies: Global Perspectives On Partnerships, Parenting and Support in a Changing World*, edited by Angela Abela and Janet Walker, 16–30. Chichester, West Sussex: John Wiley & Sons, 2014.

Nygren, Anders. *Agape and Eros*. Translated by Philip S. Watson. London: SPCK, 1957.

O'Brien, Peter T. *The Epistle to the Philippians: A Commentary on the Greek Text*. Grand Rapids, MI: Eerdmans, 1991.

————. *The Letter to the Ephesians*. Grand Rapids, MI: Eerdmans, 1999.

O'Donovan, Oliver. *Marriage and Permanence*. Grove Booklet on Ethics, vol. 26. Bramcote: Grove Books, 1978.

————. *Resurrection and Moral Order: An Outline for Evangelical Ethics*. 2nd ed. Grand Rapids, MI: Eerdmans, 1994.

Ortlund, Raymond C., Jr. "Male-Female Equality and Male Headship: Genesis 1–3." In *Recovering Biblical Manhood and Womanhood: A Response to Evangelical Feminism*, edited by John Piper and Wayne Grudem, 95–112. Wheaton, IL: Crossway, 2006.

Osiek, Carolyn. "The Feminist and the Bible: Hermeneutical Alternatives." In *Feminist Perspectives on Biblical Scholarship*, edited by Adela Yarbro Collins, 94–105. Chico, CA: Scholars Press, 1985.

————. "The New Testament Teaching on Family Matters." *HTS Teologiese Studies* 62, no. 3 (2006): 819–843.

Outka, Gene. *Agape: An Ethical Analysis*. New Haven, CT: Yale University Press, 1972.

Padgett, Alan G. "The Bible and Gender Troubles: American Evangelicals Debate Scripture and Submission." *Dialog: A Journal of Theology* 47, no. 1 (Spring 2008): 21–26.

Painter, John. *1, 2, and 3 John*. Sacra Pagina Series, vol. 18. Collegeville, MN: Liturgical Press, 2002.

Parrott, Tonya M., and Vern L. Bengtson. "The Effects of Earlier Intergenerational Affection, Normative Expectations, and Family Conflict on Contemporary Exchanges of Help and Support." *Research on Aging* 21, no. 1 (Jan 1999): 73–105.

Peterson, Eugene H. *Practice Resurrection: A Conversation on Growing up in Christ.* Grand Rapids, MI: Eerdmans, 2010.

Pierce, Ronald W. "Contemporary Evangelicals for Gender Equality." In *Discovering Biblical Equality: Complementarity without Hierarchy,* 2nded., edited by Ronald W. Pierce and Rebecca Merrill Groothuis, 58–75. Downers Grove, IL: InterVarsity, 2005.

Piper, John, and Wayne Grudem, "Preface (1991)." In *Recovering Biblical Manhood and Womanhood: A Response to Evangelical Feminism,* edited by John Piper and Wayne Grudem, xiv–xvi. Wheaton, IL: Crossway, 2006.

Piper, John. "A Vision of Biblical Complementarity: Manhood and Womanhood Defined According to the Bible." In *Recovering Biblical Manhood and Womanhood: A Response to Evangelical Feminism,* edited by John Piper and Wayne Grudem, 31–59. Wheaton, IL: Crossway, 2006.

Post, Stephen G. *More Lasting Unions: Christianity, the Family, and Society.* Grand Rapids, MI: Eerdmans, 2000.

_____. *A Theory of Agape: On the Meaning of Christian Love.* Lewisburg, PA: Bucknell University Press, 1990.

Pryor, Jan. "Marriage and Divorce in the Western World." In *Contemporary Issues in Family Studies: Global Perspectives on Partnerships, Parenting and Support in a Changing World,* edited by Angela Abela and Janet Walker, 46–58. Chichester, West Sussex: John Wiley & Sons, 2014.

Ramsey, Paul. *Basic Christian Ethics.* Chicago, IL: University of Chicago Press, 1980.

_____. *Deeds and Rules in Christian Ethics.* New York: Charles Scribner's Sons, 1967.

Rawson, Beryl. "The Roman Family." In *The Family in Ancient Rome: New Perspectives,* edited by Beryl Rawson, 1–57. Ithaca, NY: Cornell University Press, 1986.

Rekers, George Alan. "Psychological Foundations for Rearing Masculine Boys and Feminine Girls." In *Recovering Biblical Manhood and Womanhood: A Response to Evangelical Feminism,* edited by John Piper and Wayne Grudem, 294–331. Wheaton, IL: Crossway, 2006.

Roberts, Christopher Chenault. *Creation and Covenant: The Significance of Sexual Difference in and for the Moral Theology of Marriage.* New York: T&T Clark, 2007.

Rossi, Alice S. "Gender and Parenthood." *American Sociological Review* 49, no. 1 (Feb 1984): 1–19.

Ruether, Rosemary Radford. *Christianity and the Making of the Modern Family.* Boston, MA: Beacon, 2000.

---------. "Feminism and Patriarchal Religion: Principles of Ideological Critique of the Bible." *Journal for the Study of the Old Testament* 22 (1982): 54–66.

---------. *Women-Church: Theology and Practice of Feminist Liturgical Communities*. San Francisco, CA: Harper & Row, 1985.

Rusbult, Caryl E. "A Longitudinal Test of the Investment Model: The Development (and Deterioration) of Satisfaction and Commitment in Heterosexual Involvements." *Journal of Personality and Social Psychology* 45, no. 1 (July 1983): 101–117.

Schleiermacher, Friedrich. *The Christian Household: A Sermonic Treatise*. Translated by Dietrich Seidel and Terrence N. Tice. Lewiston, NY: Edwin Mellen, 1991.

Schreiner, Thomas R. "Head Coverings, Prophecies, and the Trinity: 1 Corinthians 11:2–16." In *Recovering Biblical Manhood and Womanhood: A Response to Evangelical Feminism*, edited by John Piper and Wayne Grudem, 124–139. Wheaton, IL: Crossway, 2006.

Schüssler Fiorenza, Elisabeth. *Bread Not Stone: The Challenge of Feminist Biblical Interpretation*. 10th ed. Boston, MA: Beacon, 1995.

---------. *In Memory of Her: A Feminist Theological Reconstruction of Christian Origins*. New York: Crossroad, 1983.

Scruton, Roger. *Sexual Desire: A Moral Philosophy of the Erotic*. New York: Free Press, 1986.

Shkul, Minna. *Reading Ephesians: Exploring Social Entrepreneurship in the Text*. London: T&T Clark, 2009.

Siker, Jeffrey S. *Scripture and Ethics: Twentieth-Century Portraits*. New York: Oxford University Press, 1997.

Slater, Thomas B. *Ephesians*. Macon, GA: Smyth & Helwys, 2012.

Smith, Claire. *God's Good Design: What the Bible Really Says About Men and Women*. Kingsford, NSW.: Matthias Media, 2012.

Song, Robert. *Christianity and Liberal Society*. Oxford: Oxford University Press, 1997.

Sprecher, Susan. "Sexual Satisfaction in Premarital Relationships: Associations with Satisfaction, Love, Commitment, and Stability." *The Journal of Sex Research* 39, no. 3 (Aug 2002): 190–196.

Stackhouse, John G. Jr. *Finally Feminist: A Pragmatic Christian Understanding of Gender*. Grand Rapids, MI: Baker Academic, 2005.

Sumney, Jerry L. "Ephesians." In *The New Testament and Ethics: A Book-by-Book Survey*, edited by Joel B. Green, 64–66. Grand Rapids, MI: Baker Academic, 2013.

Swartley, Willard M. *Slavery, Sabbath, War and Women: Case Issues in Biblical Interpretation*. Scottdale, PA: Herald, 1983.

Terrien, Samuel L. *Till the Heart Sings: A Biblical Theology of Manhood and Womanhood*. Grand Rapids, MI: Eerdmans, 2004.

Thatcher, Adrian. *The Daily Telegraph Guide to Christian Marriage: And to Getting Married in Church*. London: Continuum, 2003.

———. *God, Sex, and Gender: An Introduction*. Chichester, West Sussex: Wiley-Blackwell, 2011.

———. *Liberating Sex: A Christian Sexual Theology*. London: SPCK, 1993.

———. *Living Together and Christian Ethics*. New York: Cambridge University Press, 2002.

———. *Marriage after Modernity: Christian Marriage in Postmodern Times*. New York: NYU Press, 1999.

———. *Theology and Families*. Malden, MA: Blackwell, 2007.

Thielicke, Helmut. *The Ethics of Sex*. Translated by John W. Doberstein. New York: Harper & Row, 1964.

Thielman, Frank. *Ephesians*. Grand Rapids, MI: Baker Academic, 2010.

Thiessen, Elmer John. "The Vocation of the Child as a Learner." In *The Vocation of the Child*, edited by Patrick M. Brennan, 381–407. Grand Rapids, MI: Eerdmans, 2008.

Thiselton, Anthony C. *The Holy Spirit – in Biblical Teaching, through the Centuries, and Today*. Grand Rapids, MI: Eerdmans, 2013.

Thurston, Bonnie Bowman. *Women in the New Testament: Questions and Commentary*. New York: Crossroad, 1998.

Tidball, Derek, and Dianne Tidball. *The Message of Women: Creation, Grace and Gender*. Downers Grove, IL: InterVarsity, 2012.

Tillich, Paul. *Love, Power, and Justice: Ontological Analysis and Ethical Applications*. New York: Oxford University Press, 1954.

Ting, Kwok-fai. "Continuities and Changes: Five Decades of Marital Experiences in Hong Kong." In *Wives, Husbands, and Lovers: Marriage and Sexuality in Hong Kong, Taiwan, and Urban China*, edited by Deborah Davis and Sara Friedman, 147–164 Stanford: Stanford University Press, 2014.

Torrance, Thomas F. *Incarnation: The Person and Life of Christ*. Edited by Robert T. Walker. Downers Grove, IL: IVP Academic, 2008.

Turner, Elizabeth Zarelli. "Love, Marriage, and Friendship." In *Men and Women: Sexual Ethics in Turbulent Times,* edited by Philip Turner, 147–178. Cambridge, MA: Cowley, 1989.

Ulanov, Ann Belford. "Two Sexes." In *Men and Women: Sexual Ethics in Turbulent Times,* edited by Philip Turner, 19–48. Cambridge, MA: Cowley, 1989.

Vacek, Edward Collins. *Love, Human and Divine: The Heart of Christian Ethics*. Washington, DC: Georgetown University Press, 1994.

Verhey, Allen. *Remembering Jesus: Christian Community, Scripture, and the Moral Life*. Grand Rapids, MI: Eerdmans, 2002.

Waite, Linda J., and Mark Nielsen. "The Rise of the Dual-Earner Family, 1963–1997." In *Working Families: The Transformation of the American Home*, edited by Rosanna Hertz and Nancy L. Marshall, 23–41. Berkeley, CA: University of California Press, 2001.

Waldron, Jeremy. "When Justice Replaces Affection: The Need for Rights." In *Liberal Rights: Collected Papers, 1981–1991*, 370–3391. Cambridge: Cambridge University Press, 1993.

Ware, Bruce A. *Father, Son, and Holy Spirit: Relationships, Roles, and Relevance*. Wheaton, IL: Crossway, 2005.

———. "Male and Female Complementarity and the Image of God." In *Biblical Foundations for Manhood and Womanhood*, edited by Wayne Grudem, 71–92. Wheaton, IL: Crossway, 2002.

Waters, Brent. *The Family in Christian Social and Political Thought*. Oxford: Oxford University Press, 2007.

———. *From Human to Posthuman: Christian Theology and Technology in a Postmodern World*. Burlington, VT: Ashgate, 2006.

———. *Reproductive Technology: Towards a Theology of Procreative Stewardship*. Cleveland, OH: Pilgrim, 2001.

Watson, Francis. *Agape, Eros, Gender: Towards a Pauline Sexual Ethic*. Cambridge: Cambridge University Press, 2000.

———. "The Bible." In *The Cambridge Companion to Karl Barth*, edited by John Webster, 57–71. Cambridge, UK: Cambridge University Press, 2000.

Webb, William J. *Slaves, Women and Homosexuals: Exploring the Hermeneutics of Cultural Analysis*. Downers Grove, IL: InterVarsity, 2001.

Webster, John B. *Barth's Ethics of Reconciliation*. Cambridge: Cambridge University Press, 1995.

Welker, Michael. *God the Spirit*. Translated by John F. Hoffmeyer. Minneapolis, MN: Fortress, 1994.

Werpehowski, William. "In Search of Real Children: Innocence, Absence, and Becoming a Self in Christ." Pages 53-74 in *The Vocation of the Child*. Edited by Patrick M. Brennan. Grand Rapids, MI: Eerdmans, 2008.

WHO, UNICEF, UNFPA, and World Bank. *Trends in Maternal Mortality: 1990 to 2008*. Geneva: World Health Organization, 2010.

Witherington, Ben III. *The Letters to Philemon, the Colossians, and the Ephesians: A Socio-Rhetorical Commentary on the Captivity Epistles*. Grand Rapids, MI: Eerdmans, 2007.

Witte, Jr., John. *From Sacrament to Contract: Marriage, Religion, and Law in the Western Tradition*. 2nd ed. Louisville, Ky.: Westminster John Knox, 2012.

Yoder, John Howard. *The Politics of Jesus: Vicit Agnus Noster*. 2nd ed. Grand Rapids, MI: Eerdmans, 1994.

Young, Katherine P. H. *Understanding Marriage: a Hong Kong Case Study*. Hong Kong: Hong Kong University Press, 1995.

Zizioulas, John D. *Being as Communion: Studies in Personhood and the Church*. Crestwood, NY: St Vladimirs Seminary Press, 1997.

_____. *Communion and Otherness: Further Studies in Personhood and the Church*. Edited by Paul McPartlan. New York: T & T Clark, 2007.

Index

A
adoption 188–189, 256
agape, *see* love, agape
Allen, Diogenes 161
alterity 55–56, 134, 228
Amato, Paul 11–13
American Evangelism 8, 103–105, 105, 129
Anderson, Joel 90
Aquinas 17–19, 65, 74
Aristotle 163, 202, 212
Arnold, Clinton 237
asceticism, celibacy, sexual renunciation 35, 58, 181
Athanasius 171
Atkinson, Evelyn 253
Augustine 50, 51, 66, 97, 129, 135, 138, 182–183
autonomous individual, *see* individualism

B
Bahr, Howard and Kathleen 179
Balswick, Jack and Judith 242
von Balthasar, Hans Urs 1, 56, 95–96
Barth, Karl 2, 3, 47, 53–55, 60–61, 94–98, 134, 142, 144, 155, 157–158, 173, 182, 196, 200–201, 217, 232
Batey, Richard 137
Bennett, Jana Marguerite 136, 138

betrothal 34, 37–42, 47, 52, 60, 148, 183
biblical manhood and womanhood 105, 108, 110–111, 124, 126, 130–131, 144, 191
Bilezikian, Gilbert 220, 229–230
biology, biological
  difference 13, 24–25, 63, 98, 140, 142–143, 152
  family 9, 11, 33, 96–97, 134, 146, 152, 156, 180–183, 188–189, 197, 223, 253
  gender and 20–29, 32–33, 43, 45–46, 60, 63, 140, 152
  human 15, 19, 24, 29, 57–58, 61, 91, 109, 230–232, 242
  parents 18, 37, 69, 71, 81–82, 92, 149, 246
  sex and 11, 24–25, 34, 42, 58, 59, 109
Blankenhorn, David 33
Blumberg, Rae 242
body, embodiment 14, 21–28, 31–32, 49, 52, 55–56, 58, 132, 134, 167, 181, 232, 238
  as instrument 15–17, 26–30, 34, 41, 46, 53, 147
  mind and 11–15, 20, 28–32, 36, 39, 41–47, 51, 53, 55, 58, 60–61, 63, 101, 148,

151–154, 161, 189, 195, 227, 257
  technology and 19, 31, 34, 40, 41
Bonhoeffer, Dietrich 193
Breazeale, Kathlyn 89
Breidenthal, Thomas 9, 187, 191
Brock, Brian 204
Brown, Peter 58
Browning, Don 4, 8, 11, 63–94, 97–100, 132, 148–149, 158, 169–178, 208, 250

C

Cahill, Lisa Sowle 8, 31–33, 55, 174, 180, 232
celibacy, *see* asceticism
Chan, Yiu Sing Lúcás 86
Chapell, Bryan 236, 252
child, children 2, 5, 78–79, 93–94, 100, 129, 146, 152, 161
  Christ as 96, 245
  childbearing 19, 32, 41, 109, 119, 126, 142, 231–232, 241
  caring of 109–110, 125, 127–128, 131–132, 142, 150, 153, 170, 242, 247
  disciplining of 108, 246, 249
  family and 82–88, 96, 99, 125, 148, 150, 157, 218, 224, 229, 257
  growing up 19, 32, 84
  having 10, 31, 34, 49, 50–51, 68, 168
  love of 176–179, 182, 188–190, 195, 196, 199, 244, 246–249
  marriage and 36–40, 52, 54, 89–90, 92, 95, 98–99, 101, 149, 167, 171, 183, 187, 189
  obedience of 195, 222, 229, 244–246, 248
  one's own 18, 71, 76, 84, 168

responsibility toward 6, 36, 67–68, 74–75, 77, 81–83, 148
  unintended 41–43, 47
  wellbeing of 4, 11, 30–33, 37, 41, 47, 52, 63–72, 86, 92, 148–149, 158–159, 169
Christ 2, 36, 57, 97–98; *see also* Jesus
  as head 100, 102
  body of 58, 99, 137–142, 145, 150, 156, 172, 175, 191, 215, 225–256, 233, 238–239
  church and 3, 18, 30, 73, 96–97
  incarnation of 22–23, 43, 47, 56, 58, 168–174, 176, 181, 185–189, 216, 240
  life, death, resurrection, and ascension of 7, 12, 48, 59, 93, 147, 154, 159, 196, 199, 211, 216, 218, 257
  love of, *see* love, Christ's
Christians for Biblical Equality 104, 105
Christology, christological 169, 176, 186, 210, 234, 236
church
  Christ and, *see* Christ
  family and, *see* family
Clark, Stephen 110, 116, 192
cohabitation, *see* marriage
  betrothal and, *see* betrothal
Cohick, Lynn 205–206, 224, 251
Collins, Raymond 138
complementarianism 8, 11–12, 103–146, 149–151, 191–195, 200–201, 207, 225, 228
contraception 7, 19, 34, 39–42, 46, 49–52, 148, 231
Coons, John 245, 248
Costa, Mario 23
Council on Biblical Manhood and Womanhood 105

covenant 3, 52, 137, 151, 165–167, 182, 196, 222
created order, natural order 48–52, 58–59, 63–64, 92–93, 100, 118, 132–135, 143–144, 149–150, 154–155, 180, 187, 223, 231–232, 238, 240, 245
creation, doctrine of 1–2, 48, 51, 53–56, 59, 63, 83, 93–100, 108, 114–120, 133–136, 139, 146, 150, 154–155, 170, 181–183, 188, 190–191, 197, 199, 207, 223–224, 229, 231, 238, 249, 257
critical familism 11, 64–67, 70, 75, 79–83, 100, 149, 169

D
Danvers Statement 105
Darko, Daniel 210
De Vries, Roland 55
democracy 11, 64, 78–91, 99–100, 132, 149, 169; *see also* family, democratization of
desire, *see* eros
divine command 53, 54, 217
divorce 4, 6, 9, 14, 16, 18, 33, 65–66, 68, 82, 90, 93–94, 165–168
duality 1, 11–13, 60–61, 64, 94, 96, 101–103, 146–154, 189, 227, 249
dualism 11–13, 20, 22, 28–32, 39, 41, 43, 46, 51, 53, 58, 60–64, 100–101, 129, 148, 161
Dunn, James 209

E
ecclesiology 234, 236
economic
    independence 68, 73
    modern 19, 34, 125
    pattern 65, 68, 70, 128–129, 131, 145–146, 150, 153, 206
    resources 32, 229
egalitarian 105–108, 111, 113–114, 120, 124, 129, 139, 141, 143, 225; *see also* gender equality
egalitarianism 72, 99, 214
Ellul, Jacques 19
embodiment, *see* body
empowerment 90, 172, 176, 178, 196, 240–243
equal-regard 11, 63–102, 148–149, 158, 169–178, 241
eros, *see* love, eros
eschatological community 12, 136–139, 145, 190, 197, 256
eschatology, eschatological, eschaton 3, 12, 83, 88–89, 93, 96, 103, 119, 135–139, 142, 146, 150, 153, 156, 173, 183, 189, 190, 240, 249, 256
eternal begetting of the Son 122
eternal subordination of the Son 120–123, 136
eucharist 22, 24, 47, 58
evangelical feminism 105, 124
evolutionary psychology 70, 72, 76, 97, 149

F
family
    as school of love 12, 190, 197, 247
    church and 12, 57, 96–97, 104–105, 112, 115, 143, 190–191, 197, 215–216, 256
    crisis 4, 65–68, 75, 81
    democratization of 64, 67–70, 78–83, 86, 89–91, 99–100, 132, 149, 169
    definition of 8–9

dual-earner 9, 131
eschatological transformation of 150, 188
intact 64, 69–73, 80–82, 100, 149
marriage and, *see* marriage
Trinity and 36, 183, 185–189
Victorian 128–129
Farley, Margaret 8, 11, 13–22, 28–34, 43–61, 63, 67, 91, 132, 147–149, 160–162, 166–167
father 10, 36, 74–75, 80–81, 87, 92, 95, 100, 119, 139, 142, 153, 161, 177–178, 201, 214, 220, 229, 241, 244, 246–250; *see also* paternal
absent 19, 33, 65, 68, 70–72, 76
fatherhood 32–33, 46, 69, 70, 77, 177–178, 232, 241
Fausto-Sterling, Anne 25
Fee, Gordon 111, 112
female problematic 92
femininity 95, 108–109, 124, 129, 140, 144, 149
feminist 104, 169, 173, 201–204, 206, 212
Fowl, Stephen 218, 234
Frame, John 112
friendship, *see* love, friendship
Fromm, Erich 177
fundamentalism 8, 11, 104

G
Gallagher, Maggie 77–78
gender
one-sex 24–27
biology and 11, 20–22, 24–29, 43, 46, 60, 63, 142
complementarianism, *see* complementarianism
concept and conception 27, 139–140, 146, 228
difference 11, 21, 24, 31, 33
division of labor 10, 12, 125–129, 150
equality 10, 18, 72, 73, 99, 202, 211
role 12, 14, 64, 107, 110, 112, 116–117, 128–134, 142–146, 150, 153, 228
uniformity 13, 60
Giles, Kevin 121-3, 127, 143
Gillis, John 4–5
Gittins, Anthony 92
Gombis, Timothy 210
Graham, Elaine 25
Grant, George 19
Grenz, Stanley 138
Grisez, Germain 191
Groothuis, Rebecca Merrill 119
Grudem, Wayne 105, 110–112, 120–122, 194

H
Hallett, Garth 173
Hamilton, Victor 165
Hassey, Janette 104
Hauerwas, Stanley 151
Hayes, Lydia 5–7
Hays, Richard 110–111, 113, 115, 124, 203
Hering, James 212–218
Hess, Richard 118
hierarchy 46, 55, 84, 86, 105–106, 112, 118, 120, 123, 133, 137, 139, 150, 200, 208, 229, 236, 238, 241
Hoehner, Harold 226, 252
honor-shame 71–75, 205, 224
hospitality 38, 154, 255–256
household 9, 18, 69, 72, 97, 99, 109, 125, 128, 130–131, 134, 136,

139, 150, 153–154, 181, 190, 195, 197
codes 110, 115, 130, 141, 191, 192, 195
Colossian 192, 199, 213–218
Ephesian 12, 74–75, 106, 137, 192, 199–257
1 Peter 199, 218
order 71, 222–224, 226–227, 231, 233, 241, 246, 249

I
ideology 112–115, 127, 145, 203–204, 206
imago Dei 2, 47, 56, 60, 94–96, 134, 136, 156, 182
Impett, Emily 45
incarnation, *see* Christ, incarnation
individualism 5, 7, 65, 67–70, 73, 78, 90

J
Jackson, Timothy 87, 88
Jenson, Robert 186, 187
Jesus 22, 36, 71–73, 93–94, 96, 99, 113–114, 134–135, 144, 157, 163–164, 182, 193–194, 206, 208, 232, 249; *see also* Christ
Jewett, Paul 113
John, St 137, 156–157, 174
just love, *see* love, just love

K
Kass, Leon 118, 182
Keener, Craig 209
kenosis 170–171, 174, 240
Kierkegaard, Søren 87
Knight III, George W. 107, 109, 118, 125–126, 192, 194

L
Lasch, Christopher 161
Leibholz, Gerhard 78
Lesthaeghe, Ron 6–8
Lewis, C. S. 141, 180, 183
liberal democracy 11, 64, 78–86, 89–91, 100, 132, 149, 169
liberalism 8–9, 78–83, 86, 90, 96, 100, 105, 124, 171
Lincoln, Andrew 220
love
affection 21, 30, 44, 69, 91, 160, 178, 180, 238
agape 12, 22–23, 87, 98, 162–163, 184, 190–191, 256
Christ's 7, 10, 12, 73–74, 87
command of 155–158, 194–195, 220, 243
equal-regard, *see* equal-regard
eros 23, 57–58, 162, 181, 184
fatherly 177–178
free choice and 16–17, 160–161
friendship 12, 18–19, 23, 30, 44, 76, 160–169, 181, 190, 196, 199, 220–221, 249, 255–257
incarnational 12, 168–180, 190, 196, 199, 220, 240–243, 246–248, 255–257
just love 14, 21, 29–31, 60, 160, 166
marital 51–52, 59, 73, 96, 98, 162, 187–188, 238, 254
motherly 177–178
mutual 18, 42, 87–89, 157–8, 175, 187, 191, 195, 197, 212, 218, 220–221, 225, 227, 237–238, 241–242, 249, 253, 255
parental 51–52, 96, 98, 188, 247, 254
preferential 160–164, 190

romantic 44, 160
sacrificial, *see* self-sacrifice
self-love, *see* narcissism
unfolding 12, 51–52, 96, 98, 180, 187–191, 196–197, 199, 243, 247, 254–257
Luther, Martin 74

M

Mahony, Rhona 90
male headship, male authority 71, 74, 76–77, 100, 104–107, 110–145, 149–150, 192, 200, 225–257, 238
male problematic 70–78, 83, 91, 92, 97–98, 178, 241, 250
marital love, *see* love, marital
marriage
  alone together marriage 5, 6
  as contract 81–83, 90, 165–166, 188, 222
  between Christ and church 18, 30, 96, 137, 200, 215–216, 226, 233–240
  cohabitation and 4–6, 34–40
  commitment and 14, 16–18, 29–33, 37–46, 52, 54, 71, 101–102, 147, 160–161, 166–168, 180
  divorce and, *see* divorce
  eschatological transformation of 56–59, 61, 97–100, 134–135, 154, 181, 223–224, 231
  family and 8–9, 30, 33, 36, 60, 180, 188
  goods of 67, 80, 83, 129–130, 154, 183
  living apart together 6
  monogamy 18, 30, 65, 67, 71, 74, 140
  permanent 19, 30–31, 37, 65–67, 74, 80, 83, 94, 129–130, 141, 147, 154, 166
  procreation and 6, 31, 37–40, 52, 59–60, 132, 231
Marshall, I. Howard 230
masculinity 95, 108, 109, 123, 124, 129, 131, 140, 144, 149
Meilaender, Gilbert 13, 47, 48, 50, 51, 60, 61, 101, 141, 146, 147, 148, 149, 159, 160, 164, 190
Mercedes, Anna 172
Miller, John W. 75, 77–78
Miller-McLemore, Bonnie 84, 87–88
mind
  body and, *see* body
Moltmann, Jürgen 170, 174, 176, 185
Moo, Douglas 116
motherhood 29, 32–33, 46, 49, 68, 174, 232, 241
Muddiman, John 226, 239, 240
mutual belonging 8, 188, 253, 255
mutuality 12, 29, 68–69, 73, 75, 84, 87–90, 158, 160–165, 178, 185, 187, 190, 196, 205, 210, 220, 224, 256

N

narcissism 153, 177, 184–185, 188–189, 244
natural order, *see* created order
neighbor 3, 38, 87–88, 157, 158, 164, 178, 190, 194, 196, 199, 243, 256; *see also* strangers
Nygren, Anders 184, 185

O

O'Brien, Peter 239–240

O'Donovan, Oliver 7, 47–48, 54, 56, 58–61, 92, 133, 147, 154–155, 159, 168, 187, 211
one-flesh 11, 36, 94, 149, 167, 187, 188, 233, 235, 239, 243
one-sex, *see* gender, one-sex
Ortlund, Raymond 117–118
Osiek, Carolyn 203
Outka, Gene 88, 175

P
Padgett, Alan 107
Painter, John 156–157
parent
  parental love, *see* love, parental
  parenthood 98, 101, 132, 188, 223, 231, 247
  single, *see* single parent
parousia 88, 137, 191, 197, 209
paternal; *see also* father
  certainty 18–19, 65, 71, 76, 139
  investment 18, 71, 97, 149
  responsibility 72–74, 76, 250
patriarchy 10, 13, 22, 28, 32, 64–65, 67, 71–79, 91, 99–100, 113, 141, 148, 201–204, 206–212, 223–227
Paul, St 137–139, 156, 180, 183, 208, 229
Peplau, Letitia Anne 45
Peterson, Eugene 240
philia, see love, friendship
Piper, John 108–109, 126–127, 191
pneumatology 186
Post, Stephen 4, 32, 55, 184
pregnancy 32, 39–43, 46, 49–54, 60, 65, 148, 177, 229, 241; *see also* contraception
premarital sex 9, 34–35, 37, 42
primogeniture 114, 117

procreation
  sex and 11, 19, 34, 37, 39–40, 47–54, 60, 63, 132, 145, 148, 152, 180–181, 187

R
Ramsey, Paul 194–195
rational-choice 67–70, 78
reciprocity 83–89, 99–100, 148, 158, 162–166, 170, 172, 176, 178–179, 186, 205, 212, 220, 229–230
reconciliation 53, 66, 196, 214–215, 226–227
redemptive movement 207
Rekers, George Alan 109
Ruether, Rosemary Radford 128–130, 202–203
Rusbult, Caryl 167

S
Schleiermacher, Friedrich 254–256
Schreiner, Thomas 112
Schüssler Fiorenza, Elisabeth 202–204
Scruton, Roger 26–27, 140
Second Demographic Transition 6–9
self-sacrifice 72–75, 84–8, 169–177, 220, 240, 242
servants 195, 253–257
sexual difference 2, 13, 21, 24–26, 29, 31, 33, 55–56, 76, 94–95, 100–101, 132–135, 139–142, 145, 148, 227–228, 232, 241
sexual renunciation, *see* asceticism
Siker, Jeffery 203
single parent 32–33, 65, 68, 81, 92; *see also* absent father
singleness, singles 2, 59, 97–98, 101, 134, 139, 143, 146, 152, 154, 159, 188–191, 222–223

Slater, Thomas 251
slaves 71, 118–119, 186, 205, 214–216, 218–219, 222, 224, 250–254
Smith, Claire 111, 116, 120
solidarity 168–180, 185–190, 196–197, 210, 240–241, 246, 248, 255
Song, Robert 79–80
special relationship 12, 163–166, 191, 220, 246–249, 253–256
Spirit 122, 136, 140, 142, 154–155, 186–187, 189, 193, 219, 236
  gift of 138–142, 146, 150, 156
Stackhouse, John Jr. 141
strangers 38, 154, 165, 188–191, 197, 244, 256
submission, subordination
  of women 72, 74, 104–146, 149–150, 191–193, 195, 200, 202, 207, 225–232
  mutual 101, 219–231, 237, 244, 247, 249, 253
Sumney, Jerry 209
Swartley, Willard 114

T
technoculture, technology 7–11, 19–20, 28–31, 34, 40, 47–52, 60–61, 76, 148, 152
  reproductive 29, 49, 51
Terrien, Samuel 207–208
Thatcher, Adrian 8, 11, 13, 22–28, 34–47, 52–53, 56, 58–60, 63, 67, 91, 132, 147–149, 180–184
Thielicke, Helmut 2, 98, 141, 201
Thielmann, Frank 226
Thiselton, Anthony 138
Thurston, Bonnie 209
Tillich, Paul 181, 184
Torrance, T. F. 168, 171

Trinity, Trinitarian 22, 36, 43, 47, 57, 120–123, 133, 183–189, 193, 219
Turner, Elizabeth Zarelli 167

U
Ulanov, Ann Belford 184

V
Vacek, Edward Collins 162–166
Verhey, Allen 125, 151, 204
vocation, calling 2, 11, 59, 64, 95–101, 132, 134, 139, 142–145, 149–150, 154, 164, 189, 223, 232, 255

W
Waldron, Jeremy 90
Ware, Bruce 117–118, 122, 143, 193
Waters, Brent 8, 20, 28, 49, 51, 81, 87–89, 99, 166, 178, 187–189
Watson, Francis 153, 217, 220
Webb, William 207
Webster, John 155
Welker, Michael 142
witness 12, 59, 146, 154, 157–159, 162, 190–191, 195, 197, 199, 204, 217, 218, 223, 227, 238, 240–241, 248, 257
Witte, Jr. John 81–82

Y
Yoder, John Howard 205–207, 212–213, 221, 223

Z
Zizioulas, John 47, 56–61

Langham Literature and its imprints are a ministry of Langham Partnership.

Langham Partnership is a global fellowship working in pursuit of the vision God entrusted to its founder John Stott –

> *to facilitate the growth of the church in maturity and Christ-likeness through raising the standards of biblical preaching and teaching.*

Our vision is to see churches in the majority world equipped for mission and growing to maturity in Christ through the ministry of pastors and leaders who believe, teach and live by the Word of God.

Our mission is to strengthen the ministry of the Word of God through:
- nurturing national movements for biblical preaching
- fostering the creation and distribution of evangelical literature
- enhancing evangelical theological education

especially in countries where churches are under-resourced.

Our ministry

Langham Preaching partners with national leaders to nurture indigenous biblical preaching movements for pastors and lay preachers all around the world. With the support of a team of trainers from many countries, a multi-level programme of seminars provides practical training, and is followed by a programme for training local facilitators. Local preachers' groups and national and regional networks ensure continuity and ongoing development, seeking to build vigorous movements committed to Bible exposition.

Langham Literature provides majority world preachers, scholars and seminary libraries with evangelical books and electronic resources through publishing and distribution, grants and discounts. The programme also fosters the creation of indigenous evangelical books in many languages, through writer's grants, strengthening local evangelical publishing houses, and investment in major regional literature projects, such as one volume Bible commentaries like *The Africa Bible Commentary* and *The South Asia Bible Commentary*.

Langham Scholars provides financial support for evangelical doctoral students from the majority world so that, when they return home, they may train pastors and other Christian leaders with sound, biblical and theological teaching. This programme equips those who equip others. Langham Scholars also works in partnership with majority world seminaries in strengthening evangelical theological education. A growing number of Langham Scholars study in high quality doctoral programmes in the majority world itself. As well as teaching the next generation of pastors, graduated Langham Scholars exercise significant influence through their writing and leadership.

To learn more about Langham Partnership and the work we do visit **langham.org**

www.ingramcontent.com/pod-product-compliance
Lightning Source LLC
Chambersburg PA
CBHW051537230426
43669CB00015B/2629